# A GRAND ENTRANCE:
Scenes and Monologues for Mature Actors

Compiled and Edited
by
ANN McDONOUGH, Ph.D., and KENT R. BROWN

Dramatic Publishing
Woodstock, Illinois • London, England • Melbourne, Australia

### *** NOTICE ***

Professionals and amateurs are hereby warned that each scene and monologue in this book is fully protected under the copyright laws of the United States of America, the British Commonwealth, including Canada, and all other countries of the Copyright Union. Scenes and monologues may be used for audition purposes only without royalty; however, all scenes and monologues in this volume are subject to royalty payment for: professional and amateur performances, motion pictures, lecturing, public readings, radio broadcasting, television, reprinting, and translation into foreign languages.

For royalty information and permission to perform, other than auditions, please refer to the permission acknowledgment pages at the end of this book to locate the source able to grant permission for public performance. The permission acknowledgment section constitutes an extension of this copyright page.

Published by The Dramatic Publishing Company
P.O. Box 129, Woodstock, IL 60098

©MM by
ANN McDONOUGH and KENT R. BROWN

Printed in the United States of America
*All Rights Reserved*
(A GRAND ENTRANCE:
Scenes and Monologues for Mature Actors)

*Cover design by Susan Carle*

ISBN 0-87129-933-X

## ACKNOWLEDGMENTS

The editors extend their appreciation for the considerable contributions of several people whose dedication and skill aided greatly in the creation of this anthology. Thank you to Douglas Hill and Dianna Shoup who offered much-needed administrative assistance. A special debt of gratitude is extended to Gayle Sergel for her encouragement and unerring counsel. Lastly, to all the students and actors over the age of fifty-five who have shared their talent and their enthusiasm, we extend our heartfelt thanks.

# CONTENTS

INTRODUCTION . . . . . . . . . . . . . . . . . . . . . . . . . . . . . . . . ix
TIPS FOR THE ACTOR. . . . . . . . . . . . . . . . . . . . . . . . . . . . x
PREPARING THE MONOLOGUE . . . . . . . . . . . . . . . . . . . . xvi

## Monologues for Women

*Lather*, Carleen R. Jaspers . . . . . . . . . . . . . . . . . . . . . . . . 3
*The Cactus Pirate: Relative Value*, Davey Marlin-Jones . 6
*N.I.M.B.Y. (Not in My Backyard)*, Leslie (Hoban) Blake . . . 9
*Faith*, Louis Broome. . . . . . . . . . . . . . . . . . . . . . . . . . . . . 12
*Esther's Last Stand*, Adam Kraar. . . . . . . . . . . . . . . . . . 14
*The Keepsake*, Staci Swedeen . . . . . . . . . . . . . . . . . . . . 16
*Kneading*, Michael Wright . . . . . . . . . . . . . . . . . . . . . . . 19
*They Were All Good Lovers*, Mike Thomas. . . . . . . . . . . 22
*Children*, Innes-Fergus McDade . . . . . . . . . . . . . . . . . . 25
*Old Woman*, Joseph Robinette . . . . . . . . . . . . . . . . . . . . 27
*High Track*, Roger Cornish . . . . . . . . . . . . . . . . . . . . . . 29
*Bertie the Beauty Queen*, Shelly Pruitt-Wykes . . . . . . . . 33
*Summer's Last Call*, Bruce Post. . . . . . . . . . . . . . . . . . . 37
*The Late Show*, Mike Thomas . . . . . . . . . . . . . . . . . . . . 40
*My Greatest Failing*, Innes-Fergus McDade . . . . . . . . . . 43

## Monologues for Men

*Stargazer*, Kent R. Brown ........................ 47
*The Third Scourge*, Vin Morreale, Jr. ............... 50
*Progressive Passion*, Mike Thomas.................. 52
*Record Holder*, Joseph Robinette................... 54
*The Time-Share Rag*, Kent R. Brown ............... 58
*The Bonfires*, Kenneth Robbins .................... 62
*It's Half-Full*, Michael Wright..................... 64

PREPARING THE SCENE............................ 67

## Duets

*Que Sera, Sera* (1m, 1w), Katherine Snodgrass ....... 73
*Sweet Tuesday Falls* (1m, 1w), Julie Jensen .......... 81
*The Inheritance* (2w), Vin Morreale, Jr. .............. 84
*The Gallery* (1m, 1w), Loretta Novick................ 92
*Friday* (1m, 1w or 2w), Carol Wright Krause......... 99
*Sniff* (2m or 1m, 1w), Jules Tasca ................. 107
*Out on the Ice* (2m), Mark Steven Jensen ........... 114
*The Color of Heat* (1m, 1w), Saul Zachary .......... 125
*Prime Time Ago* (1m, 1w), Steven Packard.......... 133
*Death on the Doorstep* (1m, 1w), Jeffery Scott Elwell. 141
*The Tea Cozy* (2w), Joan Calof .................... 147
*Whose Turn Is It?* (2m), Phillip Potak.............. 151
*Flamingo Fantasy* (1m, 1w), Linsey Hamilton ....... 156
*Blackout* (1m, 1w), Sheryle Criswell ............... 165
*The Lost Party* (1m, 1w), Hudson Plumb ........... 172
*Gawk* (2w), Gary Garrison........................ 181
*Gray Matter* (1m, 1w), Jeanette Farr ............... 192
*The Question* (1m, 1w), Mayo Simon ............... 201
*Having a Good Time* (1m, 1w), Steve Allen......... 206

# Trios

*Scenes from the Penitentiary* (2m, 1w), Anne Harris . . 217
*The Talking Bench* (1m, 2w), Kent R. Brown . . . . . . . . 225
*The Family Tree* (3w), Karen Smith Vastola . . . . . . . . . 236
*The Grand Mommy* (3w), Adam Kraar . . . . . . . . . . . . . 244
*The Open Window* (3w), Kent R. Brown . . . . . . . . . . . 249
*Pain and Paint* (2m, 1w), Nicholas Zagone . . . . . . . . . 256
*Last Laughs* (1m, 2w), Rachel Feldbin Urist . . . . . . . . 264
*The Pickup* (1m, 2w or 2m, 1w), Kent R. Brown . . . . . 272
*The Bookmobile Doesn't Come By Anymore* (3w),
  Billy M. Pullen . . . . . . . . . . . . . . . . . . . . . . . . . . . . . 281
*Food Is Love* (2m, 1w or 1m, 2w),
  Sandra Fenichel Asher . . . . . . . . . . . . . . . . . . . . . . 290
*Carry Me Home* (3w), Angela Counts . . . . . . . . . . . . . . 299
*Mr. Wonderful* (2m, 1w), Olga Humphrey . . . . . . . . . . 306

MEMORIZING TIPS AND TECHNIQUES . . . . . . . . . . . . . . . 314
OTHER TIPS FOR PERFORMANCE AND AUDITIONING . . . 316
ABOUT THE PLAYWRIGHTS . . . . . . . . . . . . . . . . . . . . . . . 319
PERMISSION ACKNOWLEDGMENTS . . . . . . . . . . . . . . . . . 332

# INTRODUCTION

Welcome to the wonderful world of the theatre and the excitement of acting! You have committed yourself to memorizing lines, attending rehearsals, creating a believable character and entertaining an audience. This is no easy task, to be sure, but it is stimulating, energizing and just plain fun.

To help meet your obligations as an actor, we have compiled a variety of suggestions, observations and reminders intended to keep you focused on your goal: to become a better actor. You will find these suggestions dotted throughout the book. If you are a more accomplished performer, we hope these observations will serve as an artistic tune-up.

One last word before we begin. While you may not be a seasoned veteran of the stage, you are a seasoned veteran of life with many wonderful insights to bring to your acting. So, be honest about who you are and what you have achieved. Be proud of your years of experience! Celebrate your age!

Good luck and good acting!

# TIPS FOR THE ACTOR

## You and the Play

Before launching into interpreting and portraying your character, let's look first at a few basic principles and assumptions which will help guide your exploration into character analysis.

- Plays are puzzles to be solved by the entire production ensemble to include the director, the actors, the designers and the audience members.
- Analyze the play, scene or monologue with the assumption that everything is there for an express purpose—the words, the silences, the set and costume descriptions and the stage business. Playwriting is a precise craft, and in a well-written play all words and actions fit together perfectly.
- Your job is to decipher all the clues in the play, get a firm understanding of the primary and secondary plots and how they are linked and reinforce the meaning of the work as a whole. In this manner you will understand better how to interpret your character and how your character's presence influences the play as a whole.
- Pay close attention to the language your character uses to determine your character's attitude toward others and toward life in general. Is your character irascible, charming, deceitful, naive, compassionate, sullen, exuberant, insensitive, blunt or evasive? How does your character respond to pressure, to being thwarted, accepted, confused, loved or challenged?

- Just as in life, don't always assume the characters in the play are telling the full truth at any moment. They may be diverting attention, withholding key pieces of information or outright lying. Your task is to discover the underlying truth of the dramatic situation.
- Characters, like real people, are very complex. Their true nature is revealed through what they say, what others say about them and what the characters actually do.

## Characterization

Now that you have a firmer understanding of your relationship to the dramatic material you will be interpreting, let's concentrate next on creating a believable and interesting characterization. By answering the following questions precisely, you will be taking the correct steps to portraying your character with intelligence and imagination.

**What Does Your Character Want to Achieve?**

- Acting is psychology in action. Audiences expect you to know how and why people behave as they do. After all, you will be portraying a real person with a full range of desires, fears and dreams. If you don't know what your character wants to achieve, then your acting will be vague, general and lacking in definition and clarity. Ambivalence is not theatrically effective. Theatre is about passion, not about indetermination.
- Phrase your character's "want" (objective) in a single sentence, and take personal ownership of that desire. Instead of saying "My character wants a glass of water," say, instead "I want a glass of water." After all, it will be you

on that stage, not someone else. Ownership of your character's life will make you feel energized on stage.

- Avoid "wanting" states of "being" such as "I want to be happy." Theatre is about doing, not being. Try, instead, "I want to lose ten pounds so I will think better of myself," or "I want to go back to school to meet new people." The more specific your "want" is, the more purposeful your acting will be.

- If you will be interpreting the behavior of others, you should first understand what motivates your behavior. Take your own inventory of motivations. Why do you behave differently in the presence of a spouse, a former employer, a favored child, an estranged sibling? Be truthful in your assessment. Theatre is about truth, not about deception. The motivation behind an action is often more fascinating than the action itself.

- In real life, if you say, "I don't know why I said that (or did that)," you often can avoid taking responsibility for thoughts or actions. If, however, you answer "I don't know" when the director asks you why your character says or does something in the play, then you're relinquishing your special talents and insights as an artist. Take responsibility for your talent and intelligence. Dig deeply to discover your character's primary motivations.

**What Obstacles Keep Your Character From Achieving the Objective?**

- If your character easily achieves his or her objective, the audience will feel cheated. They have come to witness a struggle between two opposing energies. In effect, your character is running an obstacle course, determined to reach the finish line a winner.

• Obstacles usually fall into one of three categories. The first category includes external or physical obstacles: a blizzard, crop failure or failing health. Your character must deal with the difficulties these physical obstacles create. The second category includes the blocking character, or antagonist, who is intent on stopping your character from successfully accomplishing his or her objective: a domineering parent or spouse, a vengeful employer at work or a jealous sibling. The third category, highly prevalent in contemporary playwriting, includes your character's own failings and limitations: self-doubt, fear, conceitedness, uncertainty, arrogance, stubbornness, lack of compassion, or a moral or ethical resistance to taking certain actions

• A word about the antagonist: Don't stereotype him or her. He or she is potentially as complex as your character. Also, you may be cast as the antagonist in the play or scene, and must give that character a full life with legitimate needs and objectives. Look for ways in which the playwright has tried to humanize the "bad guy."

## What Actions Does Your Character Take to Overcome the Obstacles?

• Notice this section asks for the actions taken by your character to overcome obstacles; it says nothing about words spoken.

• At this very moment you are taking steps (actions) to improve your acting by enrolling in an acting course, attending productions, even by reading this book. You are not just saying "I wish I could be an actor." You are saying "I am reading a book on acting" and thereby "taking action." Your character should be doing the same thing—taking action to achieve an objective. Remember, the word "acting" comes from the word "action" not the word "talk."

- Consider the lines your character speaks as one of several strategies your character employs to achieve an objective. Lines are only the tips of the motivational iceberg. They represent ideas and strategies your character employs to move the obstacles aside and achieve the objective. Words will sound ungrounded and feel disconnected if delivered without an understanding of the intention behind the lines.

- Consider what character "business" you could employ that would convey nonverbally how your character feels and thinks at any given moment. Audiences are astute. They know how to read body language.

- Be selective in the number and variety of strategies your character employs. Don't take one tack and run it into the ground, such as yelling all your lines if you are angry, or whining if your are displeased. People are far more diverse in real life. We cajole, tease, bully, seduce, sweet talk, insinuate, plead, demand and negotiate our way through life every day.

**What Stakes Are Involved and What Is Your Character Willing to Give Up to Achieve the Objective?**

- We all put up with something to get something else in life. We give up our money every day, willingly and unwillingly, to buy items we need. We may give up something in order to keep a friendship or reach consensus. Your character, willingly or not, faces similar choices.

- Does your character choose to put his or her emotional well-being at risk in order to help another character? Does your character elect to sacrifice one kind of friendship in favor of another? In short, discover what will happen if your character makes one choice over another? Remember, the inner quality of most people is revealed by the choices they make. And there are consequences every step of the way.

- Discover what your character values. When those values come under attack, chances are your character will begin to take action. In contemporary drama, most of the stakes center on human relationships: a valued trust, respect or honor between two friends, siblings or a married couple.

- If you don't know how high the stakes are and what your character is willing to give up, then the audience will lose interest. Theatre, whether serious or comic in nature, is about conditions of discomfort and desperation and about people who are no longer willing to remain in those situations. If the audience believes you don't care about the outcome of the struggle, then why should they? Remember, theatre is a lot like life: no pain, no gain.

## PREPARING THE MONOLOGUE

Monologues are windows into the soul of your character. During the monologue, a private window opens, and secret thoughts and yearnings of all shapes and dimensions, as well as dark and loving memories are shared with other characters and the audience. For a moment or two, the audience is given a glimpse of the private life your character generally keeps well beneath the surface.

As actors, you must discover what your character hopes to gain by revealing that information. The answer can never be "Because the playwright wrote it." The following tips and suggestions are intended to help you prepare your monologue.

- Whenever possible, read the entire script. A monologue is a strategy your character employs to secure an objective. Discover how your monologue fits into the fabric of the script as a whole, affording you the opportunity to texture your performance with shades of subtlety and meaning.
- Never approach a monologue as if it is a story about the past. It may deal with actions that occurred in the past, but the monologue must be provoked by the present situation facing the character. It must be an attempt to progress the plot, clarify a present confusion or summon courage to take an action that will make a difference now, not twenty years ago.
- There is a tendency and a temptation, during rehearsals, to substitute lines and phrases. Make every effort to avoid this impulse. The substitutions will alter the meaning

and overall impact of the piece. Would you walk up to the "Mona Lisa" with a paintbrush and change her smile?

• Decide how the character receiving your monologue would react to what you are revealing. These responses will influence your performance. Remember, acting is reacting.

• Select fixed points on the stage or in the auditorium where the other characters in the monologue are located so that your focus does not wander aimlessly.

Don't hurry through the logical pauses and transitions. Your purpose is not to deliver a monologue, but to communicate human thought in all its variation and richness of detail.

• Avoid telegraphing what will be happening next with your character before it actually happens. Actors know what will happen next, but real people—the characters you are trying to portray—don't know what they will say or what will happen next until that moment comes.

• Avoid apologizing or stammering during your performance if you happen to forget a line. Instead, improvise until you get back on track, or, if you are really stuck, simply stop and ask politely if you may begin again.

# MONOLOGUES FOR WOMEN

# LATHER
## Carleen R. Jaspers

*(GERMAINE is a middle-class homemaker, 60-80 years of age. It is winter and she is at her sink washing her hands luxuriously and ceremoniously, creating lots of lather. She yells to someone in another room of the house throughout her discussion.)*

### Germaine *(yelling out)*

Tell him he needs to wash his hands before coming to the table. And make sure he uses soap this time. Oh, and don't just let him run his hands under the faucet either. Show him how to get a good lather worked up. Y'know Aunt Gretchen—my aunt on my mother's side, the one who used to work for that children's doctor? That short, bald fellow she used to brag about? Well, anyway, the point is that he always said it wasn't how much soap you used, it was how you used the soap. I'll never forget that. It's the friction; all that rubbing of your hands together that makes for lather; and lather and friction is what kills germs.

*(Grabs a nail brush and scrubs under her fingernails as she continues yelling.)*

And show him how to use that nail brush too. You'd be amazed, just amazed, how many worm eggs and other critters there are living under the fingernails. If you don't believe me, just swab back there sometime and put it under a microscope. It's enough to make any decent human being sick to his stomach. And, hon, tell him that even though he doesn't have to go to all this bother at his house, he's living here now. And that's how we do it in our house.

*(Loud sneeze/cough from offstage.)*

Oh, and would you ask him to please cover his mouth when he sneezes and coughs. They're plenty of freshly pressed handkerchiefs in his top drawer. I haven't had a cold—knock on wood—in four years and I don't intend to get one this winter. Also, and you're the one who'll have to show him, please ask him to...to...well, y'know, to...after he's done? I shouldn't have to see any splatters around the seat. That's not necessary, not necessary at all. If he can't be any neater, he'll have to use the bathroom in the basement, that's all.

*(Pause; she smells something unpleasant. Sniffing.)*

What's that? Do you smell something? Something... musky? Now what in the world could that be?

*(Drying her hands on the way to the window, she looks out, sees nothing unusual. She turns back and continues to yell.)*

You two aren't burning something, are you? A pipe or cigar? Incense? A scented candle? You know I can't have any kind of smoke in the house. Go in his room and put out whatever's burning.

*(She attempts to open the window with her arms and elbows, not wanting to contaminate her sanitized hands.)*

Y'know, for a second there I was back in that walk-up dump we had on the Lower East Side. And I could've sworn I was smelling that curry or whatever those people always cooked with. Isn't that funny? I haven't thought of that in forty-some years and here it is as clear as if it was yesterday. Oh God, that smell gives me the willies. Sometimes a dozen people were crammed into that apartment. No wonder they were cooking at all hours of the day. I don't know how they could stand it in there—especially in July and August with no air-conditioning! And that music! If you can call it that! That'd give anybody an excuse to drink. I can't figure out for the life of me what kind of instrument would make that kind of noise. Nothing I know of could come close. Oh God, it was ear-splitting, remember?

*(Beat; she looks agitated.)*

How could you forget that? You were there; you had to smell their cooking through the vents. It was your idea—don't you forget—to call the landlord on them about their music. I can still see their faces when the INS folks pulled up.

*(Pause.)*

I must admit, I did feel a little sorry for that young mother whose boy jumped off the roof. It was so... No matter how many times I or anybody else took a pail and brush to it, that spot just never went away. I hated like heck to have to walk by it every time I took the trash out.

*(She goes to the table, sits down and admires the linen and the china.)*

All right, now. Dinner's ready. Come and eat!

# THE CACTUS PIRATE: RELATIVE VALUE
*Davey Marlin-Jones*

*(The home of the CACTUS PIRATE.)*

## Cactus Pirate

When I was in that jail, that piss-ant Pahrump jail, for stealing cactus and the only thing between me and freedom was a fifty-dollar fine, there wasn't a friend or forgotten lover in sight.

But here I am, umpteen years later in the heart of Clark County, flush to the gills, facing six to fifteen on a second-degree murder charge, and I got relatives I never even heard of crawling out of the high-and-mighty woodwork to save my soul.

I hire me a lawyer, I make my bail, I head for my house over on Quail Ridge, I open the door, and facing me is a horse of a woman looking like the combined resurrection of Minnie Pearl and Lon Chaney, Jr.

Claims she's Alvina Pevitts, second cousin once removed of my recently deceased husband, Jimmie-Rae, and she's from someplace in Washington State. Called Moses Lake. And she's come to soothe my savage breast.

Every time she opens her mouth she tells me something good that's bad.

Here it is mid-July and she offers, "I'd like the desert if it wasn't s'dry and hot."

Goddammit, Alvina, if it weren't dry and hot, it wouldn't be the desert.

"Oh it could," she says, "but then it would be nicer."

Nicer!

"And people would want to visit."

All you gotta do, I'm thinking, to get people to visit is be accused a' plugg'n your husband and not be broke. That's what I'm thinking, but I'm not sayin' it because Alvina is not curious about what I think.

Alvina's got an answer for everything.

Even before I say something. She's got an answer and I don't even know what the question is.

I say something about likin' Las Vegas and she's tellin' me how much culture they got in Moses Lake. They got parity between culture and snakes the way she tells it. The snake part I don't doubt.

"We go to the the-ater at the church or the junior college whenever they do a musical. More people'd see them shows and feel better about that the-ater if they had more songs and scenery."

Why is it I'm facing a murder charge and it's Alvina that sounds condemned?

She goes on: "Tell us what we want to hear, what we already know." *(Bursts into.)* "Climb every mountain— And you'll neeeeeveeeer waaaaalk alone!"

Just a damned minute, Alvina. I live in a town where you can set your watch by the volcano and teach your kids to count by keepin' track of the drownin' pirates down by the sinkin' ships. They tell us what we already know and they do it with a lot of songs and scenery.

"That's just my point. They give the public what it wants. And a lot of riff-raff comes here even if it's hot and sticky."

Hot? Yes. Sticky, never. Nothing that's riff or raff sticks here long, Alvina. Then it crosses my mind, if you have to be something else than what you are to win, maybe you shouldn't win.

'Bout the time I'd dropped the line about riff and raff, Alvina is re-locking her Samsonite and asking me to call her a cab, and wonders if I'd like to come up to Moses Lake and visit a spell.

And you know, if I beat this murder rap, I might just go up to Moses Lake, plug Alvina and be a hitman for the arts.

# N.I.M.B.Y.
# (Not In My Back Yard)
### Leslie (Hoban) Blake

*(A street corner in a blue-collar Long Island neighborhood. DELLA, a clearly agitated working-class woman in her 60s, is on patrol. She's wearing a housedress and slippers, her hair in curlers, a cigarette in one hand and a clipboard in the other. She will say anything to manipulate the situation her way.)*

## Della

Will ya listen ta' what I'm tellin' ya, Mrs. Rizzo? There's gonna be addicts in there...addicts and alcoholics...there's gonna be AIDS in there...is that good fa' us, huh? We got children over here... I'm helpin' bring up two 9-year-old twins—my daughter's kids...she works inna city and I gotta get 'em ready fa' school every mornin'. We wait fa' the bus right in front'a the place where all them addicts is gonna be—now that ain't right.

Ya know, they made this decision without talkin' to the community, there wasn't no meetin's...didn't nobody ask us nothin', am I right? That's outrageous! I know beyond a doubt in my mind, if that shelter's put on this street, it's gonna be a detriment ta' the value of all the property around here. That priest in charge of the whole thing? He don't got the parish behind him...hell, he ain't even the regular priest—he's just a substitute! The old priest, Fatha'

Vincent—now, *he* was a priest, a man ta' respect. He woulda come ta' us and we coulda told him we don't want no shelter here. But when he retired they sent this here new guy, and he don't know us and he don't care about us.

Hey, I'm not saying these poor people don't got a right to some help. Ain't I a Christian and don't I know somma these guys was in Viet Nam and over in that Gulf War there? I know we owe them for that. My husband Tommy, God rest his soul, he was in the army over in Korea...and he came back a little funny too, ya know? But there wasn't no drugs back then and he got over it. Well, I mean, sure, maybe he drank a little too much—sometimes—but *drugs*—NEVER! Hell, *we* didn't know nothin' about drugs...now, even little kids are on crack and they all got guns... I mean, what's this world comin' to anyways? And they wanna put these addicts and who knows what all right here on our block? NAH, we can't let them do this ta' us. We gotta fight this here shelter, even if it means fightin' the church.

What the hell is the church doin' mixed up with a bunch'a addicts anyhow? Why don't the church just mind its own business and send clothes ta' the starvin' people in India like they used ta' and stay outta political stuff like this? Oh sure, this is all about politics, what you call your Political Correctness. And who's gonna pay for all this, huh? You and me, that's who, and then they'll just bring in a bunch of black and Porta Rican guys—hey, don't you go lookin' at me like that—I ain't no bigot...my Tommy, now, *he* was a bigot and let me tell you, I ain't like him. My daughter Marilyn—she had a colored girl at her sweet-party, *right* in our house, no matter what Tommy said—so don't you go thinkin' that's why I'm against this shelter. It ain't got nothin' ta' do with color anyways... these guys just don't belong here. Whyn't they put 'em in the Bronx or somewhere? They're gonna hafta bus 'em inta' the city ta' find work, aren't they? So why not keep 'em close ta' where they're gonna hafta go? Now, *that* makes sense ta' me.

And what about the ones with AIDS? Oh yeah, most of these addicts taday already got AIDS on account'a they don't wash out their needles before the next guy uses them... we can't have a disease like that right here, next door ta' us... we don't want them ta' come out here and infect our kids... I mean, innocent kids can catch it and die! You heard about that poor little Ryan White on *Oprah*, didn't ya? NO!!! We gotta keep them away from our kids, so that's why you hafta' sign this here petition.
*(She presents clipboard for signature.)*
It says that we're all in favor of helpin' these poor unfortunates, but not on this block. I already got everybody on the even side of the street to sign and now I'm startin' with you over here on the odd side—not that you're odd, of course.
*(She laughs at her own joke.)*
Just print your name here, signature right next to it, and don't forget the rally tomorrow. We need a lotta people to show up, 'cause we called all the newspapers and TV stations—we got signs already made and everything. I mean, we gotta stick together or we can all forgeddaboudit!!! God bless ya, Mrs. Rizzo, I knew we could count on ya. So it's tomorrow outside Our Lady at seven, and bring the kids—the more the merrier I always say.

# FAITH
## *Louis Broome*

*(FAITH, a woman in her older years, is seated in the day room of a nursing home.)*

## Faith

Oh, care here's fine. Not bad. Don't call this place a nursing home—the nurses here don't like it. Elder care facility. But everywhere is nice nowadays. When I was little, on our farm, no running water. No 'lectricity. No phone. No radio. No car. Wood-burning stove. Two mules. A cow. And chickens. Hated pluckin' chickens. Eatin's good, but pluckin', you can have it. Chores. It's all there was, as soon as I could tote a pail. Poor Kenny died of strep at 7. That was hard. Of strep! And such a gentle, lovely boy. We didn't have the drugs then, so he died. But I remember Kenny. You remember, too. He would've loved you. Every now and then we'd see a fella walkin' toward the house to ask for work. No work. It's like a game, see. There's no work 'cause there's no money—everybody knew—but hunger didn't kill their pride, so men come up and ask for work. So Momma'd send 'em to the barn and after supper, once we'd eat our fill, she'd make a plate and send my daddy to the barn. Us kids would follow, hang outside and listen. Daddy always gave 'em such respect. So kind and generous. My daddy's not what I would call religious. Can't say he believed. But somehow he could live it. One time—I remember clearly, 'cause we lost a mule the week before—a fella come to ask for work. And he was lookin' bad. His color was wrong. So thin. No shoes. They all looked bad, but he looked worse. A frightening, maybe frightened, look. But Momma sends him to the barn like all the rest, like everything's just dandy. After supper, Momma fixes up a special plate. Puts jelly on his biscuit. We saw jelly on our biscuit, birthdays maybe, maybe Christmas. Somethin's up; can't suss it out. When Daddy takes this man his plate, he brings along a blanket and a pillow—well, I never! We go out, and here's this man, he's lookin' bad. Can barely move. Has trouble talkin'. Daddy helps him eat. Ate slow. Took time to taste. But clears his plate. Then Daddy makes a place for him to sleep. And somehow we all know this man is dyin'. Not like Kenny, not so hard, but dyin' all the same. And all night long my daddy holds his hand. Same as he held Kenny's hand. And sometime in the night the stranger passed, well-fed and on a pillow and his hand being held.

You'd think it's not so much to ask, to leave this world while someone holds your hand. But all the time here, people die alone. Who'd'a thought I'd live to envy that poor man his dying in our barn.

# ESTHER'S LAST STAND
*Adam Kraar*

*(It is late afternoon and ESTHER has just learned her office is being computerized—and no one has bothered to consult her about it. She addresses her boss.)*

## Esther

Mr. Mocktinger, may I talk to you for a minute? I'm leaving. I've packed up my desk, and I'm not coming back. Don't try to stop me; I've made up my mind. You've got a computer, you've got Susan, you don't need me anymore. Please, Mr. Mocktinger, let's not pretend. I'm obsolete! You've got a micro-mini-turbo whatchamacallit now, and since you ordered it without consulting me, you've obviously got everything figured out. I never asked for anything around here, and I don't expect anything. In thirty-four years, I didn't take one sick day. Let me please just say one thing and then I'll go.

The first year I worked here, I wore white gloves, and stockings, and heels. I would never be caught dead in an office wearing blue jeans. And I don't make a big production about all the things I do for this place, like some people.

Why am I telling you this? Because I thought it would be different. I thought I would work here until... Like my husband says, till they carried me out on a stretcher. I loved this job... I loved having my own faux mahogany desk, my own paid stamp, my own swivel chair—I always appreciated that you got the special model for my size. I loved answering the phone when Susan was at lunch. "Martin J. Mocktinger, how may I help you?" Like a song, really—I sometimes answer that way at home, I can't help it.

I never minded the cigar smoke and the overtime and all the privileges you've given Susan—even though she's only been here two years, and she sits in your office and drinks coffee like she's some kind of big shot and not a junior secretary. I've never taken such a liberty in thirty-four years, I would never want to drink coffee in your office, because I'm here to work, not drink coffee. Lemme just ask you one thing: Did you ever stop to think why you did so well, starting the year I became your office manager? I never needed anything from you because I thought, even if you had no idea of all that I did—the insurance, the union forms, guarding the supply cabinet—I thought that you...respected me. Not that you'd make a big song and dance about all I did, but that, late at night, instead of worrying about some account when you were drifting off to sleep, it would come into your head for just a second, "Oh, I don't have to worry about that, Esther'll take care of it." But I guess I'm...just a foolish old woman. I guess I should've been more like Susan, taking my rewards all along; taking my sick days and my personal days and sipping coffee on your sofa. But I can't do that. I don't wanna do that. I'm tired... I'm ready.

I'm going. Here's the key to the safe. I'm not sorry I worked for you, Mr. Mocktinger. I just never dreamed it would end this way. But it's the best thing for both of us. All I ask is...just once in a while, try to remember: the accountant comes on *Thursdays!*

# THE KEEPSAKE
*Staci Swedeen*

*(MARGARET HUDSON is an elderly, heavy-set, earthy, sensuous woman. She stands center stage facing the audience holding a package wrapped in bright paper and ribbon. She shakes the gift vigorously, holding it up to her ear. She shakes it again, listens, and smiles mischievously.)*

## Margaret

It's been a long time since anyone gave me a present. And that I'm accepting it! It's a sure sign—I've lost my mind. You can see that, can't you? The funny thing is, I don't really have to think about it. Not long, anyway. Life's like a garage sale—one person's trash is another person's treasure.
*(Pause.)*
God, it's not like I have kids to be embarrassed by me. Plus the cat likes him. I mean, he can open a can of tuna as good as the next. I'm not a religious person. Certainly not in the traditional sense. And despite what he thinks, it's not for the sex—although when he finally confessed to me about the operation—I thought I'd never stop laughing. It just was so funny—and wonderful, you know—at a time when so—so many just give up, here is this goofy-looking old geezer saying—no! I want more! And I realized that I did too. So okay, neither of us looks like movie stars— But if *he* has the courage—and he makes me laugh. My god, now that's a gift.
*(Shaking the gift.)*

That's bad, isn't it? He told me to wait so he could see my expression.

*(Holds present above her head and shakes it again.)*

It's a form of *torture* when you got something wrapped this pretty sitting on the sideboard! I might be able to steam up the tape here, just take a little peek. He'd never suspect a thing. You know the kind of people I admire most in the world? The kind that can have a bowl of candy in their house and not eat it.

*(Gives gift an extra vigorous shake.)*

As kids, we had to save the wrapping paper, every year. I got so good at opening gifts—not one rip would appear, no clue that the paper had been used. Just another one of those talents you wonder if you'll ever use again,

*(Smiles.)*

I can still *act* surprised. I don't even have to *act*. I'm still astounded that—this is the kind of thing *other* people do, but not Margaret Hudson, old, conventional Maggie. I haven't been this happy since any husband died. My God, I know how that sounds. I loved Walter, but towards the end, when he was so sick—and then he went, and everyone was crying and all I felt was...relief. No one tells you that. A wave of relief. Then the great fog of loneliness rolled in.

*(Pause.)*

I thought, well, I guess that's what *this* part of life's about. So to be getting presents—I don't have to *act* surprised. I'm shocked as hell. The thing about life—ah, the older I get, the less I know—the other night I had a dream and I woke up in tears—and I realized the crying part I got down pretty good—Barney reminds me to laugh. It's that simple. That's an incredible gift for one person to give to another.

*(Starting to laugh, looking at present.)*

Oh-oh. The tape came loose.

*(Teasingly defensive.)*

It could! Let's just take a little—

*(She works the tape loose.)*

Ah, the things we learn as kids.

*(She opens the box and pulls out a champagne glass.)*

Looks like there's some champagne in my future!

*(She peers into the box again and pulls out a notecard, reads it.)*

"Dearest—accept this ring and raise a glass to..." Oh, my God. I told Dr. Lonky my eyes are not what they used to be, I didn't see any—

*(She pulls out a small ring box. Smiles.)*

What'd I tell you? I won't have to *act* surprised. Oh, no. I won't have to act at all.

# KNEADING
## Michael Wright

*(ESTER in her kitchen, kneading pie dough into balls, and rolling out other balls that have set. She has an Irish accent that has some touches of Boston in it, for this is where we are.)*

## Ester

Might be better if you stayed in the breakfast nook, there. I'm a pretty sloppy dough-slinger, or so my husband always said. Wouldn't want to get anythin' on that nice suit of yours. Anyway, to answer your question, the first time I met Llewellyn—isn't that a nice, old-fashioned name, now? Llewellyn. Welsh, he told me, that's where the name came from, his Welsh background on his mother's side. Anyhow, so, the first time was at the bank. I was just havin' one of those days when you start to think "If it gets more difficult than this, I'm steppin' in front of the next express bus I see barrelin' down the street." I was having breathin' spells, and droppin' everythin' all over the place, and I can't bend over most of the time anyway unless I want to spend the rest of the day lookin' at me shoes. Anyways, so I drops me deposit slip and up pops Llewellyn to pick it up for me. And we walk to the line together—the lines is somethin' awful anymore, now ain't they? How's your coffee, love? Good, well, so, then we start in to talkin', and this is when I find out about how he's got this grand invention—not that I understand it, mind, but something to do with a kind of universal-fittin' shoe—and he's very upset because he's had to give over a mountain of money lately to support his old auntie over in Wales, and there's a man who wants to start right in to manufacturin' this universal shoe but Lew must have the patent first, and of course all he's got in his pockets is lint. Well, I did not know him from Shamus but I loved his way of talking—had a real broad Boston sound to him—called me "Es-tah" when we got on first names—and he had the clearest eyes you ever saw, and what was a hundred dollars to me if it would help him so? And he did not do the askin', mind! It was all my doin', the entire way.

*(Beat.)*

Yes, I understand why we're talkin', Mr. Attorney-at-law, Esquire. I'm just wantin' to tell this story in me own fashion. Well, fine, if time is money, then I'll just hit the highlights, as you call it. Over the past five years, I've taken it on meself to help Lew out in a number of different ways. But it was always fifty here, a hundred there—if the fella was a con artist, as you call him, wouldn't he have tried to take it all at once?

*(Listens.)*

What? Altogether? But you know this better than I do.

*(Pause.)*

All right! Have it your way. Altogether it come to twenty-two thousand. Yeah, that's right, put on that smug look of yours: "poor old lady, taken for a ride." Well, I don't see it as any "tragedy," like you put it on the phone. I told you before, and I'm tellin' you now: I had it to give out of what Dr. Galway left me, and so what of it? Do you know how many days Llewellyn sat there, right where you are, listening to me going on and on about this and that, swapping stories with me? Do you know what it's like when your house goes silent? Have you ever talked to yourself? And I don't mean little noises or comments, I mean sentences, paragraphs, pages!

*(Pause, she fishes out a tissue from her apron pocket.)*

I mean, look, Mr. Levine, look for a minute, you got forty percent of that money back, isn't that so? Not that I even asked for it, or needed it, though the other ladies you represent did and I understand their feelin's but so okay, you got it back, but isn't it enough now?

*(Pause.)*

Your job. Aye, your job. I understand. I said I understand; I'm not the village idiot, you know!

*(Beat.)*

I'm sorry, Mr. Levine, I know you didn't deserve that. Look, look, why don't I make a fresh pot of coffee, and I'll sit down with you and we can go over this from start to finish, and I'll...I'll try to give you what you want, all right? Yeah? Good. Only...only, would you do us a favor? Do you think you could take a couple of these pies to Llewellyn for me? I mean, jail food for a man with a lovely appetite like his? Now, *that's* a tragedy...

*(She turns to make the coffee. Lights fade quickly to black.)*

# THEY WERE ALL GOOD LOVERS
## Mike Thomas

*(INEZ, 75, has outlived three husbands. She has a good sense of humor and is straightforward. She is speaking to a journalist of a small-town newspaper about her life.)*

## Inez

I've lived right here in this same house for fifty-two years. I've buried three husbands in the cemetery down the street. Two of 'em died from eating poisonous mushrooms, the third one died of a hammer to the head... 'cause he wouldn't eat the poisonous mushrooms.

*(She laughs big.)*

God, I love that joke. No, I'm just kidding with you, I lost Herschell to diabetes and Herb's heart gave out. Irving died of a stroke when he was 73 and that was too damn young. But, I'm okay with it now, I'm a tough ol' bird, always have been. My husbands were all good men, they treated me with respect, and, Lordy, the sex was good. Mmmmm hmmmm. Oh! Does that embarrass you? I'm sorry, I'm not one to dance around an issue. It was just nice to be with men who were good in the sack. I couldn't have stood going through life having to fake it or show them how to do it. All three of my husbands were damn good lovers and I'm proud to say it. Hell, that may be what wore them out. It would explain Herb's heart and Irving's stroke. But, Herschell's diabetes was his own fault.

*(She laughs.)*
I was married once, before any of them, but I don't talk about that one much.
*(Pause.)*
Oh, what the hell. I was only 13 years old and my friend bet I wouldn't marry this boy. So, I had to show her. His name was Billy Golden and he was 17 and we went out to a little country church down there in Wildcat Holler. We told that preacher we were both 18 and he believed it. Boy howdy, my mama was mad when word got back to her. She took me down the next day and got it annulled. I wonder what happened to that boy? He was real cute. When I met Herschell I was 19 and I was a waitress. He used to come in and order those mountain oysters and I'd turn red 'cause you know those are cow balls. He was 30 then and God how we used to laugh. He was a smart man too. He sold seeds to co-ops across the south. He had a college degree. He kept working, too, even after he lost both legs to diabetes. They just don't make men like that anymore. I shouldn't have married men so much older than myself, especially if I wanted them to live, but I needed some maturity. Some men are just idiots. I was married to old Hirsch the longest. I met Herb at a V.F.W. He liked to drink but he knew his limits. I had gone there with some friends and their husbands and I just thought he was handsome and so I told him. My friends were so shocked. We danced and went out a few times and he asked me to marry him one night. Things used to happen fast back then. All three husbands loved this house and I didn't care about moving. Now Irving was kind of wild when I met him, or I should say I saved him from "nursing home hell." His kids had put him away. I was doing some vol-

unteer work there and I used to just sit and talk to him and he was so damn funny, he told me some good ones. I wish I could remember some of 'em. I think I enjoyed watching him tell them as much as the joke. He had these great laughing eyes. Well, I packed him up and took him home with me and we had a great five years together. I loved all my husbands, yes sir. I'm damn glad I kept marrying and I've been lucky, I've been real lucky, 'cause men today, especially young men, are just plain stupid, and as a member of society I owe it to women everywhere to tell a man when he does something stupid or behaves rudely in public. I won't tolerate it, because I know how a man should act and treat a woman, I've lived with three of the best.

Thank you, boys. Thanks for the memories... I miss you fellas... that's all I want to say today. You can print what you heard, I'll keep the rest as a memory.

# CHILDREN
## *Innes-Fergus McDade*

*(An ELDERLY WOMAN sits surrounded by boxes and stacks of baby's clothing. However, she is not holding the clothing.)*

## Elderly Woman

No, I never did have kids. I just collect children's clothing. Not *any* clothes. Special ones... Old ones... Little ones. Like a tiny pair of overalls, all faded and worn, with little flaps and snaps. Farm clothes I guess you'd call them... For baby farmers... Not all cutie pie like what they've got at the mall. Or a little boot, an old black baby boot, sturdy and scuffed—for a fat little foot. I don't think about the children. The clothes are enough. It sounds strange but... I hang them on the wall in my apartment. Perfect little shapes with lots of space around them on a white wall.

I never wanted children. I arranged my life very well not to have them. But I do have this wonderful tiny red cotton dress—washed to death—like some very little girl would have worn a long time ago, in some faraway place like... Nebraska.

Today on the subway I saw a girl with her father. She had on a party dress and had skinny, skinny arms and legs like little white Popsicle sticks, and she was holding a present in froggie paper. She looked... astonished and... reverent. Like she was off to meet the Queen.

She shouldn't have been on that train, with all those big, frightened people, shoving and swearing. Holding her present...on her way to some...royal occasion. Much too skinny to be on that train. She should have been off somewhere. Safe.

I don't want children. All that scuffing and fading...skinny little arms...it's too much. The clothes are enough.

# OLD WOMAN
## *Joseph Robinette*

*(An OLD WOMAN in her early 70s is scolding someone who is obviously younger than she is.)*

## Old Woman

Old woman?... Old woman?! Don't you ever ask me a question and end it with—"old woman." Old is somebody that's fifteen years older than you are. So in my case that would be 87. And when I'm 87, old will be 102. I'm only 72 right now, so I got a long way to go. Old woman, my foot. You oughtta be ashamed of yourself, young man. I don't know why we have to keep reminding each other that we're getting old anyway. Even when we're young, somebody's always telling us we're getting older. "You're old enough to tie your shoes now." "You're old enough to clean up your room now." I remember when I was in the third grade, and one day at recess I was telling Bessie Coolie what I wanted Santa Claus to bring me for Christmas. Jimmy Ray Roper—who was in the *fourth* grade—heard us talking and came over and said, "You girls are old enough to know there *ain't* no Santa Claus." Bessie said she already knew, and I said I did, too. But I didn't. And I went home and cried for a week.

...Then one time when I was 11, I got to spend the night with Thelma Jean Rigins who was 12, and she asked me if I knew where babies came from. I said they got started in heaven, then the stork brought them. She said that wasn't it at all and that I was *old* enough to know the truth...and she told me. Of course, I didn't believe it, and I told Thelma Jean my mama and daddy wouldn't do something like that. And she said they did, too, and since I had an older brother and a younger sister, they'd done it at least three times. I went home and cried for another week. ...Finally, I decided if Mama and Daddy had done it *just* three times, that was okay, I guess. I knew they were probably ashamed of themselves and had asked God to forgive them.

...It never ends. "You're old enough to get a job now." "You're old enough to get married now." "You're old enough to be a grandmother now." "You're old enough for social security now." "You're old enough— You're old enough— You're old enough, old woman!"

...Oh, I know you didn't mean anything by it, young man. I guess nobody ever taught you to be a little more sensitive to your elders. But I won't hold it against you. And, yes, I will do you the favor you asked me for. I *will* eat supper with you tonight—but *not* at that table where you usually sit. That's where the *old* people eat. I never knew why you sat with them anyway. You're only 69. You can sit at that table when you're 84. Now, come on. I'm hungry. But you don't have to take my arm. I'm old enough to walk by myself, you know. Let's go.

# HIGH TRACK
*Roger Cornish*

*(She wears sweatpants and a sweatshirt, carries a gym bag and towel. She sits on a bench to change to running shoes.)*

## Martha

I have just one lung now. *(Grins.)* Don't worry, I won't bore you with Medicare talk. But there's this *thing* that happened since... Well, one medical thought. Losing a lung has made me appreciate redundancy. Two lungs, but you can live with one. Nature's almost like Boeing, isn't she? Two kidneys, two eyes, two ears, two... *(Glancing at her bosom.)* well, some losses must be harder than others. *(Bright.)* Then again, *some* losses have a bright side. Remember those old magazine ads: "The man in the Hathaway shirt"? Was he a handsome devil! Lean, trim little moustache, but, most of all, what caught you right away, that black eye-patch. He had one eye! And did he look romantic! He was my dream date, I'll tell you! But now, redundancy means I still have a lung—thank you, Mother Nature. And that's what got me walking. My surgeon said, "Start walking, build up that one lung." So I started.

My first walk was to church, about a mile. *(Laughs.)* I suppose I chose church in case it killed me! I was never a walker; my husband said I'd drive to the mailbox, if I didn't have to back up after. But I made it to church with no trouble, though I let my husband drive me home. He'd follow me all the way there, in jerky starts and stops, like a Driver's Ed student. He was afraid I'd collapse. But I didn't, and soon I was roadwalking every day— I loved it! Cut a tree branch for a hiking staff, stepped out like Mrs. Daniel Boone. I worked on strong breathing: *in* two three steps, *out* two three steps! Proud of myself. But my husband hated it. That I was *on the road* terrified him. "No proper shoulders," he'd say, "Damn transportation department won't pay for proper shoulders!" He *knew* I'd get hit by a car, which *I* knew was silly; I was a champion walker, no car could hit me if it tried. It was a constant battle. "You're gonna get hurt!" "I am not, I'm Superwoman!" And I'd pound my chest and yodel like Johnny Weismuller. But he wasn't impressed. He's really stubborn. Till one day he gets me in the car and drives over here—the Club. He hands me a membership card, shoves me on the track and says "From now on, this is where you walk!" *(Laughs.)* I started to resist, till I realized he'd trapped *himself* into some healthy exercise. After all, he'd already paid for it. He's in the pool right now.

Turns out I like the track even better than the road. No muddy shoes and no climbing over steel road guards when there's a car coming and no shoulder at all. The transportation department really is cheap! And I can walk faster! I'd never been on an indoor track before—smooth and bouncy, banked at the corners. I really stride now, and I breathe even better. I've decided to build one huge superlung, the barrage balloon of lungs! Well, my real goal is enough lung power so I can rejoin the church choir. I walk four times a week: Monday, Wednesday, Friday, Sunday—the clockwise days on the track. I like system. *(Her shoes are on.)*

Then, a couple of weeks ago, this thing happened. I had a Friday conflict, so I came Saturday, which is a counter-clockwise day, and a hockey day—down below on the gym floor. You know, little boys' roller hockey—in-line roller skates and an orange ball instead of a regular hockey puck. Well, I stepped out at a good clip, but pretty soon I felt dizzy. I tried to shake it off, but it came back, a kind of vertigo. Then I realized, "Of course, I've changed direction, I've confused my internal compass." So I slowed down and tried to change my focus by watching the hockey players down below. I tried that for about a lap, but all I could focus on was their shiny white helmets, dozens of them, shooting around the gym floor like billiard balls. And that made me dizzier than ever. I had to stop, right in the middle of the track, and lean over the railing. I was seasick! I closed my eyes, but that made me want to throw up, so I just leaned and breathed and watched the little hockey players. So tiny down there. Their helmets were wide as their shoulders, and their shirts hung below their knees. And on the shirts—their team names were the Bears and the Giants! I thought, "At least couldn't they be the Cubs and the Midgets?"

Then, as I watched them, they seemed to recede even further, as if I were looking through one of those movie lenses; they zoomed away, getting smaller and smaller. I suppose it was the vertigo, but it felt like a kind of... vision. For I suddenly thought, "This is what God sees, tiny, shiny babies skating crazy circles a million miles below, bouncing off each other like microscopic bumper cars." And then I thought, "Is this what it will be like when I die? Will I look down on microscopic creatures playing crazy games? And will I try to send them messages? 'Keep those helmets on. Tie those kneepads tight. Don't get those sticks so close to each other's faces. It's so easy to hurt each other, and so hard to make it better.' And will I know they can't hear me?" *(She does something to her hair.)* Isn't it funny, the things that go through your mind? Anyway, after a minute I was okay, and I left the track. It hasn't happened again, and I'm walking better than ever. *In* two three *four, out* two three *four!* *(Smiles.)* But I only walk the track on clockwise days. *(Flipping the towel round her neck, she exits.)*

# BERTIE THE BEAUTY QUEEN
*Shelly Pruitt-Wykes*

*(BERTIE, age 64, is employed as a live-in maid and nanny at Bristow Mansion.)*

## Bertie

When I was about...16, I guess it was, my mother talked me into enterin' this beauty pageant. I didn't want to. I really didn't want to. I didn't have all th' essentials that beauty queens was supposed to have. I didn't have the straight teeth or the naturally glowing complexion. I didn't have flowing hair or the million-dollar body. I didn't even have no friends. Oh, well, Caroline was my friend...and I shore didn't even have no beauty queen name. My name is Bertie. It's short for Albertina.

My mother said, "Bertie, you need to find something you're good at. I think you'd make a fine beauty queen." I was good at lots of things. Like whistlin' through my teeth, and immitatin' Ethel Merman. 'Course, I cain't whistle through these dentures and nobody likes Ethel Merman anymore. Most people don't even know who she is. When I realized that these talents were pretty much worthless, I thought, "Maybe Mother's right." So I told her to enter me up. When I told Caroline that I was gonna be in a beauty queen contest, she laughed. "Ooohhhh, Bertie!!" she said, "Not YOU!! You don't really think that you'll win, do you?" I don't remember exactly what my answer was, but whatever I said was good enough to convince her to enter too.

Well, the day come. Mother had me scrubbed and washed. My hair was curled up in a Shirley Temple style complete with a pink ribbon. Mother touched some mascara on my eyelashes and pearly pink shadow on my lids. Then she dabbed some pale pink lipstick on my lips. She pointed me in th' direction of the mirror. "Look at my beauty queen," she giggled. "What about rouge?" I asked. "Rouge is for disreputable women NOT beauty queens," she said. Then she pulled out a pearly pink dress with puffy sleeves and a long pink sash. It had tiny pearls on the bodice. It looked like a pink wedding dress. It was beautiful. She zipped, tied, and tucked me snugly into that dress. Then she pulled out a box of tissue. "What's that for?" I asked... I was so naive. One empty box of tissue later, I had a million-dollar body.

Rougeless, but tissue-endowed, I went to the pageant. I had never seen so many beautiful girls. All were beauty queen types. None of them had on pink wedding dresses and every last one of them had rouge. I wanted to go home. Mother shook her head. She said, "Bertie, at the end of all this you'll have a new name! We'll all be calling you "Bertie the Beauty Queen"! Caroline came over about then. She was wearing one of her mother's black silk dresses that came down and showed her bare shoulder. She had on high heels and rouge. "Ooohhh, Bertie," she squealed, "isn't this exciting!!" Then she looked at me. "Bertie," she said, "where on earth did you get THAT dress?" I stood up as straight as I could and told her that this was what all of the beauty queens wore.

A haggard lady came out of a small door on the left and made us all line up. Then gave all of us a number. I got nine. Caroline got seven. The pageant was underway. I watched as the other eight went on the stage before me. They all stood up straight, held up their heads, smiled a beauty-queen smile, and sashayed across the stage swinging their hips. Then it was my turn. I felt like I couldn't breathe. Someone gave me a push and I stumbled out on stage. I just stood there like a deer in headlights. I didn't know how to sashay. I wasn't allowed to swing my hips. I didn't even have on any rouge. I staggered across the stage as best I could. I only tripped on my dress once. The judges stared at me. One of them, the lady, gave me a smile. I liked her immediately. She wasn't beauty-queen material and she knew I wasn't either. But her smile said, "Hold your head up and smile back. You'll be all right. And, it doesn't matter that you don't have on any rouge."

About thirty, maybe forty-five minutes later, the judges brought all of us girls back out onstage and the audience clapped. Then they started naming the beauty queens. Fourth runner-up... not me. Third runner-up... not me. Second runner-up... not me. First runner-up... still not me. That was all right though. Nobody wants to be a runner-up. Then they announced the beauty queen... I still had a chance. Maybe mother was right, maybe they'll announce that "Bertie is the Beauty Queen!" The head judge, the lady, the one that smiled at me... opened the envelope and looked my way. "Our new beauty queen for this year is...

Caroline Mackenzie!" The audience roared as they placed the diamond and gold crown on her head...but I didn't hear any of the noise. It's hard knowin' that you're not beauty-queen material.

About seventeen years later I passed a little shop that sold, what you call 'em...novelties? I was looking for a Halloween outfit for my son. An' there in the window was a beautiful diamond and gold crown just like the ones that the beauty queens get to wear. It was big and glittery...just sparklin' in the sun. It blinded me to look at it...it sparkled so. I went in and bought it. Then, I wore it all the way home. In the darkness of my bedroom I took it off to get a good look...it was fake. Rhinestones that were trying to look like diamonds. The rim that held them was metal not gold. I looked down at my wedding ring. The diamond was real...and the rhinestones couldn't outshine it. The band was gold...the metal rim of the crown was a poor competitor. I keep it on my dresser to remind me of that day when I thought I had to have a crown to be a beauty queen.

# SUMMER'S LAST CALL
*Bruce Post*

(*MARGARET, 67, is speaking to her sister Rose, who, in an unexpected visit, has discovered Margaret lounging in a silk negligee.*)

## Margaret

Herb gave it to me. Eighteen months before he died. Did you know I fucked that man to death, Rose? Never mind the vulgarity, he was barren and he thought it was me and we never stopped having sex, what with the lack of children. I'm incorrigible that way. But I buried that part of my life when I buried Herb, no regrets. I almost threw this thing away several times, but I would pick it up out of the dresser, and feel the smooth silk on my fingertips, and remember how good it felt to wear it, and I would stuff it back into the bottom of the drawer.

I'd just finished my bath and I had a stew on the stove. When I lifted the lid some hot broth burst out of the pot and burned my hand. I ran to the sink to run some cold water. I looked out the kitchen window and saw him. He was hiding in the bushes, but I recognized the cowlick. I think I know what house he comes from. He's just a boy. I've noticed him staring at me from his driveway. He didn't see me at the kitchen window, and when he moved in the bushes I realized he'd been spying on me. I went back to my bedroom and, sure enough, the shade was lifted just enough to give him more than an eyeful. You know me, Rose, I anoint myself thoroughly after a bath. Well, I knew he was out there watching, and it excited me. I forgot all about my burn. I wondered what he might do if I beckoned to him. Run away, terrified, most likely. But I was flushed, dear, and very pleased to have an admirer. I went to my dresser, and I found this blue silk negligee. I held it up to myself in the mirror. I wasn't looking at the crow's feet, or the liver spots, or the gray hair. My tummy is flat, a little wrinkled, but flat, and my shoulders are straight, there's no hunch in my back, and my back still curves nicely around my fanny, which might be a little flattened. And I have good legs, shapely, with thin ankles. I pointed my toes and flexed my thigh and it was sexy. I turned to the window and walked closer. I caressed beneath my tummy and drew my hand slowly up my leg. I looked through the dark glass directly where I thought he would be, transfixed, and I gave a little smile, and I tried...I tried to wink at him. I couldn't do it.

Suddenly, Rose, I was terrified. I shut the lights and got into my bed and pulled the covers up to my nose. I lay very still. I thought I had seen his beady little eyes coming forward hungrily to meet me. I couldn't sleep I was so ashamed. I felt perverted. I could smell my own sex. It was repulsive. Trying to lure that boy. What if it had worked? What if I had seduced the child? What if people found out? I felt like a ridiculous old woman. Still, after all, there was no harm done and it's not my fault he's sneaking around spying on old ladies. I didn't invite him to watch. So I gave him a little education.

Did you know, Rose, when I told Herb I was barren, he told me I was just a cunt. I despise that word. I saved his pride by not telling him the truth, he had chromosome damage you see, and he calls me a cunt and a whore. Those were dark days for us. Now I'm so terribly lonely. I wonder sometimes if I'm becoming senile. I have so much to say and no one to say it to. Lately I've been wearing this around the house. I like the way it feels. Is that bad, Rose?

I think maybe I can get that young fellow down the street to do some work around this place. Then I'll have someone to talk to. He seems intelligent enough. And there's plenty here needs doing. I'd like to get the porch painted. There's a hole in the linoleum in the kitchen and the living room ceiling could use some spackle. My bedroom door sticks when the humidity rises.

# THE LATE SHOW
*Mike Thomas*

(*MARY is an 80-year-old woman who thinks the people on television can see and hear her. She lives alone. She is not senile, but delusional and frightened. There are times she sounds very sensible. Whether it is a movie or a talk show she is watching, it is definitely <u>her</u> movie or talk show.*)

## Mary

I see you there...
*(Straightening her nightgown.)*
I see you. You didn't come out and show yourself when my daughter was here...did you? I want you all to meet her sometime. You sure are little. How did you get so little?
*(She focuses more intently on the TV.)*
I guess we were all little once. I feel so sorry for people, so sorry for people who don't listen to you. Who don't believe in you. I believe in you 'cause I can see you. You can see me, too, I know, because sometimes you just laugh at me. I know I can be silly... My daughter doesn't believe in you and it just worries me something terrible... I'm so afraid you won't call her, to be with you when it's time, and she's a good girl. She teaches school, little ones around her all day...and she don't see it... Are you going to teach me tonight? Are you going to invite me in?... I'm scared, but I would go if you called me.

*(She closes her eyes and hums "Rock of Ages" for a few seconds.)*

Not tonight I guess... You just keep talking, I won't turn you off... I like you and that would be rude, to make you leave. I do wish you would tell me what it's like in there ...over there...up there...out there. Oh, I don't know.... Oh, I like that. I like what you are wearing. My daughter bought me this old thing... Why do you sometimes talk right to me and at other times you're too caught up with your friends to pay any attention to me? Huh?

*(She begins to threaten.)*

If you don't talk to me, I'm gonna turn that knob and you'll go away. Is that what you want? Is it?

*(She smiles at the TV.)*

No, I couldn't do that to you. That's not how I was raised, but you already know that, don't you? You know about me and my daddy, don't you? Daddy used to take good care of us. I loved him and I don't care what you thought about him. I've heard what you've said when I'm in the other room. He was a good man and he never did no wrong. Is that why you watch me now...because he told you to? I don't even know you, and he said...

*(She is lost in a memory.)*

"I will always watch over you and when I'm not around, I'll send some angels to take care of you." But I don't know you...and I know my daddy wouldn't lie... Well, I've been talking too much. I'm gonna let you talk now... You tell me what to do... Okay? You help me and I won't turn you off.

*(Pause, she listens and waits for instructions from the TV, trying not to look, but looking anyway.)*

What? What did you say? I can't hear very well anymore, you are going to have to speak up... Hello... Can I help you?... Well, you just go right ahead, you go right ahead and laugh your fool head off. You don't bother me, because I know my daddy sent you. You're not getting my money though. No, you're not. You're my sweet angels, yes you are, you're my sweet, sweet angels.

*(She begins to yawn and fall asleep in her chair as she does every night.)*

# MY GREATEST FAILING
## *Innes-Fergus McDade*

*(JEAN, an elderly woman, is sitting, purse in lap. She raises her hand to be called on.)*

## Jean

Thank you. I think *my* greatest failing is— *(She looks around the group. She gasps, covers her mouth.)* Oh, dear. I'm sorry, I suddenly— Could you call on someone else? ...Oh... Well ...I was about to say that my greatest failing was...not having had children. *(In response to one of the group.)* Thank you for that... But just this minute—the way you're all looking at me— That's not my greatest failing. Much worse than that. *(Silence.)* My greatest failing is...no sense of humor. I've never had one. ...No. I haven't! I'm just not a funny person. Around me things just kinda lose their...whatever you call it.

Some people are funny. Not even actors or show people. Ordinary people. Like Mrs. Deeder at the Beauty Lounge? The way she licks her fingers when she turns pages—lick, slap, lick, slap—with her pinkie in the air and that cute look on her face. It's just funny! Actually, that woman's got more saliva in her mouth and on that magazine by the time I get it. Everyone laughs, but...you don't want to look at her mouth too long. There, you see? That started out funny but then somehow...

Sometimes in bed at night I play a little pretend game. At my age! I imagine the gang all sitting around the family room and Monroe, my husband, says to me, "Go on, Jean, tell 'em that story. You know. The hilarious one. About the Airwick in the grand piano." Or some such. Everyone kinda rustles with anticipation and the ice cubes are chinkling, and they all look at me smiling and eager for a good chuckle, and I put down my glass, slowly, to drag out the suspense, and then I tell *the* funniest story, acting it out, with gestures and everything. Well. People start to giggle and Frank snorts—you must all know men who laugh like that—and Madge slaps at him and he snorts louder and then Madge snorts too and then everyone busts open and *hoots*. And the women start grabbing the men's drinks to avoid an accident and everyone's rocking in their chairs and Wayne is turning red and coughing he's laughing so hard, and Monroe gives my leg such a ... romantic squeeze and he winks at me, just like when we were first married and he wanted to "make music together," as he called it.

... Then everyone starts to cool down and Madge and Marge wag their fingers at me in the nicest way, and then someone repeats the last line of my story, just the way I told it, and they all guffaw one more time and then a giggle here and there and a handkerchief comes out and a good nose blow and everybody beaming at me like I just fed 'em chocolate cake. ... You know, *(A realization.)* maybe if I could have made Monroe laugh like that back when we were trying to have kids...

It's like being tone deaf. You can hear the music in your head but as soon as you open your mouth to sing... When I tell a joke it's not like chocolate cake, it's... it's cold oatmeal dripping out of my mouth, down my chin... in front of everyone. And no one's smiling. 'Cause that's not funny... is it?

# MONOLOGUES FOR MEN

# STARGAZER
## Kent R. Brown

*(It is nearing seven o'clock in the evening. MARK, dressed in casual clothes, is in his backyard preparing for a cookout. On a nearby wooden table—aged through years of rain and general neglect—sit hamburger buns, relish, ketchup, paper plates, etc.)*

## Mark

We used to spend hours out here in the summers. Dad loved to get a stack of short ribs and slather on his special barbecue sauce. And then Jimmie and I and Katie and Allan would throw down blankets and pillows. And Mother and Dad would sit in the redwood swing Dad built for their 10th anniversary so we could all be out under the stars together and wonder about the universe and God and whether I was ever going to let a girl kiss me or whether Allan would ever stop hitting me at the dinner table or whether Katie really could memorize the Bible backwards.

And Mother would tell us stories about the stars, how they were formed from God's tears. "Why does God cry, Mommy?" Katie would ask. "Because he was so happy when he created my children," she said, "that he just cried with joy."

And we'd have spelling bees! Cassiopia, Camelopardalis, Andromeda.

I loved the sound of them, the sense of enormity. How galactical it all was. We hated to spell Aquarius because Mom always launched off into several songs from *Hair*. On special occasions, when the rains came and we couldn't sleep in the backyard, Dad would read *The War of the Worlds* and we would create all the sound effects.

The night Armstrong walked on the moon, Dad bought extra-long cables and wires and Allan moved the television all the way out here. And Katie set up her telescope that Mom had gotten for her 11th birthday and we each took turns looking up at the moon. We couldn't see anything, of course, but Armstrong was up there anyway. We ended up watching the television instead. Inside that little box of tubes and lines and wires and whatnot was a man walking on the moon. Funny how reality doesn't seem to be as fascinating as fantasy.

The other day, while we were making the arrangements for Mother's funeral, I read that they've discovered the brightest star ever seen in the Milky Way. This newest, brightest star is so big that if it were here, it would fill in all the space contained within the orbit of Earth. Isn't that phenomenal? It is so powerful that it glows with the energy of 10 million suns. Astronomers think it's about 25,000 light-years from Earth. It's over there somewhere. *(Points to the sky.)* In the direction of the constellation **Sagittarius**. The Hubble telescope found it for us. They call it the Pistol Star because the shape of the glowing nebula of dust and gas around it reminded them of a pistol. There are books of hundreds of names you can choose for your baby but if a magnificent phenomenon such as a gargantuan star is shaped like a turnip, then it might be called the Turnip Star. Or how about a Rutabaga? The star is erupting great amounts of gas and losing size. They estimate it only has three million years or so to live. Our own Sun can do better than that. It has about five billion years before it goes.

Mother thought she had more time before she went, too, but she didn't. All the signs were there. "I'm bloating out just like the stars do, son," she said. "Soon I'll be a white dwarf." When a star dies, it dies in fits and starts, throbs and shudders in a kind of last gasp. All that remains, finally, is a compact, burned-out stellar corpse known as a white dwarf. But a dying star reseeds the cosmos, scatters raw material needed to create new planets, new visions. About once a year an old star dies in the Milky Way...dies with a flourish, a brightness of purpose to fuse the imaginations of others.

In a minute, Dad and Katie and Allan and Jimmie and all their kids will come out here. We're going to cook up some of Dad's famous short ribs and tell stories about Mother and look up at the stars. Dad's throat is bothering him so I've been elected to read a chapter from *The War of the Worlds*. *(Beat.)* And maybe we'll all sing a verse or two from "The Age of Aquarius."

# THE THIRD SCOURGE
*Vin Morreale, Jr.*

*(WOODROW sits in front of a small card table with a computer, its monitor turned away from the audience. He reads a few pages from his manual, looks confused, then dramatically presses a single key. We hear a loud beep indicating something has just gone terribly wrong. He groans, tosses the manual aside in frustration, then stands and addresses the audience.)*

### Woodrow

In my time, I've lived through three major catastrophes... The Great Depression... World War II... and the invention of the personal computer.

Now I firmly believe the computer was invented for the sole purpose of making me look like a dodo in front of my own grandchildren. Those little poops jabber on about gigabytes and virtual reality until my head starts to spin. It's like we're speaking two completely different languages!

To me, *RAM* is a male goat, a *chip* is something you snack on, and *Windows compatibility* means your curtains are cut to the right size. *Boot up* is how my old Army drill sergeant got us to do so many darn pushups. I ain't gonna tell you what he threatened to put his boot up if we didn't do them!

As far as I'm concerned, *Internet* is where a fish goes, and *modem* is what I did to my front and backyards whenever the grass got too tall. I up and *modem*. A *floppy disk* is what I got when I left my old Sinatra records in the sun. And *PC* is what I do after I take too many vitamins.

A *hard drive* is not some kind of memory device... A hard drive is what I had to do to get to work every morning for five years. If I didn't, I wouldn't have been able to afford to send my kids to the kind of colleges that got them those cushy jobs that let them buy those dad-blasted computers in the first place!

I try to explain all this to my grandchildren... but they just smile and shake their heads in the same exact way I used to smile and shake my head when my own granddaddy couldn't begin to understand how our old Philco television set worked.

Hell, maybe that's the thing about technology... It moves so fast, that people with old legs just can't keep up with it.

But a couple of generations from now, my smug little grandkids will have their own grandchildren smiling and shaking their heads at them over some new anti-gravity machine, or space deodorant, or some such nonsense. I'd sure like to see them take a gigabyte outa them Apples!

# PROGRESSIVE PASSION
*Mike Thomas*

*(BOB is 68 years old and has been the sole caregiver since his wife developed Alzheimer's seven years ago. He is trying to come to terms with being forced to place his wife of thirty years in a nursing home. Even though this decision is against his will, he knows that constant caregiving is wearing him down.)*

## Bob

I said I'd never do it. I told her. I looked her in the eye, held her hand and I promised her. That was our commitment. It's been seven years now, just seven years; that sounds like nothing after being married thirty. I've cleaned her up when she messed herself, I've fixed her meals and fed her. She started falling, though, more and more. The doctor said she was entering another stage. She fell and hit her head on something as she was going down. I started getting rid of all the hard furniture and padding the corners with towels and rubber bands and we were doing fine. And one day she just laid down in the middle of the kitchen floor. I couldn't pick her up, and I tried. She was lying on her side and she was conscious, but she was deadweight, she forgot how to get up, I think. And me with my back, I just couldn't do it. And all of a sudden I'd never felt more like a failure in my life. I had failed her. I sat down on a kitchen chair, put my head in my hands and cried like a baby. She was looking at me and I heard her say in a lucid moment, "It's okay, it's okay, honey." She usually just mumbled or spoke gibberish so this was big news. She actually spoke real words that pertained to the situation, and instead of getting down on the floor with her and madly hugging her, I just automatically started talking back. I said "No, it's not okay. I can't lift you. I can't get you off the floor. So, no, it's not okay." And she looked up at me and smiled and said, "I love you." I hadn't heard her say that in over three years. Her body had shut down but her mind was still speaking. It was a beautiful moment someone gave me...us.

I finally got her up with a lot of coaching and small steps. It took thirty minutes. I looked at the bruises on her arm and head as she smiled her smile. *(Pause.)* She wasn't sleeping at night either, I had to lock all the doors so she wouldn't wander off while I was asleep. I quit my job to stay home and take care of her. People said it wasn't really a marriage anymore, and that made me so mad. It wasn't any of their business. In some ways it was more of one. I felt very needed. I was able to see my unconditional love for my wife every day. I realized that day that I was doing her a disservice by keeping her at home, but, God, I do not want to put her in a nursing home. ...I just didn't know how bad it would get. Alzheimer's is death on earth. She has deteriorated so much she just sits and stares. She doesn't know who I am but she sure seems to like holding my hand. I still feel something when I hold her hand too. I know she feels it. I see it in her eyes. God, I miss her already.

# RECORD HOLDER
*Joseph Robinette*

*(A MAN in his 70's, still spry and lively, is discussing a long-time malady which has affected him since childhood. He addresses the audience.)*

## Phil

I would have made the *Guinness Book of World Records* if they'd had a category for *my* particular achievement—"World's Oldest Virgin—Male Division." ...No, I'm not impotent or sick or disinterested. I've had the desire for over 73 years. Well, more like 65 years if you want to get technical about it. I didn't get my first—you know—"physical stirrings of desire" till I was eight. That was back during the depression. It was a warm spring evening. My older sister had invited Janie Watkins over to spend the night and I peeped in on them just in time to see Janie getting undressed for bed. I'd never seen anything like it before. Maybe once or twice I'd seen my sister without anything on when she was younger, but that didn't count. Janie Watkins without any clothes on—at age 14, and with sprouting breasts—*did* count. A *lot.*

Just then my mother yelled for me to go in and take my Saturday night bath... As I was lying in the warm water, playing with my toy boat, I couldn't get Janie Watkins out of my mind. And something happened to me that had never happened before. I started to get a...you-know-what. Before long it was straight and hard as a Lincoln Log. It scared me a little at first, but then I started liking it. Needless to say, I wasn't playing with my toy boat anymore. Then a funny thing happened—I got the hiccups, real bad. And they didn't go away till the you-know-what went down.

The next time it happened was a couple of weeks later in school, when we had a substitute teacher—a real pretty lady named Miss Murphy. When I had trouble with my arithmetic, she came back to my desk to help me. As she leaned over, I felt the hiccups coming on... The only period of time when I didn't get an occasional you-know-what—or the hiccups—was when I joined the Army in 1942. Between the saltpeter and living in foxholes for three years, I didn't find too much to get excited about.

But I did make a promise to myself that I'd see a doctor about the situation just as soon as the war was over, and I did. He asked me if I ever got a you-know-what when I was asleep. I said, "How would I know? I'm always asleep." So, he told me to buy a roll of three-cent stamps and wrap a few of them around the base of my—well, you know—then check it out the next morning. If the stamps were broken apart at the perforations, that meant I'd had a you-know-what. And sure enough, the next morning those stamps were completely apart. They were also stuck to my skin. With all that postage down there, I could have sent my private parts to Peru and back. Well, the doctor said since I hadn't waked myself up with the hiccups, this was all in my head, so he sent me to a specialist who talked with a real thick accent and asked me a lot of questions about my mother. He charged me fifteen dollars and told me to make another appointment with his secretary. I didn't. I did re-up in the Army where I stayed till I retired in '78. Since then I've done a lot of hunting and fishing and gardening—but fortunately, not a whole lot of hiccupping.

But things began to change about six months ago. I was visiting an old Army buddy, Vern Maxwell, whose wife had recently passed away. Vern asked me if I wanted to go to a dance sponsored by a group he'd just joined—the Single Seniors Society. I didn't want to go, but I knew he did—and his car was in the shop—so I drove us to the dance. My only goal was to sit quietly by myself near the punchbowl, get drunk and let Vern drive us home. I was on my third glass of punch when this very attractive woman came over to me. She looked no more than 50-55 tops; she later told me she was 64—and a widow. She asked me if I wanted to dance. I didn't know how to dance, and I told her so, but she said leave it up to her. And I did. She was soft—and warm—and smelled like fresh flowers. And before long, I started feeling an old sensation again—first in the lower region, and then, of course, in the upper. I apologized for my hiccups, and she suggested we get a glass of punch—maybe that would help. So we drank and talked till everything subsided. Then she asked me to dance again. This time the hiccups started almost immediately, and I tried to break away. But she wouldn't let go, so we kept on dancing, and I kept on hiccupping, and after a minute or two she whispered softly in my ear, "You've got an erection, haven't you?" I was floored. I'd purposely kept my midsection from touching hers, hoping she wouldn't feel it—so I asked her how she knew. "Probably a psychosomatic manifestation of an early childhood experience that has caused you to harbor a subconscious guilt over the years." "My God," I said, "are you a psychiatrist?" "No," she replied, "I'm a horny old lady who reads a lot. Now, why don't we go to my place and get to the bottom of all this." And we did. I was so dazed—and delighted—and a little drunk, I forgot to tell Vern I was leaving.

I went home with that lovely, horny old lady that night, and we've been together ever since. I never did get over the hiccups. In fact, I get 'em about twice a week. I know—at my age, you don't believe it. But remember, I've got a lot of catching up to do. And she loves it when I start hiccupping. "It makes me know you're glad to see me," she says.

*(Looking at his watch.)*
And speaking of that, I've got to be going now. We're heading out for dinner with Vern and *his* girlfriend in a couple of hours. But if I leave now and get home a little early—

*(He hiccups.)*
—well, I guess you know what I've got in mind. Kinda hard to hide it.

*(He hiccups again.)*
I've really gotta go now. If I don't get home soon, I'll be hiccupping all the way out to Howard Johnson's tonight. Could be embarrassing. See ya.

*(He exits hiccupping.)*

# THE TIME-SHARE RAG
### *Kent R. Brown*

(*This time-share salesman never stops working the Johnsons. If he's not trying to get them to willingly share information about themselves, he's gathering information from how they sit, listen, reply, make eye contact and so on. In short, the Johnsons are an intricate safe and BOBBY is the consummate safecracker. But he may have met his match in Mrs. Johnson.*)

## Bobby

Hello, Mr. ... let's see here...
(*Looking at the identification card.*)
Yes, I've got it now. Joshton. Very good to meet you, Mr. and Mrs. Joshton. Ah, sorry. Johnson. Yes, I see it now...new glasses. I'm having a hard time getting adjusted to... Mrs. Johnson, I love that brooch, my mother had a brooch just like...my name's Bobby Kelly. Been here at Whispering Glades for eleven years giving folks like you the opportunity of a lifetime to have the vacation of your dreams. You folks having fun yet? Is today something, or what? Eighty-seven degrees on February 13th and where are you in from? Otanga, Oklahoma? You're pulling my leg. In the panhandle, is it? Are you sure? Get some snow there, do you? I know you do.

We've got some donuts and coffee over...no, that's completely up to you, Mrs. Johnson...no, you don't have to eat all the donuts to go on the free Valentine's Day cruise.

You two young people will absolutely love the cruise, by the way...uh, yes, it's free, free, free, Mrs. Johnson. As God is my witness. No, you can't leave right now. We have to visit our facilities first, see our beautiful vacation opportunity here at Whispering Glades because it's all about opportunities, isn't it? Really. You work hard all your life, now it's time to kick back and...after our visit here, Mrs. Johnson, our cruise colleagues will answer your every question. Oh, about two hours is all, maybe a little longer...my, but you have a full-bodied laugh, Mrs. Johnson. She must keep you moving, Mr. Johnson.

Now, you're both here for how many days? Five? Seven days, six nights, right? And you flew in? No, came by car. Drove straight through to save a hotel bill. I see. Mrs. Johnson fixed boxed lunches going eighty-two miles an hour! Didn't save on gas, did you, Mrs. Johnson? Sorry, just making a joke. Bet you've got the first dime you ever earned, don't you, Mr. Johnson? Oh, Mrs. Johnson has it.

So, you're staying at the Towers? The Shangri-La? The Tropical Palms? Oh, the Super 8 off the clover leaf. The Valentine's Day special. She can get blood out of a turnip, can't she, Mr. Johnson? So, six nights at $85 dollars a night, right? No! $41.76 with tax. Good. So $41.76 times six is around $240 for the length of your stay, Okay? $250.56, Mrs. Johnson? Thank you. Right on the money. So, let's set the average meal expense per day at, say, $75 total per day, okay? For the both of you? No? I'm wrong again? So, how much, Mrs. Johnson? Eleven dollars a day with coupons and a two-for-one senior's special at the cafeteria next to the movie theatre down on Second Avenue? Does that include Mr. Johnson, too?

No I don't know the place, Mrs. Johnson, and...well, you can write it here on the back of my notepad. Thank you, I'll keep that in mind. So $55 or so for five days for food plus $250 or so for lodging and gas at...$128? Thanks again, Mrs. Johnson.

*(Beginning to lose his composure.)*
But that's one only way, Mrs. Johnson. I caught you there. So you have to add that to the total...pardon? No, you don't have to do anything I say, Mrs. Johnson. Very sorry. She's a handful, isn't she, Mr. Johnson? No, sorry, I didn't mean anything by that, Mrs. Johnson, it's just a figure of speech.

Okay, okay, let's get back on track here, shall we? You want a relaxing vacation every year, don't you, Mr. Johnson? You don't know? I should ask Mrs. Johnson? What's the matter? Can't stand up to the old battleax? Sorry, I'm tired. Low energy in the afternoon. Think I'll eat one of those donuts. What are you writing there, Mrs. Johnson? Next year's Christmas cards? You could be dead by then, Mrs. Johnson. Could you put those up for now so we can move along here, everybody? If I don't finish my pitch here and show you how damn happy you'll be spending only airfare and $300 a week for food with a gorgeous view of Lake Winnesplache then you don't get the damn cruise, Mrs. Johnson and I'll kill whoever put you on my roster this morning, is that clear, very clear?

What did you say? Are we finished yet? Yes, Mrs. Johnson, I'm finished. You win. I'll sign anything! You must be an extraordinary man, Mr. Johnson, not to have committed suicide before now. But the day's still young! Get her out of my sight! Take the cruise. Take two cruises. And Happy Valentine's Day, Mr. Johnson. Whatever the hell were you thinking of when you married...

*(Another couple has stepped forward.)*

...oh, hello. No, I'm fine, just a little tired. Yes, you're next. You folks must be the...

*(BOBBY looks at identification card.)*

MadDougals. Well, isn't that wonderful...MacDonalds? Sorry. Must be these glasses. Have you written all your Christmas cards for next Christmas yet, Mrs. MacDonald? You have? How wonderful!

*(Extending his hand.)*

My name is Bobby Kelly and I'm here to make all our dreams come true!

# THE BONFIRES
*Kenneth Robbins*

*(HOWARD CRAWFORD LANG, 59, tells his son, Winston, about an experience he shared with a Japanese woman near the destroyed city of Hiroshima in October 1945.)*

## Howard

There was this woman, Omiya, about the same age as your mother, Winston, only prettier. Remarkable eyes. Her hair had been singed off by the firestorm following the bomb and she wore a rag around her head and carried her baby strapped to her back. Sumiko, her child. We spent time together. She didn't speak English, I didn't speak Japanese, but that didn't matter, we still talked. I took her little things for Sumiko, tins of sardines, biscuits, jam, sticks of gum. Sumiko ate the gum like it was food. Omiya finally accepted me, I think, got to where she looked forward to my visits. Only, she was sick, got sicker. She and Sumiko lived with fifty others in a lean-to built of rubble. My CO found out I was giving her food, and he ordered me to stop. I don't know why. Just stop. Something about aiding and abetting... I didn't stop, though. How could I? They needed... *(Pause.)*

Sumiko died. No more than a year old. The kid had dark spots on her tummy, and her hair fell out, and her skin turned orange and peeled off. It was the bomb sickness, they said. Omiya carried Sumiko on her back for two days before she allowed them to burn the body. I was with her when they took Sumiko to the bonfire. Those fires never went out. Only fuel they had was the bodies... My CO caught me again, my pack full of food. Ordered me confined to ship. Last time I saw Omiya, she had brown spots on her forehead and her skin was turning orange... Christ, we were sitting aboard the Circe, a cargo ship, Winston. We had more food and medicine and bottled water than we knew what to do with. And they wouldn't let us help those people. I wasn't allowed off ship again, not while we were docked in Ujina Harbor. And our supplies stayed on board with me. I don't know what happened to Omiya. But you could see the smoke from the deck. The fires never went out.

# IT'S HALF-FULL
### Michael Wright

*(BILL, 90 going on 25, is speaking to a group; he's dressed in a clown outfit, complete with make-up and a squeeze-horn attached to his belt.)*

## Bill

Good morning to each and every one of you! I am absolutely delighted to be here, not only as the chief clown welcomer to all you future clowns, but also as the oldest clown in this chapter of the Society of Do-Gooders. You are undertaking a noble purpose, my friends! Our hospital visits, soup kitchens, and food and clothing drives help thousands. Our annual participation in the Macy's Parade and numerous other parades and events all add up to nearly a million dollars in funds raised last year—just by the clown division. And think of how your resume will read: "Skills: making children smile, bringing a glow to a senior person's cheeks, driving teensy cars, and knowing how to walk in huge floppy shoes."
*(He demonstrates a little; honks his horn.)*
Now, I thought what I'd do today is try to give you fellas a little insight on what it takes to be a clown. You'll get all the other training you need from Ed and the boys back there, but I guess what I want to talk about is the heart of the clown. Some people think it's about being funny but I disagree—it's about being fun. In essence, I would sum it up as eternal optimism, seeing the glass as half-full, if you know what I mean. Because the truth is that just painting a

smile on your mug doesn't mean you're smiling. No, it has to be there in your eyes, in the way the wrinkles of your face line up, and even in the way you walk, because when you go into a hospital with little kids, believe-you-me, they'll know if you're genuine or not. Now, you take me, for example. When I get up in the morning, when I'm finally standing—and at 90 that's no small feat—

*(Flaps a shoe; honks.)*

Get it: small feet? Anyway, I get this rushing in my ears when I stand up. Most people would start worrying about their blood pressure or whatever, start reaching for the doctor's number or the glycerine pills or something but I know what I'm really hearing in there. What is it? The sound of all the toilets flushing in the complex around me, because everybody got up this morning and had a good visit! And when the air is so cold on my back I feel like I'm turning into a hunchback—why, then I know it means ice cream for desert at suppertime! Cataracts? A need to get past the peripheral—who the hell needs to know what's going on over there? It's what's right here in front of me that matters. Heartburn? Fire in the stove. Gas? A good reason to change locations. Shaky hands? Natural rhythm. Pancreatic cancer? Six months to live.

*(At the reaction of the group.)*

Oh, no, no, no, fellas, don't get upset. That's what I'm talking about right there in a nutshell! Okay, so, fine, I'm going to die, lemme see hands of who ain't? All right, so then, lemme ask you this: do any of *you* know when? Might be this afternoon after clown class, run over by some old fart like me who shouldn't be driving. Might be tomorrow, airplane falls out of the sky and you're a flapjack. Could be Saturday a week, you're poisoned at a wedding reception by some mysterious meat nobody had time to check. Guys, guys, look! Face it, everything out there is risk, but the clown? The clown is guaranteed. With the clown, all there is is happiness, silliness, and nothing but smiles. So who could be happier than the clown who knows when he's going to go and how? And what he wants to wear in the casket?

*(He does a little turn to indicate he'll be buried in his clown outfit; it gets the laugh he wants and he's pleased. After a beat, still smiling:)*

And, anyway, you don't want a catalogue of what's out there for somebody my age, believe me, and the truth is I've run my race. It's time to get off the planet and let somebody else have a turn. And it was a hell of a run, big shoes or no.

*(A beat; he's lost in thought for a moment, then smiles broadly.)*

Anyway, that's how I see it.

*(He honks his horn. Blackout.)*

# PREPARING THE SCENE

Regardless of how challenging and fulfilling performing a monologue may be, most actors prefer acting in a scene or in an entire play. After all, audiences come to witness two or more real people—not celluloid images—locked in a struggle of conflicting desires. But good scene work is far more than delivering well-memorized lines. It must be infused with a sense of reality, of immediacy. It must reverberate with behavior the audience believes is true to life. The following suggestions will aid in breathing life-like reality into your scene work.

**Look for the Power Shifts in the Scene**

• Good drama is like an exciting athletic competition. No one really wants to watch a lopsided game. We want the contest to be close with the lead changing frequently before the final outcome is known. Audiences come to watch a struggle of wills, a contest of two energies coming into conflict with one another.

• Make your acting more life-like by discovering those moments in the scene when power, influence and/or dominance shifts from one character to the other. See who has the upper hand in an argument or who has the high ground. Chances are the arrival of new information will stimulate the shift in energy and power.

• Determine how your character feels and thinks about the power shifts. What does your character do to gain an advantage so the objective will be more successfully achieved?

## Look for the Love in the Scene

- When you are playing a scene full of anger and hurt, avoid yelling all your lines. This approach lacks texture and nuance and forces the actor to keep plowing through the scene like a locomotive.
- Chances are, a scene about anger or hate is really a scene about lost love of one kind or another. Most of the pain in life comes in the departures we've experienced: the loss of loved ones, the loss of youth or physical or mental prowess, the loss of feeling close and needed by someone. We respond by feeling defeated, perplexed, angry, frustrated, amazed or frightened.
- We seldom yell when we are deeply angry. We might talk slowly, in a disarmingly quiet voice, or speak condescendingly or even laugh defensively. We often search for the right word to describe how we feel and then become more frustrated at our inability to find the precise expression. Consequently, a fight scene may really be a love scene gone bad. What we are really doing is trying to understand what went wrong so we can fix it, reestablish a positive connection with someone.

## A Word or Two About Comedy

- Actors often mistakenly say, when cast in a comedy, "Oh, good, this will be easy. No work and lots of fun." Well, you should certainly have fun, but comedy is far from easy. Don't make the error of thinking that comedy is light, fluffy and trivial. Good comic writing examines very serious issues. *The Odd Couple* by Neil Simon, for example, is a serious play about how selfish behaviors can destroy a solid and wonderful friendship.

- Audience members constantly deal with petty and absurd problems in their lives—irritating next-door neighbors, irascible in-laws, and so on. They have come to the theatre to see how other people, you and your fellow characters, solve your problems and survive a series of mishaps.

- When you play a character in a comedy, be sure you go through the same character checklist you do when cast in a serious drama. Be sure you know what your character wants and what the stakes are. Even though comedy puts the spotlight on character foibles, you should not think you (your character) is funny. The humor comes when the audience recognizes believable characters caught in an absurd or wacky situation who continue struggling to reestablish a sense of balance.

- Good comic lines derive from the ironic viewpoint the characters have of themselves, their predicament and the prospects of surviving the situation.

- Most of us are unaware of our annoying, endearing or funny habits, phrases and attitudes. As a three-dimensional character in a "real" make-believe situation, be sure you don't telegraph the "funny" moments to the audience.

# DUETS

# QUE SERA, SERA
*Katherine Snodgrass*

## CHARACTERS

ANNE: An older leading lady.
MICHAEL: A younger leading man.

PLACE: Anne's New York apartment.
TIME: New Year's Day, 1997.

AT RISE: *MICHAEL follows ANNE into the room. She is tipsy, he is not. She waves an open champagne bottle.*

ANNE. Oh, the room is spinning, spinning!
MICHAEL. Sit down, Anne.
ANNE. HAP-py New Year! Champagne for every— Oops!
MICHAEL. Anne. Sit.
ANNE. Oooh, I'm a doggie. Grrr-uffff! The couch is circling. Uh-oh!
MICHAEL. Sit, Fido.
ANNE. Grrr-ufff-rufff! Look, I'm in the window and I'm wagging my tail.
MICHAEL. Cute.
ANNE. Arf-arf! Quick, who sang that?
MICHAEL. Sang what?
ANNE. That song, that song! Where the doggie is so happy. *(She kisses him and begins to unbutton his shirt.)*

MICHAEL. This is a song I should know?
ANNE. I'm wagging my taaaay-ill.
MICHAEL. I should know this song?
ANNE. Grrrr-uff.
MICHAEL. It's something from the fifties, isn't it?
ANNE. Is it?
MICHAEL. The All-Important Decade of which I have no personal recollection and, therefore, no valid opinion of its worth. *(That stops her.)*
ANNE. Pardon me?
MICHAEL. That's what you've been trying to tell me all night, isn't it? I didn't live through the Renaissance which, of course, was the 1950s, so basically, I'm unpresentable to your battery of friends—the youngest of which, I might add, was 70, if he was a day. And if I just knew who Munkolani was—
ANNE. Mantovani.
MICHAEL. —then I could pass as your date, I could be a contender. However, I wasn't born until 1960, that's six-0, which, by the way, doesn't mean you have to apologize for my youth every time you introduce me. It just means I don't give a damn about Doris Day, I never thought Sid Caesar was funny, and I don't remember where I was when Kennedy was shot because I was three, count 'em, THREE YEARS OLD! *(Silence.)*
ANNE. I wish you hadn't told me that.
MICHAEL. Don't tell me you didn't know.
ANNE. How could I? I thought everyone loved Sid Caesar.
MICHAEL. Not this superficial, brain-dead product of the video cartel, but then, I don't know what's funny without *Show of Shows* and Carl Reiner to hit me on the head with it!

ANNE. Oh, we've been playing catch-up on the kinoscopes.
MICHAEL. No, WE—that is, you and I—have been humping like bunnies for the past three weeks, so when I want to catch up on the olden times, I go ask my mom. *(Pause.)* I'm sorry.
ANNE. Oh.
MICHAEL. I didn't mean—! I'm sorry.
ANNE. Well, it's true. I suppose I could be your mother. I've played Juliet. What was she—13? Fourteen?
MICHAEL. You couldn't be—
ANNE. I played Clytemnestra once at the Public, but I hated that Orestes.
MICHAEL. You couldn't be my mother in real life—
ANNE. No, actually, I *could*. If I had just met Bobby Bettis when I was 11—
MICHAEL *(overlapping)*. No, no, no, I didn't mean—
ANNE. —who knows, under the stars—
MICHAEL. I'd never think of you as my mother!
ANNE. —with a little hooch from his father's stash—
MICHAEL. WILL YOU LISTEN TO ME? *(Silence.)* Is the room still spinning?
ANNE. I wish.
MICHAEL. Seriously, then. Who am I to you?
ANNE. Who—who—who do you want to be?
MICHAEL. We've been...dating, right?
ANNE. Right.
MICHAEL. We...get along, right?
ANNE. Right.
MICHAEL. I want to know what I can expect in the future. *(He waits.)* Do you think we *have* a future, or...?
ANNE. Or...am I just interested in your body? *(Pause.)* I *am* interested in your body, but... What's your name again?

MICHAEL *(moving to leave).* I'm gone.

ANNE. Mikey, I'm kidding!

MICHAEL. No. *(Turning back.)* No, it's not "Mikey." I prefer the adult version at this juncture. "Mike" or "Michael," but no "Mikey."

ANNE. I'm sorry, I'm sorry, I didn't mean to hurt your feelings. But you and I, we have virtually nothing in common. *(Looking at him.)* Well...almost nothing. I mean, you grew up with the Brady Bunch, I was weaned on Imogene Coca, and don't say "Who's that?" You work nine to five, you haven't even seen me on stage, and...! Age doesn't mean you lose your fear, you know. If anything, you get more *afraid* because you're closer to...losing your teeth.

MICHAEL. Your teeth look fine.

ANNE. They should, they're not mine. Oh my God, I'm living a cliché! You'd think, after thirty years in this business, I'd be living a better play! "Older woman seduces younger man who leaves her weeping, heartbroken, on the edge of despair." *Merde,* it's a melodrama!

MICHAEL. Tennessee Williams.

ANNE. Oh, please, that is such a male fantasy! Blanche did not seduce Stanley.

MICHAEL. I meant *Sweet Bird of Youth.*

ANNE. *Sweet Bird of*—!! Oh, and since when do you know so much about it, anyway? You seem to have picked up quite a few theatre tidbits in Joseph's office. You'd think my own agent would protect me from— So now he's getting you to read plays? I thought you were his accountant.

MICHAEL. I didn't— What I mean is, maybe he falls in love with her.

ANNE. Joseph?

MICHAEL. No, the younger man. With the older woman. He's not that much younger, remember. She just thinks he is.

ANNE. Oh, believe me, she knows to the day.

MICHAEL. I'm not that much younger than you.

ANNE. Well, of course not.

MICHAEL. I'm 42.

ANNE. Your driver's license says—

MICHAEL. I lied. *(Beat.)* You checked my driver's license?

ANNE. You lied?

MICHAEL. I'm 42. That would make me 9 when Kennedy died. I was in Mrs. Hoag's fifth-grade art class drawing "John Glenn In Space" when the news came down the pike.

ANNE. You *lied*? To the motor vehicle department. Why?

MICHAEL. I'm not the only one embarrassed about my age.

ANNE. I am not embarrassed about—!

MICHAEL. Tell me about our future, Anne.

ANNE. What? I don't know, I haven't let myself think about—

MICHAEL. But now that I'm old enough to be taken seriously? *(Pause.)*

ANNE. I apologize for my friends. They're asses.

MICHAEL. They're not the only ones.

ANNE. No, they're not. *(Pause. She sits.)*

MICHAEL. Are you feeling sick from the champagne?

ANNE. I'm having a Chekovian moment.

MICHAEL. In all good conscience, I should tell you everything. I mean, about working at the agency.

*Duets* 77

ANNE. I knew it. You're not an accountant.

MICHAEL. No. I mean, I *am* an accountant and have been for ten years. But I'm not just a C.P.A.

ANNE. You're working in an agent's office, you're embarrassed about your age, you're reading Tennessee Will—! Oh my God, my God! YOU'RE AN ACTOR!

MICHAEL. No, no, don't worry, it's nothing like that. Really.

ANNE. N-n-no? You're not—?

MICHAEL. No. Really.

ANNE. No lying now! You're *not*—!

MICHAEL. NO.

ANNE. Oh, thank you! Thank God.

MICHAEL. I'm a playwright. *(Silence.)*

ANNE. A playwright. For the theatre? *(Beat.)* Is this your way of telling me you're in AA?

MICHAEL. No, no.

ANNE. Oh, no, I see. You're the one sitting in rehearsals with that condescending smirk of superiority on your face. You're that tobacco-stained slob who smokes in the dressing room and gives me line-readings *after* we've opened.

MICHAEL. Well...I'm trying to be.

ANNE. And you can stop this second, because—! But wait! Oh, no, wait! Writers are notorious for—! Their lives are fodder for—! Oh my God, you're writing as we speak! Aren't you, aren't you, don't deny it!

MICHAEL. I don't know. *(Beat.)* Of course not!

ANNE. Did you think I could help you, is that it? That if you went out with me, that somehow I could—I could—

MICHAEL. No! No, I never thought you'd be interested in my plays. I wouldn't dare hope—! You couldn't help me get them produced anyway.

ANNE. Oh, really! And why is that?

MICHAEL. They're Absurd. *(Beat.)* That's with a *capital* "A." Beckett, Ionesco, Pinter—

ANNE. I'm familiar with "absurd."

MICHAEL. And I did so see you on stage. In *Six Characters*. You had on this black dress that was slit up to here and flame-red hair that ran down your back. It was like... like...

ANNE. A wig?

MICHAEL. —like a torch! And when you spoke, fire came out of your mouth. You spit it at the other actors. You were brave and unforgiving, the most beautiful thing I'd ever seen. When you left the stage, the light left with you, and when you came back, I couldn't take my eyes away. I still can't. I had to give it my best shot. *(He starts to go, she stops him.)*

ANNE. Michael... The fifties were boring, as I recall. I don't miss them much.

MICHAEL. Don't you? Not even Sid Caesar?

ANNE. My parents made me watch him. *(Beat.)* Are you really 42?

MICHAEL. Yes. *(Absolutely.)* And no. Reality on stage is subject to change depending on— *(She waits.)* I'm 36. I was 3 when Kennedy was shot. I didn't lie to the motor vehicle department for fear they'd make me stand in line. I'm a playwright. I have a day job and I thank God for it because it's how I met you, but I write for the stage. I believe in the power of words, and I revere actors as the heart and the soul of the theatre. I revere one actor in particular.

ANNE. She's afraid, you see. Afraid that one day she'll wake up in the morning and she'll see you watching her in the mirror, and...and I won't be fiery or pretty or even brave, but I will be me, and I'll see in your eyes that it's not enough. I'm afraid in the end I'll have no one.

MICHAEL. I can't tell the future, Anne, but I know everything about the present. You don't have to be afraid. Not now. Never with me. Tell me this, if you're so worried. The truth. *(Beat—because this is important.)* Where will you be...if I can't write a good play? *(Silence. A holding of breath.)*

ANNE. I am going to be...so in love with you. *(They touch as lights fade.)*

# SWEET TUESDAY FALLS
## *Julie Jensen*

### CHARACTERS

FLORA ROOTS: Mid-60s.
MACEL: Mid-60s.

PLACE: Rural America.
TIME: The present.


AT RISE: *MACEL's adult son, Collis, has just embarrassed his mother by appearing naked in the bushes outside the front window during the visit of FLORA ROOTS, the town's first-grade teacher.*

FLORA ROOTS. Macel, he's right out here in these bushes by the porch.
MACEL. I know where he is.
FLORA ROOTS. I can see him. *(Pause.)* You better go get him.
MACEL. He knows the way in.
FLORA ROOTS. He's out there naked, Macel! You act like that's all right with you.
MACEL *(exploding)*. Nobody ever asked me if what they was doin' was all right with me.
FLORA ROOTS. They don't ask, Macel. You have to tell them.
MACEL. Warren never asked me if he could fill that yard up with all those motors. Ten thousand assorted car parts.

FLORA ROOTS. All the more reason you should be firmer with Collis.

MACEL. You should see all the radios he left. The drawers are full of radios. Top of every closet, there's radios. The basement's full of them. Their boxes taped together, no knobs, faces gone, plugs cut off.

FLORA ROOTS. And that's exactly why you've got to get firmer with Collis. You don't want to make the same mistake twice in a row.

MACEL. Those motors are still out there. You go out there with a shovel, anywhere in that back yard. You'll hit a rusted generator or a rusted alternator.

FLORA ROOTS. I was never in your back yard, Macel.

MACEL. It's full of generators and alternators.

FLORA ROOTS. But, Macel. Collis is standing in your *front* yard.

MACEL. Well, it'll be sundown soon.

FLORA ROOTS. You're not leaving him out there till then.

MACEL. He's leaving himself out there till he leaves himself in.

FLORA ROOTS. Not the right use of those words, Macel.

MACEL. Sorry.

FLORA ROOTS *(long pause)*. I hope this is at least teaching you something, Macel. That you've got to do something about him.

MACEL. What do you suggest, Flora Roots?

FLORA ROOTS. Well, send him away.

MACEL. You can't send your children away.

FLORA ROOTS. You can if they're behaving like this!

MACEL. Where would you have me send him?

FLORA ROOTS. Out of town.

MACEL. I already sent him to the Navy. And what happened to him there?
FLORA ROOTS. He got kicked out.
MACEL. Yes, he did.
FLORA ROOTS. So what's next?
MACEL. That's up to him, I think.
FLORA ROOTS. But he is out in your yard stark naked.
MACEL. And Jess was lost on the post office lawn this afternoon.
FLORA ROOTS. Jess is an old man. Collis is still a boy.
MACEL. He's 28.
FLORA ROOTS. Macel. He's faced this way now.
MACEL. It's better if you just ignore him, Flora Roots.
FLORA ROOTS. What if someone comes by?
MACEL. I told him not to go out there today.
FLORA ROOTS. He's looking right at me, straight in the eyes.
MACEL. You're staring straight at him, Flora Roots.
FLORA ROOTS. He's not four feet from me, Macel.
MACEL. I'm going in the kitchen now, Flora Roots, and serve up some sherbert and pecan sandies. Would you care to join me?
FLORA ROOTS. You're just going to leave him? Out there?
MACEL *(calling to Collis)*. Collis, you can come back in when you're dressed. Join us for refreshments if you'd like. *(MACEL exits. FLORA ROOTS remains frozen at the window. Blackout.)*

# THE INHERITANCE
## *Vin Morreale, Jr.*

### CHARACTERS

WILMA: Late 50s.
CATHERINE: Early 60s.

PLACE: Anywhere.
TIME: The present.

AT RISE: *A simple kitchen. WILMA sits at a worn kitchen table. CATHERINE stands by the counter, her back to WILMA. By their postures, we can sense the tension between them.*

CATHERINE. Would you like some coffee, Wilma?
WILMA. You know I don't drink coffee.
CATHERINE. Oh, that's right. I forgot. Tea? With lemon and honey?
WILMA. Just lemon. I'm watching my figure, in case you haven't noticed.
CATHERINE. I noticed. *(An awkward silence as CATHERINE places two cups on the table. She fills them with hot water from a well-worn teapot. In WILMA's, she places a tea bag. In the other, she spoons some instant coffee.)* It is good to see you again, Wilma.
WILMA. Really? That's funny.
CATHERINE. Why is that funny?

WILMA. It is the same thing you said to me the last time I was invited over here. And that was twenty years ago.
CATHERINE. Has it been that long?
WILMA. The last time was when Daddy died.
CATHERINE. There must have been some...
WILMA. There wasn't. But as to my comment, I was wondering why, if it is so good to see me, you wait until two decades pass before we get together?
CATHERINE. Is that entirely my fault?
WILMA. Not entirely. Mostly, would be more accurate.
CATHERINE. You never change, do you?
WILMA. Actually, I've changed a lot. It's you who never changes, Catherine.
CATHERINE. You think so? That's funny. I could have sworn becoming a widow, teetering on the edge of bankruptcy, and fighting a four-year bout with cancer might have changed me a little. *(With a hard smile.)* But I'm probably wrong. You always were so much more perceptive than me. *(Pause.)*
WILMA *(not knowing what else to say)*. This is good tea.
CATHERINE. Thank you. I dropped the bag in the water myself.
WILMA. Why do we do this, Catherine?
CATHERINE. I don't know. Because we are sisters, I suppose. Natural antagonists, linked by an accident of genetics.
WILMA. Cute.
CATHERINE. Thank you.
WILMA. I meant to call you when you were in the hospital.
CATHERINE. I got your card. What was the postmark? Denmark?

WILMA. Detroit.

CATHERINE. Ah, that explains why you were unable to visit. Two tankfuls of gas can be so expensive.

WILMA. I was wrong about you not changing. You have developed quite a talent for sarcasm.

CATHERINE. It keeps me sane. All alone in this big, empty house.

WILMA. I can imagine.

CATHERINE. And how is your life? Roger and the kids?

WILMA. Roger left me for a 23-year-old bimbo. I thought you heard.

CATHERINE. I did. I just wanted to hear it from you... *(Lowering her head.)* I...I'm sorry.

WILMA. That's okay. I need my ego lacerated by my sister every couple of decades.

CATHERINE. I really am sorry, Wilma.

WILMA. Right.

CATHERINE. I guess...I guess knowing you've been through some tragedy too gives us something in common.

WILMA. I suppose the same parents and the fifteen years growing up together wasn't enough for you?

CATHERINE. Let's not do this.

WILMA. I was thinking the same thing. However, I figured it would be more polite to finish my tea before I left.

CATHERINE. That's not what I meant. Please let's not tear each other apart anymore. We aren't little girls fighting over Daddy's and Mommy's affection.

WILMA. Or running from it.

CATHERINE. Or running from it. We can't change the past.

WILMA. I know. But I'm not ready to let it go yet.
CATHERINE. Wilma... You are 55 years old.
WILMA. Fifty-eight.
CATHERINE. Fifty-eight. The point is... when *will* you be able to let it go?
WILMA. I don't know if I ever can.
CATHERINE. Of course you can. You just don't want to. Anger is a great motivator in life. But it is also poison. It makes even the great things you've accomplished seem inadequate.
WILMA. What do you know about what I've—?
CATHERINE *(cutting her off)*. I know everything you have accomplished. Graduated magna cum laude from one of the top engineering schools in the country. You earned a master's degree in engineering back when women in the profession were looked upon as oddities...
WILMA. Or freaks...
CATHERINE. Or freaks... But the point is, you did it. With no support from Mom and Dad... you did it. You made a name for yourself and a career. Then you eloped with Roger, because you didn't want any of the family to spoil your day. You gave birth to twin daughters... Darlene and Deborah... my only nieces, whom I have never seen...
WILMA. I sent you photos...
CATHERINE. Once. When they were 5.
WILMA. You never wrote back.
CATHERINE. You didn't put your return address on the envelope. I took that as a rather blatant hint.
WILMA. It wasn't.
CATHERINE. It was. Why deny it? As I said, the past is over.

WILMA *(softly)*. You would like them. Darlene especially. She is just like you. Practically perfect in every way.

CATHERINE. I was only perfect in your eyes, Wilma.

WILMA. And in our parents' eyes.

CATHERINE. Was that my fault?

WILMA. Wasn't it?

CATHERINE. No. No, it wasn't. Yet, you have wasted our entire lives torturing me, as if I had stolen them away from you. Well, here's a news flash, Wilma. Mommy and Daddy are dead. They have been for twenty years. Isn't it time to drop the sibling rivalry?

WILMA. That's easy for you to say.

CATHERINE. Is it? Is it easy to have that same door slammed in your face year after year? To know that your only living relative still hates you for something that you never did understand? *(Desperately.)* Listen, Wilma. I don't know why Mommy and Daddy lavished everything on me. I have no idea why I was their favorite, and you weren't. I don't know the reasons for any of that. And I don't even know why they left the house to me and not you. I never asked them for it!

WILMA. But you didn't refuse it.

CATHERINE. No, I didn't refuse it... Jonathan was just starting his business at the time. We, uh, didn't have a lot of money.

WILMA. I didn't have a lot of money either.

CATHERINE. I know that. I...I should have borrowed against the house and given you half. It would have been the fair thing to do.

WILMA. It would have. But you didn't do it.

CATHERINE *(taking a deep breath)*. That is why I am doing it now.

WILMA. What?

CATHERINE. I want you to have the house.

WILMA *(stunned)*. You're kidding.

CATHERINE. No, I'm not. I have had it longer than I deserved. It's your turn now.

WILMA. You mean... you are giving me this house?

CATHERINE. It's just a house, Wilma.

WILMA. The only one you have ever lived in.

CATHERINE. While you have been able to travel all around the country. Maybe it's my turn to do that for a while.

WILMA. Two years after bankruptcy and suddenly you have enough to become a jet-setter? A world traveler?

CATHERINE. Look. I'm an old woman now. I've lost my husband. We never had any children. All I have left... All I have is my memories. They don't take much room.

WILMA. Catherine...

CATHERINE. I don't need this much space. I don't need much of anything anymore.

WILMA. I can't take your house.

CATHERINE. It's not my house. It's Mom and Dad's. Now it's yours.

WILMA. I don't want it.

CATHERINE. You don't have a choice. The paperwork is all drawn up. *(She moves to the counter and picks up a manila envelope. She tosses it on the table in front of WILMA. WILMA stares at the envelope, she opens it slowly, examines the paperwork inside.)* It is perfectly legal. I had a lawyer draw it up last week.

WILMA. This isn't what I wanted.

CATHERINE. It doesn't matter. It's yours now.

WILMA. Stop being so damned noble and listen to what I am saying! *(She hesitates, then:)* I don't want the house because I don't need it anymore either... Roger is living in Omaha with his new Barbie-doll wife. Darlene and Deborah have their own families now, and I only hear from them on Mother's Day and Christmas. One ten-minute phone call each. That's all. *(Softly.)* I am 58 years old and completely alone. What makes you think I need this much space any more than you do?

CATHERINE. But you deserve it. This house is your inheritance. Either now, or when I die.

WILMA. What do you mean, when you die?

CATHERINE. Come on, Wilma. Let's face facts. I beat the last battle with cancer. It took everything I had left inside, but I beat it. When it comes back...

WILMA. *If* it comes back...

CATHERINE. If it comes back...I don't think I'll have the strength to fight it anymore. Or a reason to.

WILMA. Catherine...

CATHERINE. But none of that has absolutely anything to do with my giving you the house. Everything is already set in motion. It's officially yours as of the first of next month. No liens. No mortgages at all. The house is yours, free and clear. *(They stare at their cups. Neither one speaks for a while. WILMA is the first to break the silence.)*

WILMA. Okay, Catherine. You win. I will take the house.

CATHERINE. Good.

WILMA. However, I do have one condition.

CATHERINE. Why must you always look a gift horse in the—?

WILMA *(cutting her off)*. My condition is that you agree to stay here, also.

CATHERINE. What are you talking about?

WILMA. You can't expect me to clean up this big old house all by myself? Not even you could be that inconsiderate.

CATHERINE. So hire a housekeeper.

WILMA. And spend what little money I have left? Nothing doing.

CATHERINE. So you're saying...

WILMA. We'll handle it this way... I'll live on the bottom floor. You take the top floor. We share the kitchen, basement and whatever bathroom is closest at the moment. If I want to pee in your bathroom, you can't stop me.

CATHERINE. This doesn't make any sense.

WILMA. It makes perfect sense. I will own the house and you will be sort of a permanent guest. You know, one of those annoying relations who come by to visit and you can never get rid of? We can be like that.

CATHERINE *(trying to hold back the tears)*. Wilma...I don't understand... Why are you doing this?

WILMA. Because, Catherine...maybe I've finally realized what my real inheritance is. *(Wipes her eyes with a napkin.)* Now stop your blubbering and make me another cup of tea. *(CATHERINE looks at her sister and wipes the tears from her eyes. She rises, crosses to the kitchen counter. Her back to WILMA.)*

CATHERINE. Lemon and honey?

WILMA. No honey. I'm watching my figure, in case you haven't noticed.

CATHERINE. I noticed. *(Stage lights fade out.)*

# THE GALLERY
*Loretta Novick*

### CHARACTERS

MAN: Late 50s to early 60s.
WOMAN: Early 50s.

PLACE: An art gallery.
TIME: The present.

SETTING: *An art gallery exhibition room. Two benches and a few chairs are positioned so the public can sit comfortably and contemplate the paintings. Abstract paintings in pastel colors hang on the walls.*

AT RISE: *The MAN is discovered sitting on a bench, holding an art pad. He is sketching one of the paintings. He is gray-haired, well-built, wears a turtleneck sweater and gray pants. After a moment, the WOMAN enters. She is supple, attractive, and wears a belted sweater, straight skirt and boots. She moves from picture to picture and tilts her head a bit while viewing one of the paintings. The MAN is intrigued by the WOMAN and begins to sketch her. A long pause.*

MAN. Having any luck?
WOMAN. What?
MAN. I asked if you were having any luck.
WOMAN. With what?

MAN. Getting picked up. This is considered a pick-up spot.
WOMAN. You must be cuckoo.
MAN. Oh, so you came for the art. *(Waves arm to take in mediocre abstractions.)* Maybe you can explain it to me. Especially *(Mimics her previous head tilt.)* looked at sideways.
WOMAN. If you must know, I'm here because it IS empty. Meaningless.
MAN *(at a loss for words)*. A-ah.
WOMAN. It's kind of soothing, emptiness. Preferable to grief. This has actually been proven—scientifically.
MAN. Really?
WOMAN. In a double-blind test—300 widows in Columbus, Ohio, were asked, "Would you rather hurt or feel nothing?" Nothing won, 270 to 30.
MAN. You're pulling my leg.
WOMAN. A little. *(She notes his sketch pad.)* What's that?
MAN. I was sketching you over there. *(Looks at pad.)* Not bad.
WOMAN. I'm not interested in your talents.
MAN. How about the story of my life then? A tale of a man left alone in the world by the woman he loved.
WOMAN *(shows some interest)*. But it's different for a man.
MAN. Is it?
WOMAN. Of course. I'll bet that you weren't a widower for five minutes before the nice lady down the hall knocked at your door and asked if there was anything— just anything—she could do for you.
MAN *(appearing to consider)*. Actually, it was about an hour.

*Duets*

WOMAN. And, of course, you said no because—well, because she was too old and you knew you could easily have a woman half her age.

MAN *(doing arithmetic in the air with finger).* Yeah, that's about right.

WOMAN. So, why are you here? Why aren't you—??

MAN. At the Plaza Hotel, with my Bimbo of the Week?

WOMAN. Something like that. *(Turns away.)* I don't really need the sordid details.

MAN. Just a *minute*. Why sordid? Athletic. Good fun. I'd say it's very American. *(She moves to exit.)* Wait. Don't go. I will tell you a pitiful tale. As sad as the ancient mariner's. And you *will* take pity on me. Please? *(She sits, her body stiff.)* A man finds himself alone in the world—at a certain age. Along comes a woman. I'll call her Phyllis. She was the first. Very bright. Always said the complimentary thing, but not too obviously. Great clothes. Good hair. And she knew all the best restaurants and even when to go to get the best service.

WOMAN *(rolls her eyes).* A paragon. Did you go to those places where chocolate pudding is always mousse?

MAN. Oh, yes. And the sauces are now salsas.

WOMAN. And there's no more lettuce, just mesclun and frisee?

MAN. Don't forget the sorbet!

WOMAN. And did they sear the tuna and blacken the swordfish?

MAN. Both at once. *(They laugh.)* Actually, she was a fabulous cook. And she ran a business.

WOMAN. For heaven's sake, what happened?

MAN. She wanted to get married.

WOMAN. Uh-oh.

MAN. Not because she wanted me. She wanted a baby, right away.

WOMAN. I thought she wasn't obvious.

MAN. Only about that. We'd be watching something on television, or standing in a lobby and suddenly, she'd stop still as if she were listening—to her clock ticking.

WOMAN *(ready to defend Phyllis).* Well, really! Why shouldn't she think about a baby? She wants to have a child.

MAN. Well, I want peace on earth, but do I get it?! *(Stops short.)* I'm sorry, that was mean-spirited.

WOMAN. You didn't love her.

MAN. And she didn't love me.

WOMAN. Then it's not a very pitiful story, is it?

MAN. Okay. But here's another one. Diane. I'll call her Diane. She's half my age. Works out at the gym.

WOMAN. You go to a gym.

MAN. Only when I'm getting ready for the marathon.

WOMAN. I AM impressed. You ran the marathon.

MAN. Three times. The last was my Personal Worst. Also my final. But that's another story. Back to Diane. She was fun and decent, but she exhausted me. God, the energy of youth.

WOMAN. Probably good for you.

MAN. Did you ever try to climb a rock face? With a pack on your back? I had to quit before my heart gave out. *(Pauses.)* You know, all this talk is making me thirsty. Would you consider having a cup of coffee?

WOMAN. Absolutely not. You know what will happen? *(He shakes his head.)* We'll go down the block to that nice cafe and we'll have coffee. And you'll be charming—and funny—and then you'll take my phone number. On Tuesday, you'll call me and ask me out. Nothing fancy, nothing too private, maybe a short concert. Afterwards, we'll shake hands and say goodbye. And a few days later, you'll call and say, "It's a beautiful day, let's go for a boat ride." And we will, and it will be. And then, getting off the boat, I might take your hand—and ask you over for dinner.

MAN *(smiling happily)*. I'll accept.

WOMAN *(rising)*. You'll bring wine, but you'll be casual. You'll tell me a crazy story, something that happened on the bus. And we'll laugh while I light the dinner candles. Then we'll have a lovely dinner and—we'll talk some more—and then—I'll touch your face. And we'll kiss— And I'll fall in love with you *(Pauses.)* And then you'll get SICK—and you'll DIE!

MAN. That was *some* cup of coffee. *(WOMAN breathes deeply to calm herself, then begins to exit. Her knee twists, she falters.)* You okay? *(She nods. He helps her to a bench. She clutches her knee.)*

WOMAN. You wouldn't happen to be an orthopedist?

MAN. No.

WOMAN. I'm in denial. I call it a twisted knee. It's probably arthritis.

MAN. I've got that in two fingers. Gives me an excuse to stop playing golf. I hate golf... Hey, time takes its toll, to coin a phrase. My elbow gets twinges I can't explain.

WOMAN. My neck gets stiff more often. And I think my left ear has lost some hearing. Or is it my right?

MAN. I just got a partial bridge.

WOMAN. My dentist says I'll need one soon.

MAN. I've got an enlarged prostate.

WOMAN. You win.

MAN *(breaking a silence)*. Was your husband sick a long time? *(She nods.)* Cancer? *(She nods again.)* He died peacefully? At home? *(She hesitates, nods.)*

WOMAN. You know what the worst day was? The very first day, when that smug doctor came out of the examining room and said... you know, as if he's auditioning for TV—the cool doctor everybody hates— *(Imitates doctor's voice.)* "I won't lie to you, he has maybe a year."

MAN *(impatiently)*. And you expected him to be *caring*? You wanted him to sympathize? You think that would have made things easier? Forget it.

WOMAN. Is that what happened to you?

MAN. I'm not a widower. My wife isn't dead. She left me. *(Pause.)* We married very young. The kids moved out two years ago. Apparently, the nest was too empty. So she went off with her judo instructor. She called me from the airport. "I'm not ready," she said, "for evensong." Or was it vespers? *(Angry.)* She's telling me I'm in my bloody twilight years and she doesn't want any part of it.

WOMAN. You shouldn't have retired.

MAN. I'm not retired. I'm a lawyer. And don't make jokes.

WOMAN *(after a pause)*. Nobody's perfect.

MAN *(wry smile)*. You know, you'll wake up one day and say, I'm ready to begin living again. But why procrastinate?

WOMAN. Procrastination is the gift of time.

MAN. I thought it was the thief of time.

WOMAN. Not in my book. *(Pause.)* I lied to you. About my husband. He didn't die peacefully. He'd been sick about two months, and he got depressed. And one day my daughter came to visit, with her husband. He's a police detective, he had his gun with him. Well, my husband got hold of it and locked himself in the bathroom... and shot himself.

MAN. I am sorry. I hope you don't feel guilty about it

WOMAN. I try not to. But I get angry. Those bastards of disease! Those thieving monsters that sneak into your body and grab away your life—

MAN. Hey, want to hear a story?

WOMAN. Sure.

MAN. It's the latest woman. Tracy. A classic story. You know, an older man must be a richer man. So she latched onto me.

WOMAN. What kind of latch did she use?

MAN. Every kind. She was very cute. I took her out twice. And then one night, we were in a restaurant and I looked into her eyes and there it was, printed right on her eyeballs, the entire pre-nuptial agreement, with all the dollar signs.

WOMAN. Were you surprised?

MAN. Well, my ego was bruised.

VOICE *(on loudspeaker)*. Your attention, please. The gallery will close in five minutes.

WOMAN *(rises)*. I have to go. *(Looks at him, then turns away.)*

MAN. No coffee? *(She exits. He picks up his sketch pad, looks at it. WOMAN appears in doorway.)*

WOMAN. You were right. It *is* the thief of time. *(He smiles, walks toward her.)* I know a place where they make terrific chocolate pudding.

MAN *(at her side, smiling)*. What's your name? *(Lights fade.)*

# FRIDAY
## Carol Wright Krause

### CHARACTERS

MRS. PACKER: An old woman.
FRIDAY: A Meals on Wheels volunteer, 40s.

PLACE: Mrs. Packer's modest living room.
TIME: The present, at noon on a Friday.

AT RISE: *MRS. PACKER enters from kitchen with two glasses of cider on a tray. She moves stiffly, with difficulty. She puts tray on coffee table and peeks out front window, half-singing, half-muttering a flat tune.*

MRS. PACKER. Friday, Friday, Friday. Friday, Friday, Friday. *(She exits into a hallway and comes out with an empty light bulb package; removes the light bulb from the room's only lamp, puts the bulb in the package and exits into hallway with it, sing-muttering.)* Today is Friday. Today is Friday. Today is Friday. Friday, Friday, Friday. *(She returns with a crumpled paper bag from which she pulls a grayed bulb. She shakes the bulb near her ear, listening for the burned-out filament to rattle, then screws it into the lamp and adjusts the lampshade.)* Yesterday was Thursday, yesterday was Thursday. I don't like Thursday. Thursday, Thursday, Thursday. *(She goes to the window, folding the bag, and peeks out; opens her door and unlocks the*

Duets 99

*storm/screen door, takes her purse from the coffee table, checks its contents and stuffs it under the sofa.)* I like Friday. I like Friday. I like the heck out of Friday. Friday, Friday, Fri-day.

*(She exits into hall carrying the bag and returns empty-handed. She begins her song again as she peers out the window, but stops abruptly and exits into hall as we hear a car pull up and honk. FRIDAY appears at the screen door, banging on it and shouting. FRIDAY is a brisk woman in a business suit and running shoes. She carries a covered foil dish and small paper bag.)*

FRIDAY. Mrs. Packer! Meals on Wheels! Mrs. Packer? *(No response. She bangs again.)* Meals on Wheels! Mrs. Packer? *(She enters tentatively and listens.)* Mrs. Packer? *(She quickly closes the front door and leaps aside, as though expecting to find someone behind it.)* MEALS ON WHEELS! *(She whips around to scan the room.)* Oh, boy. *(She takes the meal into the kitchen and returns, shouting congenially.)* Say something so I'll know you're okay. *(She exits into hall, tentatively.)*
MRS. PACKER *(offstage).* Boo.

*(FRIDAY yelps; strides back into living room with forced cheer, followed by MRS. PACKER.)*

FRIDAY. So! How are you today, Mrs. Packer?
MRS. PACKER. Good, thanks. How are you, Friday?
FRIDAY. Fine. I have four more lunches to deliver, so I'd better collect and run.

MRS. PACKER. Four? Shouldn't take long. Did you open my milk?
FRIDAY *(exits into kitchen)*. No, but I'm happy to.
MRS. PACKER. My hands, you know. Stiff.
FRIDAY *(offstage)*. Happy to.
MRS. PACKER. What is it today?
FRIDAY. Salmon croquettes.
MRS. PACKER. Hey. Set out the catsup. Got to have catsup with salmon croquettes.
FRIDAY. Okay.
MRS. PACKER. Got to. Ever try them that way?

*(FRIDAY reenters.)*

FRIDAY. All set. Now, I do need to collect today.
MRS. PACKER. Are you sure? I think I paid Thursday.
FRIDAY. The route sheet says I'm supposed to collect, as usual.
MRS. PACKER. Oh. Cider?
FRIDAY. No, thanks. I think I've explained to you, I volunteer on my lunch hour, so time is tight.
MRS. PACKER. Oh? Well, I've got my purse here somewhere. *(She rotates in place, looking around the room.)* Sit, while I look. The cider's good. Cinnamon stick in it.
FRIDAY. I'm sorry. I just don't have time.
MRS. PACKER. Take one minute. Sit. Don't rush so much.
FRIDAY. Let me help you look.
MRS. PACKER. No, I'll look. Would you turn on the lamp so I can see?
FRIDAY *(attempts to turn on lamp; it doesn't work. She suspects why)*. How strange. Your lamp doesn't work.

MRS. PACKER. Bulb burned out and I can't change it. My hands, you know.
FRIDAY. Please, let me do it for you. Then I've got to go.
MRS. PACKER. Sit. I'll get a bulb.
FRIDAY. Let me. Where are they?
MRS. PACKER. I can—
FRIDAY. Where?
MRS. PACKER. Hall closet. *(FRIDAY exits into hall.)* Can you peel my apple, too? My hands—
FRIDAY *(offstage)*. No apple today.
MRS. PACKER. An orange is worse.
FRIDAY. You'll be fine.
MRS. PACKER. A pear, I bet. Very hard to do.

*(FRIDAY, bulb in hand, sweeps through the living room and into kitchen; emerges with a banana, triumphant.)*

FRIDAY. Banana.
MRS. PACKER. My hands—
FRIDAY. Banana, Mrs. Packer. *(Puts banana on tray and goes to lamp.)*
MRS. PACKER. How are your kids?
FRIDAY *(replaces bulb)*. Growing up fast.
MRS. PACKER. Everything is fast. How's your job?
FRIDAY. Fast.
MRS. PACKER. Hey. I like fast, sometimes. Not all the time, but sometimes. I like fast-breaking news, fast-rising yeast, fast-acting—
FRIDAY *(turns lamp on, holds old bulb in hand)*. Where's your trash can?
MRS. PACKER. —antacids.
FRIDAY. I sure don't see a trash can anywhere.

MRS. PACKER. Just give it to me. I might have a use for it.

FRIDAY *(handing her the old bulb).* I bet. Now, let's find that purse. The other lunches are getting cold and people are waiting.

MRS. PACKER. I don't care. Anyway, they're not waiting for lunch. They're waiting for you.

FRIDAY. Where did you see it last?

MRS. PACKER. Just like I do.

FRIDAY. The purse. Where did you leave it?

MRS. PACKER. I want my turn.

FRIDAY. Mrs. Packer, I'd like to chat, but—

MRS. PACKER. I want my full turn.

FRIDAY. Okay. Talk. Talk while I look for your purse.

MRS. PACKER. No. You talk.

FRIDAY. I talk all day.

MRS. PACKER. So do I, but nobody talks back. I want you to talk. Talk to me, Friday.

FRIDAY. Okay. Sure. My car's oil light is coming on, my 16-year-old cried last night because I wouldn't buy her a $400 dress for the homecoming dance, my secretary is going on maternity leave, and my dog is incontinent. Where is your purse, Mrs. Packer?

MRS. PACKER. I stashed it under the sofa. *(Silence. They eye each other.)*

FRIDAY. Every week. The energy you spend.

MRS. PACKER. You're the first person I've seen since Thursday.

FRIDAY. Yesterday?

MRS. PACKER. That's when Thursday comes! *(FRIDAY retrieves the purse and hands it to MRS. PACKER, who opens it.)* Got change for a hundred? *(FRIDAY stares at her.)* I could make out a check if only I could find my glasses.

FRIDAY. You're wearing them.

MRS. PACKER. Phooey. *(Takes out a couple of bills; gives them to FRIDAY.)*

FRIDAY *(hands MRS. PACKER a receipt from her pocket).* Your receipt.

MRS. PACKER. Thank you.

FRIDAY. You're welcome. Have a good afternoon, Mrs. Packer.

MRS. PACKER. You have a good afternoon, too, Friday. *(FRIDAY gets halfway out the door.)* That was my son in the paper, you know.

FRIDAY. Pardon?

MRS. PACKER. That was my son who embezzled all that money. In the newspapers?

FRIDAY. No.

MRS. PACKER. Yes. Didn't you see the name? Packer. Big as life on the front page.

FRIDAY. I saw it. That man is your son?

MRS. PACKER. Yes.

FRIDAY. I'm sorry. Have you seen him?

MRS. PACKER. No. He doesn't want to see me. He blames me.

FRIDAY. Blames you? For his crime? Surely not.

MRS. PACKER. Oh, yes. Yours will blame you for their problems, too, eventually. And you'll do what I do. You'll let them. You may even invite them to.

FRIDAY. Mrs. Packer, would you like us to notify your social worker?

MRS. PACKER. No, I hate her. I really do. Rubs me the wrong way.

FRIDAY. The Meals on Wheels people could refer you to a counselor. How about that?
MRS. PACKER. Counselors, social workers, referrals. Phooey! I need a friend. Can you get me one? Not one of those "home companion" baby-sitter types, mind you. Most of them are either thieves or morons. I eat 'em for breakfast. Ask around. And not some sick, deaf granny who cries all day and talks about the good old days before refrigeration and Poly-Grip. I need somebody still in it. Somebody interesting. Somebody alive. Got anybody like that, Friday?
FRIDAY *(after a pause)*. Maybe. Look. Call your son. I can come back after work and take you to see him.
MRS. PACKER. That would be nice. But you have so little time. I couldn't impose.
FRIDAY. I'll manage. Please call him. He is your son, Mrs. Packer, and I suspect he is feeling alone now.
MRS. PACKER. Cider?
FRIDAY *(realizing)*. Hacker. The embezzler's name was Hacker.
MRS. PACKER. Misprint.
FRIDAY. Do you have a son?
MRS. PACKER. Someplace. *(FRIDAY turns to go.)* Stay. It's a good story. He went bad right after I refused to buy him a $400 dress for homecoming.
FRIDAY. Every week, something weird.
MRS. PACKER. Look, come after work anyway. I like you, Friday. I don't do this every day. Just Fridays. I plan it all week.
FRIDAY. You're good.
MRS. PACKER. Damn right.

FRIDAY *(goes to MRS. PACKER; takes cider. They clink glasses in a toast; FRIDAY chugs hers)*. Good cider. *(Peels back banana; hands it to MRS. PACKER.)* Next Friday.

MRS. PACKER. I'll be here. *(FRIDAY exits. MRS. PACKER smiles as she takes a bite of banana. Curtain.)*

# SNIFF
## *Jules Tasca*

### CHARACTERS

RAYMOND COFFIN: An older man.
MAN: A nameless patient, middle-aged.

PLACE: The game room of the Morrisville State Psychiatric Hospital.

TIME: The present.

SETTING: *Some games and a few chairs and card tables suggest the setting.*

AT RISE: *A MAN sits and stares out at the audience. After a beat, RAYMOND COFFIN enters. He looks at the MAN. Pause.*

RAYMOND. Hello... Hello... I'm Raymond...

*(The MAN nods and waves a small hello.)*

It's nice... It's nice... they have a game room like this. Isn't it? It's a... a nice accommodation... *(Pause.)* I'm... I'm Raymond Coffin... I'm Raymond...

*(The MAN nods again. Pause. RAYMOND walks around and stops at a table on which is a checkerboard.)*

Say, how about a game? How about a game of checkers? What say?

*(The MAN shakes his head.)*

This is a game room. This is the hospital game room and checkers is a game. And you're in the game room doing nothing. How about some checkers?

*(The MAN rises.)*

You'll play?

*(The MAN shakes his head.)*

Oh, I know why you won't. You're trying to be courteous and not show it. But I know why you won't play. Yes, I do.

*(The MAN turns to him.)*

You won't play because you can smell it. You can smell it, can't you?

MAN. Huh?
RAYMOND. Oh, don't deny it. Just don't deny it. Even though I just had a hot shower—a long hot shower—and I put on an unscented deodorant and baby powder—and I didn't rush down the stairs, and took the elevator, so I wouldn't sweat...I stink...I stink anyway, don't I?

*(RAYMOND sniffs his armpits.)*

You smell it? Of course you do. I'm sorry. This is not something I can control. I told the doctor this. I can't stop it.

It started... It started with my wife. She began sleeping in the guest room. I couldn't figure out why, after thirty-two years, she took to the guest room. Oh, I called her on it. Okay, yes, I did. And she blamed the whole thing on herself. Menopause. Menopause, she said. Hot flashes and sweats. And the woman wouldn't come near me for sex. We used to fight over it. It was about that time when I started to smell it—smell me. She couldn't admit it, but the reason she took the guest room, my man, is that she couldn't bear the smell that oozed outta me. But I could detect it. Oh, I know, it's a horrible smell. When I took off my shirt or my pants or my shoes there was a stifling odor. Then... then... I began to notice that my daughter didn't come to visit as often as she did. Or she'd come during the day to see my wife when I wasn't home. I noticed that when she did come in the evening, she'd give me a quick kiss and not the usual longer hug... and the grandchildren... the grandkids didn't want me to hold them anymore. My daughter said it was because they weren't babies anymore, and they didn't like sitting on anyone's lap. But I know it's this stink on me, coming from me, that made them back off... Oh, don't even ask, my friend, of course, I went to my doctor. Then to a specialist. A dermatologist. Yes, I did. The specialist told me the same thing as my family doctor. He told me I had no odor. Do you believe it? Do you? You, who stand there in my reeking presence? Huh? Do you believe this dermatologist told me I had no unusual body odor?

*(The MAN begins to leave.)*

Oh, go ahead, go. I know... I know I've made your nose a sinkhole.

*(The MAN stops and watches RAYMOND sniff his armpits and his hands. Then RAYMOND unbuttons his trousers and pulls them down a bit as if to air them out.)*

Whew... It comes from all over my body.

*(He pulls his trousers back up.)*

My condition is so bad that the dermatologist lied to me. Oh yeah, he lied. I could smell the bad smell of myself right in his office. He had no cure for it, so he told me I had no particular odor. That's when I knew it was real serious. You understand me? At meetings, at work, I'd make suggestions and people would hardly glance at me or consider what I said. Can't blame 'em I guess... Who's gonna consider a suggestion from a man who stinks. I'm sure that after meetings, they got together and had a lot to say about me, about the smell. Young turks now, all of them. But not one of them had the guts to say anything to me about the odor, because I'm older. Not one... then... then I lost my secretary. Oh, I know why. She couldn't breathe deep around me. The smell. After all those years of having my own secretary, I had to use the secretarial pool. Like a rookie. Don't even wonder—yes, I went to other dermatologists. You bet. A whole yellow page full of 'em. They all said the same thing, because they have no cure for such a condition as mine. You have no unusual body odor, Mr. Coffin, they said. What can a doctor do when a man's giving off the smell of rotten meat and that doctor can't stop it? Nothing... I changed my diet. I took vitamins. Ginseng root. Herbs. I drank only pure cranberry juice. I slept with potpourri spread all over the bed. I prayed to Almighty God. Yes, I did. I swear, I did. I prayed, Oh, Jesus, how I prayed.

*(RAYMOND sits.)*

I started to go to the movies during the day when nobody was there, so nobody, you know, would have to put up with whiffing me. Because when I went at night, people around me talked. I could hear them talking during the movie, talking about how I smelled up the place. The doctors told me this was all in my head; that's what they said, that I imagined it all, the smell, my wife's change toward me, the situation at work, all of it. One day when I went to a movie, the theater was empty except for a woman sitting in the middle of this big empty movie house. I walked down the aisle and sat down next to her. That woman, my friend, got right up and moved away from me—far away—to another continent of that movie house. And the doctors told me I imagined it all. Oh, hey, I don't blame the woman. Odor is a warning device. If it smells bad, your nose is telling you to keep away.

*(RAYMOND raises his foot and sniffs it.)*

God, it's really bad today. When I get nervous, it really gets bad. I become a regular sewer.

*(RAYMOND rises.)*

They all finally forced me to see a psychiatrist.

*(RAYMOND laughs.)*

A psychiatrist. What in hell does a psychiatrist know about a body that fills the air with the perfume of decay? What can they do for me here? Look, I thank you, buddy, for putting up with the smell.

*(RAYMOND sniffs his armpits again.)*

I guess it's best we didn't play checkers. I'd get all excited and sweat. It'd get worse. You'd be sick to your stomach before the first king appeared on the board. Right now this whole room has my smell in every corner. I know what you'd like to say: it smells like somebody just lifted a manhole cover... Almighty God, let this cesspool in me stop.

*(RAYMOND puts his head in his hands.)*

Go. Go. Leave me in this stench, go ahead. I'm used to it. Go, I said. You're not gonna hurt my feelings...

*(Pause. The MAN sniffs back a clogged nose.)*

MAN *(in a nasal tone)*. Look, Raymond. I have a head cold. I can't smell anything. I'm leaving because you're upsetting me. I'm here to rest. Rest. Your problems are upsetting me. That's why I'm going. I smell absolutely nothing...

*(The MAN blows his nose and exits. Pause.)*

RAYMOND. Even through his head cold, he couldn't stand the stink.

*(RAYMOND sniffs.)*

Jesus Christ, it's never been this bad... never...

*(He proceeds to smell his armpits and his hands and his feet as the lights fade.)*

# OUT ON THE ICE
*Mark Steven Jensen*

### CHARACTERS

KNUTE: A tough fisherman in his 60s. He lives in a small town somewhere in Minnesota. His best friend is Bob.

BOB: Another tough fisherman in his 60s. He lives on a farm. His best friend is Knute.

PLACE: A lake in Minnesota. The water is frozen solid. An ice-fishing contest is taking place, and Knute and Bob have staked out a claim to take part in the contest. The surrounding ice is filled with other fishermen, icehouses, pickup trucks, snack tents, and snowmobiles.

TIME: The present. A cold January day.

NOTE ON DIALECT: The characters speak with a Midwestern Scandinavian accent. This accent is common in northern and central Minnesota, particularly in the regions around Brainerd and Fargo.

NOTE ON PERFORMANCE: Since Knute and Bob are fishing, their dialogue should occasionally be interrupted by long pauses. These pauses are indicated by the "they fish" stage direction.

AT RISE: *A frozen lake. KNUTE and BOB sit on lawn chairs; they dangle lines through holes they've cut in the ice. Both wear heavy winter clothes. Two tackle boxes, a cooler, and various other pieces of ice-fishing paraphernalia are near them. They say nothing for a time.*

KNUTE. T'at Bronco's gonna be ours t'is year, Bob.
BOB. Yup. Hope so. *(They fish silently.)*
KNUTE. You get a look at her? All smooth and shiny black, red stripe decal running down her sides, black leat'er interior. Bucket seats. 'magine driving around in that t'ing. Comes with one of t'ose AM/FM stereo cassette CD players! Tammy Wynette would really sound good t'en. Plus the back seat flips down too. And t'at engine. Boy! Eight cylinders, overhead cam, five hundred plus cubic inches. A beaut, a real beaut! Even comes with t'em new puncture-resistant Firestone tires—
BOB. Sh, t'ere, Knute! I got a nibble. *(They sit still. Then BOB yanks hard on his line.)* Yup, he's hooked! Get t'at pail over here! T'is is the one, Knute, t'is is the big one!
KNUTE. Yeah, could be the fish t'at wins us t'at Bronco.
BOB. Oh, he's sure a fighter, boy!
KNUTE. Get t'at bugger outta the lake, now t'en!
BOB. Yeah. Just making sure he's not getting hung up under the ice, y'know, we gotta be careful 'bout t'ings like t'at.
KNUTE. Okay, I see him. Now pull him on t'rough.
BOB. Yeah, I got 'im past the bottom of the ice. Here he comes. *(BOB pulls out a tiny perch.)* Well. Considering his size, he sure was a fighter. *(KNUTE rips the perch*

*off BOB's line and throws it in the pail.)* How many of t'ose perch we caught so far anyway?

KNUTE. Must be a whole school of t'em stupid little buggers down t'ere. Won't be getting t'at Bronco at t'is rate.

BOB. Now don't go saying t'at, Knute, y'know t'em fish are biting pretty good t'is year. I betcha we got a good chance at winning t'at rig. I don't see very many of t'em other guys around here pulling in as many perch as we are. Where t'ere's perch, t'ere's nort'ern pike.

KNUTE. DNR must've seeded the whole lake down with this little scrap.

BOB. We'll get t'at Bronco. Day's young yet.

KNUTE. You get two choices with a lake, Bob. You eit'er get a lake with a few big fish or a lake with a buncha little fish. What kind of lake do you t'ink we have t'is year? Judging by what's in the pail t'ere, t'is year the lake's fulla perch.

BOB. I don't know, I've been watching ol' Ivan Pooch over t'ere and he hasn't caught a damn t'ing.

KNUTE. Twenty years we've been coming to t'is contest, Bob! Twenty long years!

BOB. More than t'at. When we first started going, little Bobbie used to come along with us. He wasn't more t'an 6 or so t'at first time. Heck, now's he's a big shot down t'ere in Minneapolis. Oh man, how the time goes.

KNUTE. I want t'at Bronco, Bob.

BOB. Heck, you're tellin' me.

KNUTE. Every year t'ere's a new shiny Ford, and every year some fancy punk drives off with her!

BOB. Well, t'at's the way it goes, y'know. But the weather's good today, sun's out and it's predner

warmed up to twenty degrees. I brought some brew along if you're getting a little t'irsty t'ere, Knute. The whole cooler's chuck full.
KNUTE. Maybe later.
BOB. Yup, okay. Help yourself whenever. *(They fish.)*
KNUTE. Bob. I got a way we can win.
BOB. Oh you do, do you? Well, I said my prayers last night, too, Knute.
KNUTE. I brought somet'ing with. Somet'ing t'at'll let us win for sure.
BOB. Some sorta secret lure?
KNUTE. Nope.
BOB. Oh?
KNUTE. It's a nort'ern, Bob.
BOB. Nort'ern? Whatcha saying here?
KNUTE. A big one. Bugger's still half alive. Nearly twelve pounds. *(BOB says nothing.)* It'd be an easy t'ing to do. We just hook him on a line, toss him down a hole here. T'en give out a hoot and a holler and pull the darn t'ing back up here again. Half the lake be watching us because of all our shouting. We'd win t'at Bronco.
BOB. You're such a kidder, Knute. You don't got no fish along.
KNUTE. It's in the cooler.
BOB. T'ere's beer in t'at cooler.
KNUTE. I unpacked the beer.
BOB. Ah! You're fulla bull.
KNUTE. Take a look t'en.
BOB. Jeez, Knute.
KNUTE. Take a look, for Pete's sake.

BOB. You've got Bronco on the brain, t'at's what you got, Knute. Bronco on the brain. All right, let's see t'is here mighty fish— Oh jeez!

KNUTE. Just like an aquarium, ain't it? Only you can't see t'rough the sides. T'at way the contest officiators couldn't see my little ace t'ere. Is t'at a contest winner or what?

BOB. Jeez. Oh jeez, oh jeez, t'at's bad. Oh jeez.

KNUTE. Sit down here and pretend somet'ing's biting your hook. Old Ivan is getting suspicious. He's looking over here.

BOB. Where'd you put my beer, Knute?

KNUTE. Hurry, Bob, somet'ing's BITING YOUR HOOK!

BOB. Dammit!

KNUTE. Quick! Hook 'im! Hook 'im! *(BOB runs to his line. To Ivan.)* OH, DAMMIT, HE GOT AWAY. *(To BOB.)* Sit down and act pissed.

BOB. Yeah, okay.

KNUTE. LOOK OUT, IVAN, BOB HERE JUST MISSED THE CONTEST WINNER! HE'S HEADING YOUR WAY! *(To BOB.)* Ivan's practically deaf, ain't he?

BOB. You mean to say you plan on cheating here, Knute?

KNUTE. Too proud to get himself a hearing aid, t'ough. Ivan is just too proud, it's his whole trouble.

BOB. They catch us with t'at fish and we're banned from t'is contest for life.

KNUTE. What about the Bronco, t'ere, Bob. The prize! We'd look pretty sharp behind the wheel of t'at t'ing.

BOB. Oh jeez. Where'd you buy the nort'ern?

KNUTE. T'at fish farm down by Henning.

BOB. No! The owner of t'at place is probably out here fishing right now. He loves promoting t'is contest.

KNUTE. T'at's why you gotta catch it for us, Bob. With t'at fish farmer around, knowing my luck, he'll remember where I was yesterday.
BOB. I catch it... No, nope. I ain't agreeing to not'ing like t'at.
KNUTE. You and I never win Bob, we've never won a t'ing.
BOB. I wanna fish, Knute. Just fish.
KNUTE. Need somet'ing nice in my life, Bob. Somet'ing fancy. My whole life is scrap. Scrap house, scrap truck, scrap TV, scrap business. After t'irty goddamn years of trucking, me and the missus got scrap to show for it. Scrap!
BOB. Forget about t'at north'ern. Fish.
KNUTE. T'is ain't about being right or fair, it's just about... Guys like us can't get t'ings the normal way. I mean, boy, the situations you've been in. All t'ese years. I know you, Bob. I know you. I've seen you cry, Bob. Just t'at once, during your auction sale. All the equipment driving off the place, bank took away your dad's land—
BOB. SHUT UP T'ERE KNUTE OR I'M WALKING BACK TO THE TRUCK! *(Awkward moment.)*
KNUTE. Okay. We'll do t'is the traditional way.
BOB. I just wanna fish.
KNUTE. Fish t'en! Forget about it! *(They fish.)* Cripes almighty. Now not even t'em little perch are biting.
BOB. Maybe t'ey got scared off by a buncha nort'erns.
KNUTE. Probably so. *(They fish.)*
BOB. Where'd you stash my beer?
KNUTE. Under the workbench in your garage.
BOB. I like a little beer when I fish.

*Duets*

KNUTE. Yup. Beer's nice. *(They fish.)*
BOB. T'ink somet'ing would bite sooner or later.
KNUTE. Ho, you'd t'ink so.
BOB. T'ey were biting here pretty good a little bit ago. You haven't seen old Ivan Pooch pull out anyt'ing yet?
KNUTE. Only t'ing he's pulled out is a fresh can of Copenhagen. *(They fish.)*
BOB. What would we do with t'at Bronco? Would you have it one week and t'en I'd have t'other or what t'ere?
KNUTE. I'd buy your half from you.
BOB. Buy half?
KNUTE. It's worth t'irty t'ousand. I'd get a loan and pay you fifteen. I get the Bronco, you get fifteen t'ousand free and clear.
BOB. You'd put yourself in pretty deep debt t'ere.
KNUTE. Hell, what's a little more? Finally get to drive somet'ing decent. Tired of t'at worn out Toyota. The wife doesn't like driving it much eit'er, but she'd sure drive all over the country in the Bronco.
BOB. Fifteen t'ousand...
KNUTE. I get worried too, y'know, when she's driving t'at old pickup around in the winter. Especially when I'm out hauling beef to Chicago. Heater don't work too good on it, and t'en I'm not here. Call her every night when I'm gone. Wanna make sure t'at she's... well, t'at she's... t'at she didn't have any trouble with the pickup.
BOB. Fifteen t'ousand's a lot of money for you, Knute.
KNUTE. For a Bronco? Hell no. T'at's cheap.
BOB. For a Bronco, t'at's cheap, sure yeah.
KNUTE. Can't get much more t'an one of t'em roller skates with wheels for fifteen t'ousand.

BOB. Yeah, t'at don't buy much these days. Hey t'ere. Look! Ivan's caught somet'ing! I see him, he's pulling a fish up.
KNUTE. Ivan?
BOB. Get out your binoculars.
KNUTE. Hang on, hang on.
BOB. Is it big?
KNUTE. Cripes almighty. It ain't small.
BOB. Oh jeez.
KNUTE. Yup, t'at's a contender. Real long, good-looking nort'ern. He's heading for the judge's tent to register it.
BOB. Oh jeez, oh jeez, oh jeez!
KNUTE. He's big, but he's not as big as what's t'ere in the cooler.
BOB. Oh, jeez!
KNUTE. Our nort'ern's got about t'ree pounds on him. At least t'ree. Wonder what old Ivan would do with a Bronco?
BOB. Ah, he won't get it. Somebody else'll pull in a nort'ern pike t'at'll make that one look like a bullhead.
KNUTE. Yup, probably so. Somebody else. Somebody else. *(They fish.)*
BOB. Fifteen t'ousand. Sure could do a lot with t'at.
KNUTE. Oh yeah?
BOB. Yeah.
KNUTE. Like what?
BOB. Living room needs new carpet. T'at weave we got right now is looking pretty t'in. The wife's starting to t'row rugs over it, it's gotten so, what does she call it, pilly. Little nubs everywhere. Looks terrible. You should know, you've seen it.
KNUTE. Oh, I don't, no, I haven't...

BOB. You sure know what I'm talking about, you've seen it.
KNUTE. Bob. I don't t'ink it's my place to talk about another man's carpet.
BOB. You're a good guy, Knute. *(They fish.)* Now would be the time to put on your nort'ern, while Ivan's gone.
KNUTE. I wasn't going to say not'ing, but yeah, t'at's true.
BOB. He's the only one close enough, y'know, to, to really see us. If we were to...
KNUTE. Sounds a little bit like you want to do it?
BOB. No, oh no, no. I was just saying t'at now would be the time, if we were to... With, with t'at nort'ern.
KNUTE. Yup, Ivan's not going to catch too many fish like t'at today. So t'at he takes another one up to the judge's tent again, t'at is.
BOB. Yeah. But, jeez, we could still get caught.
KNUTE. Well, t'ere's the problem, of course. Not t'at we'd go to jail t'ough. We'd have to give back the Bronco.
BOB. You'd have to give back the Bronco, you mean t'ere.
KNUTE. And you'd have to give back my fifteen t'ousand.
BOB. I'd wait on spending it till spring, anyway.
KNUTE. Smart move.
BOB. I've always been smart. Just ain't ever been lucky. *(They fish.)* Ivan's not heading back yet, is he? Take a look.
KNUTE. Nope, he's still in the tent. *(They fish.)*
BOB. So. We put the nort'ern on my hook t'en?
KNUTE. Yeah. Pull your line outta the hole and I'll get him set for you.
BOB. Do it quick.

KNUTE. Yeah, I ain't gonna be slow about it. T'row me your line. *(KNUTE opens the cooler.)*
BOB. Make sure you dig in t'at hook good.
KNUTE. Yeah, I'm not releasing t'is expensive mother for some other fool to catch.
BOB. Yeah, okay t'en, hurry up t'ere, jeez, you're pokey.
KNUTE. Yeah, yeah, okay, t'ink he's hooked good.
BOB. Oh jeez, finish it, someone's walking out of the tent.
KNUTE *(holds up the northern pike)*. We're actually doing t'is. Cripes almighty.
BOB. Is he hooked deep enough?
KNUTE. You sure about this here?
BOB. Well...Ivan's coming.
KNUTE. Yeah.
BOB. I don't know. *(They are frozen. Then:)* Toss it down my hole. Ivan'll see us pretty soon. *(KNUTE drops the fish into BOB's ice hole.)*
KNUTE. Boy. We're committed now.
BOB. Yeah.
KNUTE. Well...Ivan's close enough. You start pulling him in and I'll start shouting.
BOB. Yeah.
KNUTE. Start pulling on your pole!
BOB. Okay, yeah, okay. *(BOB does.)*
KNUTE. C'mon, it's the catch of your life. Get excited.
BOB. Yeah. HEY KNUTE! I'VE GOT MYSELF A BIG ONE.
KNUTE. IS HE A FIGHTER?
BOB. OH YEAH, HE'S A FIGHTER!
KNUTE. I'LL GET THE PAIL READY!
BOB. YEAH, YOU BETTER GET THE PAIL READY. *(BOB rolls up his line.)* Hell, Knute, what do I do now, t'en? T'is hasta look good.

KNUTE. I don't know. Yell. Yell... He's a big one!

BOB. He's, HE'S A BIG ONE, KNUTE!

KNUTE. Louder!

BOB. HE'S BIG! DON'T KNOW IF I CAN GET THE BUGGER OUT! *(KNUTE helps BOB pull out the fish.)* Ivan's looking t'is way, ain't he?

KNUTE. Oh, he sees it. NOW T'AT'S A FISH! C'mon, Bob, we've got to head towards the judges' tent and weigh in t'is contender.

BOB. Yup. We better... You'll give me a test-drive in the Bronco today, won't you?

KNUTE. We'll be driving in t'at beaut all night, Bob, all night.

BOB. Yeah, I suppose.

KNUTE. Okay t'ere t'en?

BOB. Yup. Okay. *(They exit.)*

# THE COLOR OF HEAT
*Saul Zachary*

### CHARACTERS

SIMON DUFFNEY: A man who has a public life, a private life and a *very* private life, with a moat between each. He loves his wife in the encrusted manner of the long-married, but has made a habit of protesting the fact.

JANICE DUFFNEY: His wife, an inquisitive, materialistic, gentle woman with a sometimes rough delivery. She feels constantly on one foot with her husband, but has developed her powers of balance so that only a little of what he says throws her off anymore, or so she thinks.

PLACE: A hilltop.
TIME: *The present, a beautiful, rare day in May.*

AT RISE: *SIMON and JANICE have decided to enjoy a picnic in this idyllic setting.*

SIMON *(taking a deep breath before plunging into the exertion of verbalizing).* If somebody snaps his fingers, let's say, our heads will turn in the same direction. But whether we see the same things is anybody's guess. You're you and I'm me. So why should our memories be the same? Because we've been married for sixteen years? Makes no sense. Even Siamese twins don't share everything in common. And *we're* not even in each other's skins.

JANICE *(stung, her eyes starting to brim).* You say that now, but we were—that day on the beach.

SIMON *(wryly).* In a way, I suppose. Don't start crying. I haven't got any tissues.

JANICE. I'm not crying... Were you very disappointed?

SIMON. Disappointed? I was relieved, oh was I relieved! I was no more disappointed than you were, I guess. When your expectations get out of hand, the real thing is bound to be a bit of a letdown, I suppose...

JANICE. I wonder how it is with them. *(SIMON turns and looks down the hill. Without breaking his gaze he places the folded beach chairs he has been holding on the ground and stands motionless for a long moment, transfixed.)*

SIMON. Who knows? I'm—I'm out of my element here. Ask me about plant sites, mortgages, commission checks—I can talk faster than you can listen. But something happening in a field three hundred feet away that has nothing to do with me—what can I say? For all I know they might be two little naked dolls some kid left behind. Who knows? In heat like this you don't know what you're seeing. So a couple of juvenile delinquents are belly to belly in the clover—why should it get me riled up? None of my business... How quiet it is! Why isn't anything moving out there? Everything looks like it's pressed behind glass—notice? *(Pointing upward.)* Even that one little cloud—look how confused it looks. Poor thing, what are you waiting for? Move!

JANICE. Maybe the cloud wants to watch them too. *(Pause.)* I'm sorry, what did you say?

SIMON. I didn't say anything.

JANICE. Simon.

SIMON. Yes, dear?

JANICE *(timidly)*. Would you believe it, I have never seen another couple...doing it. Of course this is going to sound foolish any way I put it, so if you want to be sarcastic, here's your chance. Had I remembered my glasses... *(She stops, at a loss as to how to continue.)*

SIMON *(coaxingly, a faint smile on his lips)*. Come on, come on.

JANICE. Could you be my eyes, Simon, and tell me what you see? *(He looks at her penetratingly, though what she says seems to come as no surprise. When he speaks, his voice is softer than it has been.)*

SIMON. Be happy to... I see a tangle of arms and legs. First glance you'd think you're seeing some sort of sea plant, all wavery and underwater-looking 'cause of the heat lines coming off the grass. *(He rubs his eyes to get a better focus.)* They're both very dark, very sunburnt, about 20, I'd say. Looks as if they're wearing white bathing suits, but it's just the distance. The boy's lying across her; she's pretending to be asleep, got one arm flung out on the grass... Not moving at all, maybe they are asleep. No, I didn't think so—what's he up to? *(He chuckles. Little by little JANICE gets drawn into the scene SIMON describes. As she listens she grows calmer, her movements less random and self-conscious until she is herself watching the couple in her mind's eye, her frozen posture barely suggestive of her involvement and a complete confirmation of it.)* He's tickling her shoulder with a blade of grass. She's not going to be bothered, brushes it away; she thinks it's a fly... Ah, he's doing it again. He's got her scratching now, Oh-oh! She's opened her eyes, grabbed some grass of her own, she's tickling *him*! They're rolling over, he's got her wrist. They're laughing—do you hear?

JANICE. I hear.

SIMON *(laughing contagiously)*. Who's boss now? Now she's got you, mister. You should see—she's bouncing up and down on his chest, tickling him to pieces. That's it, girl! Give him a taste of his own medicine. Oh, he finally got her wrists pinned to the grass; I think the bout's over. Oops—wrong again! The girl is wild; she's biting his chest—not hard—little nips to make him let go. *(More subdued.)* He's wrapped his arms around her back. Now she's slid down his body; she's lying full-face on top of him. They're kissing. Hardly moving except for his hands making figure-eights on her back. ...She seems a trifle uncomfortable, lifts her upper body, kind of flinches. She's opening her legs... I think they've begun. Her legs are spread like a starfish; she's settling again on him. Oh yes, they've begun. Slowly, ever so slowly, taking their pleasure in small sips... there's a squirrel! It's standing upright about five feet away from them, watching. Absolutely fascinated. Strange creatures, these human beings. They don't see it, of course. They're dead to everything, everything except each other and a few indelible facts, like maybe her lips are dry and there's a ladybug in her hair and her body has a mind of its own...

JANICE. Simon.

SIMON *(hoarsely)*. A mind of its own. *(Pause.)*

JANICE *(sitting on the grass)*. Simon?

SIMON *(turning to her)*. Yes, dear?

JANICE. Simon, how is it with us?
SIMON. What do you mean?
JANICE. Can't we...do the same?
SIMON. Here?
JANICE. Yes.
SIMON. Now?
JANICE. Yes. If you'd like to, I would. Very much.
SIMON *(ambivalently)*. All right. *(He goes to her, drops to his knees and kisses her, somewhat hesitantly. Their kiss becomes more passionate and they sink into the grass, still embracing.)*
JANICE *(touching his face)*. ...I see myself in your eyes. Two of me.
SIMON. Guess I'll just have to make love to both of you. *(They kiss.)* What are we whispering for?
JANICE. My husband is around here someplace.
SIMON. So's my wife.
JANICE. I didn't know you were married. *(Sighing, "The Heroine.")* Oh dear, I've been led astray again.
SIMON *(and he, "The Villain")*. My intention exactly. *(A long kiss.)* Lady, where'd you get the freckles?
JANICE. Supermarket. They were on "special."
SIMON. Very becoming...
JANICE. Simon, do you love me? *(Taken off-guard by her question, SIMON does not answer immediately. When he does, it is with the grinding shyness of a man long unaccustomed to expressing such thoughts.)*
SIMON. ...Cuts and bruises not withstanding, I—I'm afraid I love you with all my heart.
JANICE. Afraid?
SIMON *(nodding)*. A *little* afraid. Don't ask me why...

JANICE. Let's not talk anymore. *(She offers her lips. He kisses her quickly, ardently, pressing her down.) Squirming:)* Excuse me. Something— What— What's sticking me in the back? *(She sits up and starts fumbling around behind her.)* It's probably a rock. *(She produces a pair of eyeglasses.)* Look! Look what I found, Simon! My glasses! They were probably under the blanket all along. I had a *feeling* I took them along with me this morning.

SIMON *(trying to draw her back to the previous moment).* That's wonderful.

JANICE *(putting on her glasses, jumping to her feet).* Now I can see 'em for myself!

SIMON. Janice! *(He stands up.)*

JANICE *(scampering off a few feet).* I'll only be a minute. *(Giggling.)* Besides, maybe I can learn something. Kindly remove yourself, Simon. You're blocking my view.

SIMON. Janice, will you please stop.

JANICE. Such an impatient man! *(She darts playfully out to the side.)* Now I've got 'em in my sights. *(Pause.)* WHAT IS THIS? WHAT KIND OF A STORY HAVE YOU BEEN FEEDING ME, SIMON?

SIMON. I don't understand.

JANICE. The hell you don't! They're not making love; they're not even touching each other. *They're reading magazines!* Like two goddamn strangers in the subway reading magazines!

SIMON. You shouldn't have looked. *(Wearily turning back to the beach chairs again.)* Take the blanket, will you?

JANICE. Take it yourself. *(Looking at him with newfound curiosity and wariness.)* I want to know why you ran off this—this porno movie for me. I'm your wife, you don't have to seduce *me*. You have your rights. Just ask.

SIMON *(mumbling to the ground)*. Had nothing to do with my "rights."

JANICE. Then what then? If I had any brains I wouldn't ask—God knows what you'll come out with next! Once in a while you read stories in the paper about women who find out their husbands are killers or spies or have five mistresses. I never could believe they were as dumb as all that. Now I'm not so sure! You never know, not even after sixteen years. *Mister, what is your name? Who are you?* 'Cause anybody who could dream up such a story—don't look at me! *(Crossing her arms over her bathing suit.)* I feel like a sink full of dirty dishes. Why'd you do it? WHY?

SIMON *(woodenly)*. I—I just wanted to see if we were still alive. If we had something besides a house with six air-conditioners. It gives me no joy to say it, Janice, but we are dull people. Dull and predictable. Our ears close as soon as the other opens his mouth to speak, happens all in one motion. And with good reason. There was once a time we would have laughed at people like us, right in our faces we would have laughed because we knew in our snotty young way we could never become such...zombies. Here's an irony for you, Janice—we managed.

JANICE. So I'm a zombie. Nobody's perfect. Is there a point to all this?

SIMON *(eagerly)*. The point is, when those two came along we became alive! All the static disappeared. You listened to me. Really listened. And I could hear your heart beating— *(Pointing off.)* "That's us! That's us! That's us!"

JANICE *(pulling away from him)*. Bullshit! You lied and I caught you.

SIMON. It wasn't a lie! We were like them once. We made love out of love, not because there was nothing to watch on TV. You're the one with the memory—what about our third date, Janice? Bayshore, the empty beach? Aren't we the same people we were then?

JANICE. No, we're supposed to be mature adults now. Stop trying to change the subject. How many times have I asked you what you're thinking? Never once in sixteen years did you tell me the truth, huh? Huh? But today I found out—by a fluke.

SIMON *(shaking his head)*. Static...

JANICE. Men like you should be very carefully watched. From this day on, I promise you, you will be.

SIMON. All I'm getting is static.

JANICE *(secure now behind an emotional wall)*. You're a dirty old man, my husband!

SIMON *(takes the beach chairs and starts to leave)*. I'll wait for you in the car.

JANICE. Only one thing in your head—

SIMON *(almost sorrowfully, but with a mechanical smile)*. Spots—I told you, Janice. Pinkish and gray and blue spots. That's all. *(He leaves. JANICE starts collecting their things, angrily brushes off some grass still adhering to her, glances down the hill at the couple. Her face softens for a moment and she unconsciously runs the tip of a last blade of grass down her shoulder and arm, shivers suddenly at the contact and begins to scratch her arm. She scratches harder and harder until she is raking her skin with her fingernails, choking back her tears and uncontrollably scratching as the curtain falls.)*

# PRIME TIME AGO
*Steven Packard*


### CHARACTERS

MOTHER: 50-70 years of age.
FATHER: 50-70 years of age.

NOTE: Neither should be slender or obese. Both should be as average and as unremarkable as possible.

PLACE: The American Midwest.
TIME: The present.


SETTING: *A living room. The decor should reflect or represent the assortment of furniture, pictures and knickknacks which MOTHER and FATHER have accumulated in thirty to fifty middle-class years of life in the same house. Behind the sofa is an ironing board on which rests a steam iron and a damp, wadded-up long-sleeved shirt. Downstage of a recliner is a console television set. The set should be on, but the volume should be inaudible to the audience and not disruptive to the dialogue; the screen should be visible to MOTHER when she is at ironing board or sitting on sofa and to FATHER, sitting in the recliner throughout the play.*

AT RISE: *MOTHER is standing behind the ironing board. She is dressed in a flowered pink cotton nightgown, a pink cardigan sweater, and pink mules. Her hair is set with pink plastic curlers and, perhaps, a pink bandana. FATHER is sitting in the recliner, focused on the television screen, drinking beer and eating potato chips. He wears creased brown dress pants, a brown plaid shirt and white socks. On his head is a cap with the emblem of a seed or feed company, farm-implement dealership or something similar. His boots are on the floor beside the recliner. MOTHER wets the tip of her finger with her tongue, tests the plate of the steam iron and begins to iron shirt.*

FATHER. Eighty-two degrees in Denver tomorrow.
MOTHER. What, dear?
FATHER. Weatherman just said it was gonna be eighty-two degrees in Denver tomorrow. In February! We still have snow on the ground...
MOTHER. When I was at the Sears yesterday, they had all the spring clothes out already.
FATHER. Eighty-two degrees.
MOTHER. They had a blouse I liked. It was the prettiest shade of pink and had little mother-of-pearl buttons. Twenty-seven-ninety-five.
FATHER. Seems like we've had more snow this winter than we did last year.
MOTHER. They had one in my size and I tried it on. It looked very nice.
FATHER. Good for the crops, though. Two years ago we had almost no snow. Then it was so dry all summer. The crops didn't do very well.
MOTHER. I thought about getting it, but I'm hoping they put it on sale.
FATHER. The price of wheat went up so high.

MOTHER. Such nice material. It's that cotton/Dacron blend that always washes up so beautiful. Wears so well, too. Still, twenty-seven-ninety-five...
FATHER. I don't think the price ever went down, even though they had bumper crops last year.
MOTHER. Seems like so much for just a blouse. And that's the kind of thing they never put on sale.
FATHER. Prices just seem to go up and up and up.
MOTHER. I *could* get the blouse when we go to town on the weekend.
FATHER. Prices never go down. Even when there's no reason to keep 'em high.
MOTHER. Of course, if I do that, I *know* the blouse will go on sale the very next week.
FATHER. The government raises taxes "temporarily" to get through some crisis...
MOTHER. And if I wait for the sale, it'll be gone.
FATHER. ...but when the crisis is over, the taxes never go down.
MOTHER. If I found the same pink material, I *could* sew the blouse myself. *(Beat.)* It couldn't be that hard.
FATHER. There was a time when a person felt he was gettin' something in return for the taxes he paid in.
MOTHER. I used to make all my own clothes. When the kids came along, I had to do it because we didn't have the money to buy ready-made. When we first got married, I sewed to save money. The truth is, though, I liked sewing. I made some nice things.
FATHER. New roads, bridges, things a person could *see*.
MOTHER. Nice dresses for the girls. The year we went to Canada, I made matching blouses for us to wear on the

trip. The girls were so cute, I don't think Alice was even three, yet. Remember, dear? Our first big family trip.

FATHER. Used to be able to take a trip now and again. Go to the movies on a Saturday night. Taxes weren't so high back then. A person had enough left over in his paycheck to raise a family and be comfortable.

MOTHER. Then we almost didn't go to Canada. You made such a fuss about the shirt I made for you from the left-over material. I thought it would be a good surprise. *(Beat.)* We haven't been anywhere since we went to Canada.

FATHER. Now the government takes every nickel it can get its hands on and a person can't hardly afford to eat no more.

MOTHER. I always thought I'd sew the girls' wedding dresses. All my sewing projects seem to have sad endings. I think Alice still blames me for Tommy Peterson.

FATHER. Tommy Peterson was the best quarterback that ever graduated from Buchanan High School.

MOTHER. Only he didn't graduate, dear. That's why he couldn't take that football scholarship.

FATHER. A real waste. There was one football player who should have gone pro.

MOTHER. The week before the prom, a girl at school—if I remember, it was Linda Hotchkiss—told Alice that nobody was wearing rose-crushed velvet to the prom, that's what they'd worn the year before. I'd spent weeks on that dress. Weeks and weeks. It turned out so beautiful.

FATHER. There was one boy who could've put this town on the map.

MOTHER. When I think back on it, I think maybe she *was* as sick as she said, she was that upset about the dress.

FATHER. Tommy Peterson could have been a national hero. Could've played for any team in the NFL.
MOTHER. If she'd gone to the prom, maybe Tommy wouldn't have run off with Linda and things might have been different, who's to say? Who's to say about anything? After all, *(Gesturing toward FATHER.)* I got my quarterback.
FATHER. I still think enough of him, I get all my gas at Peterson's.
MOTHER. At least Alice didn't end up with four kids, fifth on the way, and tending bar 'way over to Fairview till one every morning 'cause Tommy can't support his own family. God has not been kind to Tom and Linda Peterson, but I don't think anybody in this town can wonder too long about that.
FATHER. Pay a coupla cents a gallon extra, but I like doin' business with Tommy.
MOTHER. Nowadays I never seem to have time to sew. I did enjoy it, though.
FATHER *(yawns)*. Nobody I'd rather talk football with.
MOTHER. Knitting, though, I never had the knack for that. Remember—when I used to go to Miss Gildred across the street?
FATHER. Nice to stop at Peterson's even when I don't need gas. Grab a beer, sit, talk football. *(Yawns.)* Usually a couple of us up there. I know Gimpy Russell practically lives up there since Edna had her stroke and there's always Lucky-Strike Bales hangin' around... *(Yawns.)*
MOTHER. Every time I saw her I used to think how beautiful her sweaters were. I'd always say to her how beautiful her sweaters were. I'd say, "Your sweaters are so

Duets 137

beautiful." I said that to her at a Ladies' Aid meeting once and she looked at me and smiled and she said, "Oh, dearie, it's nothing. Anybody can knit sweaters."

FATHER. A regular social club, Peterson's Garage...

MOTHER. I said to her, "Oh, I couldn't knit sweaters like that. I can't even knit a pot holder."

FATHER. ...oughta call it Peterson's Clubhouse.

MOTHER. She said to me, "Oh, don't be silly, anybody can knit. It's so simple."

FATHER. His wife don't think much of it, though. Thinks he don't get enough work done. I don't think I'd get much done, either, some woman like that naggin' at me all the time...

MOTHER. I said, "Oh, Miss Gildred, I don't think it's as simple as all that." That's what I said to her. I said, "I don't think it's as simple as all that." Then I said, "It would take a saint to teach me to knit and I'd bet a dollar there isn't a saint who could do it!"

FATHER. When the noon siren goes off and Linda comes to work, we all head up to the Corner Tap for lunch.

MOTHER. She said, "Oh, my dear, I must show you how easy it is. There really is nothing to it."

FATHER. Nothing like the Hot-Lunch Special and a beer at the Corner Tap to put me in the mood for a nap. Just thinkin' about it... *(Yawns.)*

MOTHER. So I said, "Oh, Miss Gildred, you can't teach me how to knit. Why, I'm all thumbs!"

FATHER. 'Specially if it comes with a big wedge of pie. Peach, cherry, blueberry, rhubarb...

MOTHER. She said, "You just come to my house next Tuesday afternoon and I'll have you knitting in no time." So the next Tuesday I went to her house.

(*MOTHER drapes ironed shirt over upstage end of ironing board and crosses to downstage end of sofa to pick up hanger. She notices the comforter, and, laying the hanger on ironing board, picks up the comforter to hold it as she sits on the arm of the sofa.*)

FATHER. Is there anything better than home-made rhubarb pie and a scoop of vanilla ice cream? (*Yawns.*)

MOTHER. I never did learn to knit, but I have missed her so much since she died. (*Beat.*) When I was cleaning out the upstairs closet this morning, I found this comforter she knit for my birthday one year. (*MOTHER hugs the comforter before replacing it on sofa. Through the following dialogue, she picks up the hanger and crosses behind the ironing board to shirt which she puts on hanger, buttoning the top button.*)

FATHER. Or apple pie—à la mode—with a slab of sharp cheddar cheese?

MOTHER. How many times did I go to her? Do you remember, dear?

FATHER. Or blueberry, so warm that the ice cream just melts (*Yawns.*) down the sides of it... (*MOTHER hangs shirt from edge of ironing board. During the following speech she shuts off and unplugs the iron, arranging the cord neatly over the ironing board.*)

MOTHER. Every Tuesday afternoon. We sat in her sewing room on those little tufted chairs. She'd serve tea with that delicate china tea set that had been in her family since before they came over from Europe. "The old country" she called it. And those small, sweet cakes. It was all so quaint. And *so* lovely. As if I'd walked into another time. (*FATHER has fallen asleep during the beginning of MOTHER's monologue and will remain asleep through blackout. MOTHER continues to speak as she exits to hang shirt offstage.)* Then we'd start on the knitting lesson and that was always a disaster. *(Reentering.)* I remember the third Tuesday I went. I got so knotted up in the yarn—she had to cut me free with a scissors. A little gold-plated sewing scissors. *(Noticing FATHER is sound asleep, MOTHER pauses to regard him. After a moment, she picks up a sofa pillow and punches it, frustrated and angry. When she is in control of herself, she continues.)* I was in tears I was so embarrassed. *(MOTHER sits on the sofa. During the following, she takes comforter to hold it in her lap.)* She was so calm, as if it happened every day. She stroked my hair and kissed my cheek—she was so soft—and made me feel so comfortable. My memories of those Tuesday afternoons are like that. Soft and comfortable. The second month, I started going to her house on Tuesdays *and* Thursdays. You never knew about that, did you, dear? About going to Miss Gildred's on Tuesdays *and* Thursdays. You were still working then and after a while I was sorry you even knew I was going on Tuesdays. When you'd come home and ask me how the knitting was coming along, always teasing me about it. *(MOTHER stands and addresses the sleeping FATHER. Bitterly:)* There was no reason for you to know. *(Angrily.)* I wish you hadn't. *(MOTHER angrily shuts off the television set. She turns to FATHER who is still sleeping. Softly:)* We always had tea and the little cakes. *(Beat.)* But after the third lesson, the time she had to cut me loose with those little gold scissors, we never did any more knitting. *(MOTHER exits with the comforter. Blackout.)*

# DEATH ON THE DOORSTEP
*Jeffery Scott Elwell*

### CHARACTERS

HERBERT: The husband.
LOUISE: The wife.

PLACE: Any city.
TIME: The present.

SETTING: *A fashionable living room of a fashionable house in a suburban neighborhood. All the requisite accouterments of the upper middle class are in place: wet bar, an uncomfortable looking sofa, an untouched baby grand piano, several chairs and a number of occasional tables.*

AT RISE: *LOUISE is seated in a chair. HERBERT, vodka gimlet in hand, looking out the window, entices his wife to look out the window. She does so, but fails to grasp the importance of what she sees.*

LOUISE. It's only a man. A black man. Really, Herbert, I don't see anything wrong with a black man walking in our neighborhood.
HERBERT. He's not walking, Louise. He's staring. At me. I saw him earlier today outside my office building.
LOUISE. You're saying he's following you?
HERBERT. He could be.

LOUISE. Oh, Herbert. Every black man is not Willy Horton.
HERBERT. I know that. I voted for George Bush, didn't I? And where is our kinder and gentler nation, I ask?
LOUISE. I think I'll go out and invite the young man in. He looks thirsty. *(She heads for the front door.)*
HERBERT *(rushing to block her way).* Don't you dare.
LOUISE. You're being childish.
HERBERT. You don't know anything about him.
LOUISE. And how am I going to find out if you won't let me past?
HERBERT. We don't need to find out.
LOUISE. He might be a neighbor.
HERBERT *(looking out the window).* I don't think so.
LOUISE. Really, Herbert! Have you been taking your medicine lately?
HERBERT. As regular as Amtrak.
LOUISE. Your anti-prejudice pills?
HERBERT. I don't need them anymore.
LOUISE. Says who?
HERBERT. Says me.
LOUISE. That's ridiculous. B'nai B'rith and the American Medical Association say they increase one's tolerance toward difference. I could never get through your family reunions without them.
HERBERT. I take too many pills.
LOUISE. That's not for you to decide, dear.
HERBERT. I'm tired of everybody but me deciding what's best for me.
LOUISE. Now don't be difficult, dear.
HERBERT. I'm not the one being difficult. Now get me the portable.

LOUISE *(not moving).* And what do you plan on doing with it?

HERBERT. Calling the police. *(He sees that LOUISE is not moving to get the phone and starts across the room.)*

LOUISE. I won't have you embarrassing us. *(She starts across the room to the front door and opens it.)*

HERBERT. What the hell do you think you're doing?

LOUISE. Inviting in this nice young man. *(Calling out.)* Yoo hoo! Excuse me, young man... *(HERBERT dashes across the room and pulls LOUISE back in, at the same time slamming the door shut.)*

HERBERT. You're going to get us killed.

LOUISE. You're showing your age, Herbert.

HERBERT *(winded from his run).* What?

LOUISE. You're a stereotypical septuagenarian...

HERBERT. I don't have to listen to this ridiculous babble.

LOUISE. No, you don't. You could invite the nice man out there inside and we can all talk about something much more pleasant.

HERBERT. Don't you ever read the papers?

LOUISE. I read them all the time. So?

HERBERT. So? How many times have you read about attacks on the elderly?

LOUISE *(freeing herself from his grip).* Is that what we are? Elderly. God help us if it's come to that.

HERBERT. Was it you who just called me a septuagenarian, or have I lost my mind?

LOUISE. Correct on both counts, dear. *(Crosses to the window and looks out.)* He's still there.

HERBERT. Of course he's still there. Where else can he get this much entertainment for free? Open the door, call out to him, close the door, look out the window. I'm sure he must be exhausted by now, I know I am.

LOUISE. Don't exaggerate, dear.

HERBERT. I'm not exaggerating. Is he still out there?

LOUISE *(looking out)*. Yes. *(She waves to him.)*

HERBERT. Don't do that!

LOUISE. Are you paranoid?

HERBERT. No. Are you insane? Waving at him?

LOUISE. I'm just being friendly.

HERBERT. You need to be friendly with strangers who look like that?

LOUISE. There you go with your prejudices again. What's wrong with him?

HERBERT. You can't see?

LOUISE. I see an attractive, thirsty, young black man in a suit standing on the sidewalk in front of our home.

HERBERT. And you don't find this unusual?

LOUISE. What I find unusual is your behavior.

HERBERT. My behavior! My behavior is unusual?

LOUISE. Yes.

HERBERT. It doesn't bother you that I saw this man outside my office building?

LOUISE. Not at all. If I'd been outside your office building today, I would have seen both of you.

HERBERT. But I'm your husband!

LOUISE. We all have our crosses to bear.

HERBERT. This isn't funny.

LOUISE. No, you're right, it isn't. It's sad. I can't believe I've been married all these years to a closet bigot.

HERBERT. I'm not a closet bigot!

LOUISE. No, you're certainly out in the open now.

LOUISE *(not moving)*. And what do you plan on doing with it?

HERBERT. Calling the police. *(He sees that LOUISE is not moving to get the phone and starts across the room.)*

LOUISE. I won't have you embarrassing us. *(She starts across the room to the front door and opens it.)*

HERBERT. What the hell do you think you're doing?

LOUISE. Inviting in this nice young man. *(Calling out.)* Yoo hoo! Excuse me, young man... *(HERBERT dashes across the room and pulls LOUISE back in, at the same time slamming the door shut.)*

HERBERT. You're going to get us killed.

LOUISE. You're showing your age, Herbert.

HERBERT *(winded from his run)*. What?

LOUISE. You're a stereotypical septuagenarian...

HERBERT. I don't have to listen to this ridiculous babble.

LOUISE. No, you don't. You could invite the nice man out there inside and we can all talk about something much more pleasant.

HERBERT. Don't you ever read the papers?

LOUISE. I read them all the time. So?

HERBERT. So? How many times have you read about attacks on the elderly?

LOUISE *(freeing herself from his grip)*. Is that what we are? Elderly. God help us if it's come to that.

HERBERT. Was it you who just called me a septuagenarian, or have I lost my mind?

LOUISE. Correct on both counts, dear. *(Crosses to the window and looks out.)* He's still there.

HERBERT. Of course he's still there. Where else can he get this much entertainment for free? Open the door, call out to him, close the door, look out the window. I'm sure he must be exhausted by now, I know I am.

LOUISE. Don't exaggerate, dear.

HERBERT. I'm not exaggerating. Is he still out there?

LOUISE *(looking out)*. Yes. *(She waves to him.)*

HERBERT. Don't do that!

LOUISE. Are you paranoid?

HERBERT. No. Are you insane? Waving at him?

LOUISE. I'm just being friendly.

HERBERT. You need to be friendly with strangers who look like that?

LOUISE. There you go with your prejudices again. What's wrong with him?

HERBERT. You can't see?

LOUISE. I see an attractive, thirsty, young black man in a suit standing on the sidewalk in front of our home.

HERBERT. And you don't find this unusual?

LOUISE. What I find unusual is your behavior.

HERBERT. My behavior! My behavior is unusual?

LOUISE. Yes.

HERBERT. It doesn't bother you that I saw this man outside my office building?

LOUISE. Not at all. If I'd been outside your office building today, I would have seen both of you.

HERBERT. But I'm your husband!

LOUISE. We all have our crosses to bear.

HERBERT. This isn't funny.

LOUISE. No, you're right, it isn't. It's sad. I can't believe I've been married all these years to a closet bigot.

HERBERT. I'm not a closet bigot!

LOUISE. No, you're certainly out in the open now.

HERBERT. His race has nothing to do with my attitude. I'd react the same way if it was a Caucasian man stalking me.
LOUISE. Who was talking about race?
HERBERT. You were.
LOUISE. No, I wasn't. I was talking about the man's clothes. He's wearing a very cheap broadcloth suit.
HERBERT. You're paying attention to his clothes. The man is stalking me, your husband, and you notice what type of suit he's wearing?
LOUISE *(peering out)*. It's difficult to tell from this distance. I could give you a much better analysis if you'd let me invite him in.
HERBERT. No! And you stay this time. *(He dashes across the room and grabs the portable phone from the bar. LOUISE stays at the window.)*
LOUISE. You're going to make a fool of yourself.
HERBERT. We'll see. *(He punches in 911 as he walks back to the window.)*
LOUISE. The man is doing nothing wrong.
HERBERT *(listening as it rings)*. Then he has nothing to worry about. *(Someone answers.)* Hello...yes, I'd like to report a suspicious-looking man lurking around our house... No, he hasn't threatened me... *(Looking out window.)* No, he doesn't appear to have a weapon... Look, this man followed me home from my office building... No, he never said a word... What am I supposed to do, go outside and confront this black man who followed me... NO, I haven't taken my anti-prejudice pill today! *(LOUISE flashes a smug grin. Ignoring his wife:)* The man's race has absolutely no bearing on my— NO, I AM NOT A BIGOT!! I'm merely concerned

*Duets*

about my safety and my wife's and I was hoping you might be able to come out and find out why this person is following me... Yes, I'm sorry, too! *(Slams down the phone.)* Of all the...

LOUISE. Now, Herbert. Don't go getting all overexcited. It isn't good for your heart.

HERBERT. Now you're concerned about me? *(Blackout.)*

# THE TEA COZY
## *Joan Calof*

### CHARACTERS

GERTIE COHEN: Age 86.
RUTH COHEN: Gertie's daughter, 55.

PLACE: Gertie Cohen's living room.
TIME: The present.

GERTIE. Let's have a tea party. I want to buy something for the teapot, to keep it warm. What's it called?
RUTH. I won't be your dictionary anymore.
GERTIE. What's the word?
RUTH. I know what you mean.
GERTIE. I'm old. I can't think of it.
RUTH. You've done this for forty years.
GERTIE. But you're so clever.
RUTH. I draw the line at sentence completion.
GERTIE. Line? All the times I worried about you and...
RUTH. Stop. You're just as smart as me...smarter!
GERTIE. You think I'm clever?
RUTH. Yes.
GERTIE. Tell me the word. I'm your mother. You'll never know how much I love you. There's nothing I wouldn't do for you.
RUTH. You're looking good, Mom.
GERTIE. You like my hair?
RUTH. Yes.

GERTIE. I put on gel and curlers, in the morning. It dries fast. White hair suits you, too.

RUTH. I stopped dyeing it.

GERTIE. I showed a picture of you to Sadie. She said, "Does Ruthie bleach her hair?" I tell her no. She says, "Oh, I didn't know she was that old." I never tell your age.

RUTH. I do.

GERTIE. Not to my friends?

RUTH. Not your age, my age!

GERTIE. Same difference. My age is none of their beeswax. So what's the word? *(RUTH is silent.)* Your hair looks *tsepatlt*. Comb it. And what are you doing wearing those clothes that could fit a baby elephant. Show your figure.

RUTH. It's comfortable.

GERTIE. What's comfortable got to do with it? Show your figure. It's just a bigger version of mine. Now I have a stomach, but you should have seen me at Thomas Beach in my bathing-beauty days. I had bigger *tsitses* than you. Now I'm smaller. Like my nails? I finally got them to grow. Gelatin capsules and Sally Hansen "Hard as Nails."

RUTH. I don't want long nails.

GERTIE. Feel my skin. What's wrong with you, you don't want to touch your own mother? You didn't even hug me when I came in. *(RUTH hugs her mother. GERTIE doesn't hug back, stands with arms hanging limply at her sides.)* A kiss too! *(RUTH gives her mother a reluctant peck on the cheek.)* See, it's soft as silk. Glycerine, rose water and lanolin, every night. Try it.

RUTH. I have some stuff.

GERTIE. I'm only trying to tell you my secrets before I go.
RUTH. Stop that!
GERTIE. Since Daddy went, I don't care.
RUTH. Not even about your clothes and skin and nails?
GERTIE. You're making fun of me again. What's the name of that teapot thing?
RUTH. Time to get dressed. Company's coming.
GERTIE. I brought another outfit. My purple. Which one should I wear?
RUTH. They're both fine.
GERTIE. Who can I ask if I can't ask you?
RUTH. Stop.
GERTIE. Twenty years I took care of Daddy. Twenty years I was depressed. Twenty years I haven't been myself. You're all I have. I'd do anything to make you happy.
RUTH. Then make your own damn decisions.
GERTIE. This visit is a nightmare. Why can't we get along like other mothers and daughters?
RUTH. You should only know how other mothers and daughters get along.
GERTIE. What do you mean?
RUTH. Never mind.
GERTIE. I hate when you say that. What are you trying to say? Spit it out.
RUTH. Never mind. Nothing.
GERTIE. Stop that. It drives me crazy.
RUTH. Look, I'm a very good daughter to you.
GERTIE. I can't hear you.
RUTH. I'm a very good daughter to you, and don't you forget it!
GERTIE. Don't yell. It hurts my feelings.

RUTH. And what about my feelings?
GERTIE. I can't say anything without you jumping down my throat. If that's how you feel, you can just go home.
RUTH. Fine.
GERTIE. So should I wear the purple tonight? Does the neck show my wrinkles? I could wear a turtleneck.
RUTH. You look fine.
GERTIE. Does it make me look fat?
RUTH. It hides your middle.
GERTIE. Could I wear dangling earrings like you?
RUTH. Your neck's too short.
GERTIE. So what is that thing for the teapot?
RUTH. It'll come to you.
GERTIE. You're mean.
RUTH. Mean?
GERTIE. Obstreperous.
RUTH. If you know obstreperous, you'll find the other word.
GERTIE. Daddy used to say it. I don't know what it means. So what is that teapot thing?
RUTH. Tea cozy!
GERTIE. It was on the tip of my tongue the whole time. *(Blackout.)*

# WHOSE TURN IS IT?
## *Philip Potak*

### CHARACTERS

AL: A grandfatherly figure.
WALTER: Al's best friend, a little older.

PLACE: A community center.
TIME: Mid-afternoon.

AT RISE: *AL and WALTER are playing checkers.*

AL. I taught my grandson checkers.
WALTER *(a mixture of pride and one-upmanship).* My granddaughter beats me at checkers.
AL. You're not very good at checkers.
WALTER. If you didn't take so long to move, I might remember what my strategy was.
AL. That's *my* strategy.
WALTER. It's not fair, you taking advantage of my memory lapses.
AL. Don't blame me because you played kick-the-can with Methuselah. *(They play checkers. AL says something under his breath.)*
WALTER. You're mumbling. Are you talking to yourself or are you just mumbling?
AL. I don't mumble.
WALTER. Are your teeth in right?
AL. Of course my teeth are in right.

WALTER. Then what did you say?
AL. I said move. *(WALTER looks at the board. He squints and looks up at the lighting.)*
WALTER. The lights in this community center are terrible!
AL. It's your eyes. You got old eyes.
WALTER. My eyes are fine. It's those iridescent lights.
AL. Fluorescent not iridescent.
WALTER. Whatever... It's the supervisor's fault. Damn snot-nosed politicians.
AL. Supervisor stuporvisor. You got old eyes. It goes with the rest of you. It's a set.
WALTER. Maybe I should run for town supervisor.
AL. At your age, maybe you should walk.
WALTER. You're no spring chicken, yourself, Albert.
AL. *Fred.* Al-fred. We've been friends a hundred-fifty years and you don't even know my name.
WALTER. Iceberg, Steinberg... What the hell's the difference?
AL. Anyway, Mr. Smarteepants, you couldn't run for supervisor, you're both Republicans.
WALTER. There's Republicans and there's GOP, and never the twain shall meet.
AL. You know, sometimes I'm better off playing checkers alone.
WALTER. Then you would be playing solitaire.
AL. Aah, be quiet and move. *(They play checkers for a couple of beats.)*
WALTER. You know what the problem is?
AL. You're the problem!
WALTER. Let me repeat the question, Mr. Buttinski. Do you know what the problem is?
AL. Which problem?

WALTER. *The* problem.

AL. I got all kinds of problems: plumbing problems, back problems. The Cubs are never gonna win a pennant, what the hell problem are you talking about?

WALTER. The problem is all those brain surgeons in the legislature can't make a decision.

AL. Look who's talking. You can't decide whether to have oatmeal or corn flakes.

WALTER. This is from someone who spreads butter with a spoon.

AL. It wasn't butter, it was margarine!

WALTER. Whose turn is it?

AL. You only say that when it's my turn. *(They play checkers.)* I know you're gonna be crushed when I tell you this, but I'd get more votes than you any day of the week and twice on Sunday.

WALTER. Hogwash.

AL. Balderdash.

WALTER. Poppycock.

AL. I'd make one heck of a governor. King me.

WALTER. What's the first thing you would do?

AL. I'd fire you.

WALTER. I don't work for you.

AL. Then I'd hire you so I could fire you.

WALTER. What time zone you been hidin' in? You don't fire people anymore, you "downsize" them.

AL. Downsize? What the heck is that, weight-watchers?

WALTER. Yeah, *dead* weight-watchers... *(Laughs at his own joke.)*

AL. You call that funny? That's not funny.

WALTER. You tellin' me you know funny? You don't know funny. You think Phyllis Diller is funny. Let me tell you something, Moms Mabley is funny. Phyllis Diller is just skinny.

AL. Let me tell you something. You don't get votes by making fun of your constituents' sense of humor. And Moms Mabley isn't funny, she's dirty.

WALTER. Dirty can be very funny—unless you're over the hill like you.

AL. You're older than me.

WALTER. Age has nothing to do with being over the hill.

AL. It's statements like that that make me really wonder about you.

WALTER. Talk about the kettle callin' the pot black.

AL. You'd never get elected with that attitude.

WALTER. Like you would, Mr. Commissioner of Checkers?

AL. The best people for public office don't want nothing to do with it. That's why you're so interested in it.

WALTER. I'd be better than that crooked Eyetalian who should be in jail with the rest of the swindlers. He's as corrupt as the day is wrong.

AL. Long.

WALTER. No. He's from Louisiana.

AL. He's corrupt as the day is *long*.

WALTER. That's what I'm saying.

AL. Who are we talking about?

WALTER. I don't remember his name. But he should be behind bars.

AL. You know *we* pay for all those people in jail.

WALTER. Yeah, but you won't even buy me a Ballantine.

AL. A valentine? What the hell's the matter with you?

WALTER. Ballantine. Ballantine. Beer. When was the last time you had your ears checked?

AL. You'd make a perfect politician—you don't make any sense.
WALTER. Why do I waste my breath?
AL. Whose turn is it?
WALTER. Memory is the first thing to go.
AL. Speaking of going, where's the bathroom?
WALTER. I forget. Ask that kid.
AL. That kid's my grandson. Wanna see a picture of him?
WALTER. HE'S STANDING RIGHT OVER THERE, WHY WOULD I WANT TO SEE A PICTURE OF HIM???
AL *(short pause).* I taught him to play checkers.
WALTER. My granddaughter *beats* me at checkers.
AL. You're not very good at checkers.
WALTER. Well, if you didn't take so long to move... *(Fade to black.)*

# FLAMINGO FANTASY
*Linsey Hamilton*

### CHARACTERS

DONALD: *A businessman in his early 60s. He is overdressed in a Western-style suit, bollo tie, and cowboy hat. He smokes a cigar.*

MARSHA: *An attractive woman some years younger than Donald. She is dressed in a revealing black-sequined dress, a size (perhaps two) too small and wears too much make-up.*

PLACE: *A bar (P.O.V. bartender) at the Flamingo Casino in Las Vegas, Nevada.*

TIME: *Last Saturday night/Sunday morning.*

AT RISE: *MARSHA sits at a bar playing video poker, smoking (perhaps a bit awkwardly), sipping a tropical drink and wearing very dark sunglasses. DONALD, in cowboy hat and suit, enters, notes her, straightens his tie, then casually sits next to her and smiles for a long moment. MARSHA glances at him, smiles, then returns to her game.*

DONALD. A pretty thing like you shouldn't be alone. *(Pause.)* This is one hell of a town, doncha think? *(Pause.)* Say, that's a hungry machine you have there, little lady. *(Pause.)* Never been much of a gambler myself. *(Pause.)* How about you?

MARSHA. Depends on the game.

DONALD. From all I hear, this is the town for games. *(Pause.)* Think maybe I'll try my luck. *(Pause.)* What do you think, darlin'?

MARSHA. I think a man will never really know, unless a man takes a risk.

DONALD *(pause)*. So, little lady, do you happen to know where a man could find a...room?

MARSHA. A room would cost a bit. It's the busy season and there are several conventions in town.

DONALD. My friends call me generous.

MARSHA. And my friends call me hospitable.

DONALD. I just bet they do. So...?

MARSHA. Four hundred dollars.

DONALD. FOUR HUNDRED DOL—four hundred dollars?

MARSHA *(sultrily)*. It's a wonderful room.

DONALD *(pause)*. Of course. Yes... But first— Would you... Do me a favor, darlin', and take off those glasses. I just gotta see your eyes. Yep, just like I imagined...they're... *(Looking past her and suddenly becoming a Midwestern Estate Planner.)* ...pink.

MARSHA. Pink?

DONALD. That woman over there has pink hair.

MARSHA. What the hell are you talking about?

DONALD. It's incredible! She has pink hair and pink attire. Pink...

MARSHA. For Chrissake, Donald, concentrate! You're going to ruin everything.

DONALD. Hunh? Oh! *(By rote.)* Just as I imagined, they're azure blue, like the desert sky...

MARSHA. Forget it. *(She angrily feeds quarters into the machine and continues to do so.)*
DONALD. I'm sorry, honey, but... Just take a look.
MARSHA. Why do I even try?
DONALD. Mother had an acquaintance who had pink hair.
MARSHA. Oh God, let's not start on Magda again. Please?
DONALD. Magda was like strawberry ice cream. It was bizarre, but—at the same time—whimsical.
MARSHA. I told Janelle this wouldn't work.
DONALD. Janelle? Wait! Where are you going?
MARSHA. To call our grandchildren.
DONALD. It's two a.m. in Minneapolis. Now, what about Janelle?
MARSHA. If I'm not going to have any fun for my anniversary, I might as well get some rest.

| DONALD | MARSHA |
|---|---|
| You discussed our intimate life with my personal secretary? That's fascinating, sweetheart. Maybe we should call a board meeting while we're at it. Hey! Janelle can do the whole presentation! | Oh for Chrissake. When will you get it? |
| Slides, computer graphics—charts! We can all examine the steady downward curve of my sex life and note the slight but obvious correlation between the advent of the '90s and the slow decline of my personal vitality! Would you enjo— | It was a simple plan, Donald. A little fun for once, that's all. Hell, I was willing to do all the work. Everything! All *you* had to do is focus, but no. Was that too much to ask? FOCUS. Oh my God. Honey... Donald, look... Donald! *(Whispering.)* The Pink Lady is coming this way. |

DONALD. Hunh? Ah, magnificent. Didn't I tell you she was all pink?

MARSHA. You didn't tell me she was so tall. She must be over six-foot-one.

DONALD. You know? I find it rather compelling—all that pink.

MARSHA. Great. I spend two hundred and fifty dollars for this dress and you find *that* sexy?

DONALD. I didn't say sexy, did I? It's simply that she exudes a certain—confidence.

MARSHA. "Exudes"?

DONALD. She makes a statement. Just like Magda.

MARSHA. That's sounds like one of your mother's words. "Exudes."

DONALD. I mean, you'd really have to know who you are to take that kind of risk, wouldn't you?

MARSHA. That's always been the problem with your family, Donald.

DONALD *(dreamily)*. Magda used to baby-sit me sometimes.

MARSHA. You're all pretentious...and old. My brothers warned me not to marry an older man.

DONALD. On cold days she'd make me hot-pink lemonade and wrap me in soft pink blankets...and we'd pretend that we were...

MARSHA. Old and sexless.

DONALD. Sexless? That's a bit severe, don't you think, Marsha?

MARSHA. Sorry. Maybe the fact that I can't breath in this dress is making me *exude* hostility.

DONALD. Speaking of which, couldn't you have bought that dress secondhand?

MARSHA. Wonderful, a second-hand dress for a second honeymoon.

DONALD. You are well aware that I have been under a certain strain lately: Losing those accounts, all those little female MBA's nibbling away at my pie—panting for me to retire.

MARSHA. Then ask my brothers for a raise... A little raise. I am their only sister, you know.

DONALD. Can you comprehend the effort it takes to concentrate under such pressures?

MARSHA. IT'S AN EFFORT TO MAKE LOVE TO YOUR OWN WIFE?

DONALD. Will you please lower your voice?

MARSHA. YOU THOUGHT LAS VEGAS WOULD HELP YOU CONCENTRATE?

DONALD. SHHH! *(Pause.)* It's just that the four hundred dollars threw me a little.

MARSHA. For Chrissake, Donald, you said you wanted exotic!

DONALD. AND THIS EXOTIC LITTLE TRYST IS COSTING ME A GODDAMN KING'S RANSOM. *(Silence.)* And what, excuse the expression, "working girl" your age would command such a fee?

MARSHA. Uh huhn. *(Pause.)* And just what am I worth, Donald? Two hundred?

DONALD. Here we go.

MARSHA. One hundred?

DONALD. Ever since our son got married, there's no reasoning with you.

MARSHA. Maybe fifty?

DONALD. Is it being a grandmother that makes women act like this, Marsha?

MARSHA. Is fifty too much, Donald?

DONALD. Mother changed after our kids were born. Remember?

MARSHA. Why don't you just toss me a twenty and we'll find a broom closet?

DONALD. Excuse me. Just how many quarters have you used?

MARSHA. Maybe you can get the nice, soft, pink lady, who, by the way, happens to be a man—for less.

DONALD. I... What?

MARSHA. She has an Adam's apple, Donald, and, for all I know, soft, pink fuzz all over her alluring six-foot-one body. *(Beat.)* Think about it.

DONALD. Just what are you insinuating?

MARSHA. Don't be naive. "Naive"—do you like that word, Donald?

DONALD. Thirty years of marriage, and you imply that I'm gay?

MARSHA. Not gay, sweetheart—just queer.

DONALD. If this is your way of heightening my ardor, you should reconsider your tactics.

MARSHA. *My* tactics? You're the one who needs his wife to dress up like a hooker.

DONALD. This whole fiasco started as *your* idea. Yours and Janelle's apparently.

MARSHA. You said it sounded intriguing.

DONALD. I said it sounded interesting! I also find the *Wall Street Journal* interesting.

MARSHA. Hey, why don't I just spank you with the *Wall Street Journal*? Maybe that'll crank your chain!

DONALD. Vulgarity does not compensate for inarticulateness—and stop squandering quarters!

*Duets* 161

MARSHA. I'm looking for the payoff, Donald, a little return for my efforts. Is that too much to ask?
DONALD *(pause)*. I think we'd best go to our room before I say...
MARSHA. I think you mean *my* room?
DONALD. You cannot be serious.
MARSHA. The deal was I was to take you to a strange room, remember?
DONALD. Fine, I'll book my own room.
MARSHA. Fine. Your luggage is at the front desk.
DONALD. Fine! *(Pause.)* But I want you to know that your attitude is antithetic and alienating and—and emasculating.
MARSHA. Ooh—go read a dictionary or something! *(DONALD marches off. MARSHA watches out of the corner of her eye. After a moment DONALD returns.)*
DONALD. Two intelligent adults should be able to discuss their relationship with a modicum of...
MARSHA. Speak English, Donald.
DONALD. Possibly I was a bit precipitate. *(Pause.)* Okay, I'm sorry I called you vulgar.
MARSHA. Thank you.
DONALD. You're welcome. *(Pause.)* What exactly is our room number?
MARSHA. So. What did she say?
DONALD. Say? Who?
MARSHA. The Pink Lady, Donald. What did she say?
DONALD *(long pause)*. She said I looked like a man in need of liberation.
MARSHA. Well, I'm sure you'll both be very whimsical together.

DONALD. You were right about the Adam's apple. *(Pause.)* What do you think this means?

MARSHA. It means she's a man, Donald.

DONALD. No, I mean, why would he—she, say something like that to someone like me?

MARSHA. I bet she could tell that you only like the very best.

DONALD. No, you don't get it, she wasn't propositioning me— It's like she knew...

MARSHA. Knew? Knew what?

DONALD *(pause).* Nothing. Honey, please. Can't we just go upstairs?

MARSHA. *Wellll*...that depends... *(She feeds in another quarter and the machine suddenly pays. She smiles at DONALD.)* This is a busy season and there are several conventions in town.

DONALD. I, uh— *(Pause.)* No problem, little lady. My friends call me generous. *(MARSHA casually puts on the dark glasses.)*

MARSHA. Five hundred dollars.

DONALD. What?!

MARSHA. Six hundred dollars. *(Pause.)* Think of it as liberation. *(He struggles, then grimly pays her the six hundred dollars. MARSHA graciously rises and begins to collect her things. DONALD looks back toward the Pink Lady, and thinks a moment.)*

DONALD. Say, little lady, just what sort of lingerie does a hospitable woman like you possess?

MARSHA. Lingerie? Well, I've a wonderful little red satin number. Or a black lace if you—

DONALD. I guess I was looking for something more in the line of...pink.

MARSHA. Pink.

DONALD. Hell yes. Something with a little sparkle?

MARSHA. I really don't have—

DONALD. No? Well, I'm sure I saw the perfect thing in one of the shop windows.

MARSHA. I wouldn't be caught dead wearing sparkling pink lingerie.

DONALD. Now, darlin', who said anything about *you* wearing sparkling pink lingerie?

MARSHA *(pause)*. What? *(Beat.)* What?!

DONALD. Hey now, a person will never really know unless a person takes a risk. And a person's never too old to take a risk. Right, darlin'?

MARSHA. You're out of your mind if you thi—

DONALD. Just imagine the payoff, little lady—the handsome return on your effort? *(Pause. He gestures "After you." She hesitates.)* Oh, relax, darlin'. I bet you'll learn to like me in pink.

MARSHA. Donald...please...

DONALD. In fact, I'm gonna wager you'll adore me in pink.

MARSHA. I won the quarters back, didn't I?

DONALD. Yessirree, little lady, for six hundred dollars, I guarantee that you'll be downright passionate for pink... All. Night. Long. *(DONALD and a stunned MARSHA exit stage right. The lights fade.)*

# BLACKOUT
*Sheryle Criswell*

### CHARACTERS

HARRY: Age 75.
RUTH: Age 73.

PLACE: South Florida.
TIME: The present.

SETTING: *The interior of a small Florida condo. There are two candles on a side table at R and a "Yahrtzeit" candle on a rolling tea cart at L. (A Yahrtzeit candle is a candle in a little glass that burns for approximately twenty-four hours. It is used to remember a close Jewish family member who has died; and is lit every year on the anniversary of the passing.)*

AT RISE: *It is a Saturday night in November, the start of the rainy season in south Florida. We hear loud thunder and heavy rain and see flashes of lightning. HARRY is sitting in his Lazy-boy watching TV, and we hear the HBO theme music as he is preparing for an exciting evening of movies. He is wearing bright-colored trousers, a shirt and golf sweater, also in a bright color but not necessarily matching his slacks. RUTH walks into the living room and hands him a mug of tea and then sits on the sofa. She is dressed in nice but colorful slacks, a top to match with some glitter sewn on, metal-*

*lic-colored flat shoes and a fair amount of expensive-looking jewelry.*

RUTH. Your gas any better, Harry?

HARRY. A little—maybe the tea'll help. I don't know why we eat at Solomon's—for the whole twenty-two years since we moved here, I never ate in there one time without getting gas.

RUTH. So who tells you to eat the stuffed cabbage and those pickled tomatoes—shouldn't you learn by now it doesn't agree with you?

HARRY. Yeah, but it's good.

RUTH. So suffer! *(HARRY sips the tea noisily. RUTH is filing her nails.)* Sounds good, must be musical tea. *(Long pause.)* Isn't that something, Markey and Sarah are going to have a baby? Did you ever think you'd live to be a great-grandfather? *(HARRY gets up and walks around.)* What's the matter?

HARRY. Nothing. I got a cramp in my knee.

RUTH. So go see Stanley on Monday.

HARRY *(still pacing).* He don't know about knees, he only knows about ass-holes. If I got polyps I'll see Stanley, what I need is a chiropractor.

RUTH. Call Miriam, she's got a terrific gal over in Tamarac.

HARRY. I should go to a lady doctor? What, you want some beautiful young thing seeing me naked? Then she'll hug me so she can crack my back?

RUTH. How do you know she's beautiful? Maybe she's ugly as sin. Besides, you wouldn't know what to do if she hugged you.

HARRY. You think so, huh? *(The lights suddenly go out.)* What the hell? You got a candle somewhere, Ruthie? I can't see a goddamn thing here. I'll trip and break my neck, then I won't need a lady chiropractor, I'll need traction and a body cast.

RUTH. Calm down, Harry. I got candles right here. *(She lights the candles as HARRY paces.)*

HARRY. My favorite movie of all time and the goddamn lights go out.

RUTH. Harry, stop complaining already. I'm sure it will be on again another night.

HARRY. No, it won't, they don't show it that often. You know that.

RUTH. I don't know anything of the kind, and I could very easily live out all the rest of my life in perfect happiness without seeing *The Terminator* one more time.

HARRY. That's because you don't have any taste in movies.

RUTH. Have it your way.

HARRY. So that's it?

RUTH. What's it?

HARRY. That's all the candles you got?

RUTH. Sit down, Harry. The only other candle I have is your mother's Yahrtzeit, but that's not until Wednesday.

HARRY. So where's the flashlight?

RUTH. I'll see if the flashlight's in the kitchen. Okay?

HARRY *(sits on the sofa)*. Never mind. Light the Yahrtzeit, light it, my mother's dead a long time, she don't know what day of the week it is anymore. *(RUTH lights the candle and HARRY goes to the window and looks out at the rain.)* Everything is dark, everybody must be out. *(Pause.)* Look at it out there, black, not a light in the whole damn development. *(Pause.)* They'll decide to turn on the power, everything'll be over. *(Pause.)* Well, I may as well go to bed now, except I wouldn't be able to find the bedroom. *(Pause.)* I'll never get used to the wind, it's like hurricanes all the time. *(Pause.)* You can't sneeze around here without the power going out. *(Pause.)* They built the whole state of Florida out of cheap materials, you know that, Ruthie?

RUTH. If you don't stop complaining, I'm not talking anymore.

HARRY. Well, if I live here a thousand years, I'll never get used—

RUTH. The only way your gonna live here a thousand years is in Forestview in plot number eight-three. And when they do the archeological dig, they'll find your bones and put a tag on you that says, "fine specimen of a twentieth-century crabby old Jew."

HARRY. Very funny. *(Silence.)*

RUTH. So, now what?

HARRY. So now we're gonna miss the movie. Son of a bitch! *(RUTH laughs.)* What's so funny?

RUTH. I was just thinking, now we're gonna have to talk, and who knows what else.

HARRY. What do you mean talk? We never talk? We talk all the time, we've been talking for fifty-six years.

RUTH. No, I mean really talk, about things.

HARRY. Things!

RUTH. Yes, things, like politics and art and religion...

HARRY. I don't like politicians and we're Jewish—next subject.

RUTH. What about the kids.

HARRY. What about the kids?

RUTH. Sam and Joany just bought a house in Asheville—in town—right next to the Jewish Community Center and one street over from the Unitarian Church.

HARRY. How convenient. Are they gonna flip a coin or what?

RUTH. You know these kids today—they don't think religion is important anymore.

HARRY. Obviously, since not one of four children and six grandchildren married a Jew. We're the last, Ruthie, you know that, don't you? When we go, and they talk to their children about religion ten, fifteen years from now, they'll all tell them, "You know, your great-grandparents were Jewish," and all the babies will say "What's Jewish?" And they'll say, "You know that old guy who tells jokes on the Comedy Channel, Billy Crystal? That's Jewish!"

RUTH. Judy married a Jew, that son of a bitch.

HARRY. Ya, but she divorced him and married an Italian, so what good is that? *(Long silence.)* So, now what do you want to talk about?

RUTH. Sex.

HARRY *(stands up, surprised)*. What?

RUTH. Sex—is your knee hurting?

HARRY. No, my back, where's my pills?

RUTH. I'll get 'em when the lights go on. *(Silence as HARRY paces and RUTH watches him.)* SEX.

HARRY. Why do you keep saying that word?

RUTH. Because, I think maybe you forgot it.

HARRY. S-E-X. See, I didn't forget. *(Pause.)* What are you getting at?

RUTH. It's been a long time, Harry. Sitting in the dark is very romantic.

HARRY. It's not so long.

RUTH. Three years is long, Harry.

HARRY. It hasn't been three years—what's the matter with you?

RUTH. It most certainly has. I remember exactly the day. It was—

HARRY. I'm not interested.

RUTH. So, what does that mean? You never plan to have sex again until you die?

HARRY. We're old, Ruthie. Old people don't have sex, it's—it's...

RUTH *(stands)*. What? It's what? It's obscene, it's dirty, it's what?

HARRY. No, that's not what I'm saying. I'm saying it's—difficult.

RUTH. For who? *(Pause.)* Don't you ever feel sexy anymore?

HARRY. Sure I do, but I try to ignore it, it goes away.

RUTH *(goes to HARRY)*. Why do you ignore it if you feel sexy? I'm here all the time—as long as it's not on Friday when I go to the beauty parlor or Tuesday when I play bridge—otherwise, I'm here. And tonight—Saturday night—date night, remember that?

HARRY *(turns away)*. I don't know, Ruthie, what if I can't do it anymore?

RUTH. How you gonna know you can't, if you don't try. Besides, I'll help.

HARRY *(sits on the sofa)*. That's embarrassing.

RUTH *(laughs)*. Embarrassing? After fifty-six years? I know your body as well as I know my own. What could be embarrassing? *(She sits close to him and kisses his ear. He pulls away a little, she persists, he finally succumbs. He turns toward her and gives her a peck.)* You call that a kiss, buster? *(She kisses him hard.)*

HARRY *(pulls away).* Hey, come up for air, will ya. I don't have good breath control anymore at my age.

RUTH. Shut up, Harry, and kiss me again. *(They kiss as the lights fade and we see them slowly sinking into the sofa. The lights fade to black and all we see are the candles and in the dark we hear:)* Don't mess up my hair, Harry, I just had it done yesterday. Wait, I'll take off my earrings. *(Pause.)* Don't catch your ring on my sweater, Harry. It was eighty-nine dollars on sale. I don't want to pull the threads.

HARRY. OUCH! Be careful—my back. OY!

RUTH. Shift—shift a little.

HARRY. I can't—my knee... *(The candles wink out.)*

# THE LOST PARTY
*Hudson Plumb*

### CHARACTERS

LAINE: Griffith's wife, in her upper 50s.
GRIFFITH: In his upper 50s.

PLACE: The Great Northwest.
TIME: The present.

SETTING: *A comfortably appointed cabin.*

AT RISE: *With his fishing gear in hand, GRIFFITH returns to the cabin earlier than LAINE anticipated.*

LAINE *(surprised to see him)*. You're back early.
GRIFFITH. Tssh! Unbelievable. *(He hangs the fly-rod on some pegs above the doorway.)*
LAINE. What?
GRIFFITH *(moving closer to her)*. It's unbelievable.
LAINE. Grif, watch it, back up.
GRIFFITH *(seeing the pile of dirt)*. Oh. Right.
LAINE. What happened?
GRIFFITH. Well, I guess there's a first for everything. *(He hangs his vest on a hook.)*
LAINE. For what?
GRIFFITH. I get down there, and I pull up to the dock, and there's my party climbing into a boat that is exactly like mine, except the engine's bigger. And Peter's

standing alongside, and his *son* is at the wheel. Decked out in brand new, spanking new gear—neoprene waders, graphite rod—and suddenly I'm remembering all the times Peter called me this fall. "What's the best rod to get? And by the way, what kind of jet works best on the Klamath?" Etcetera, etcetera. So I just look at them like, what's all this? Peter comes over and says, "Grif, listen, you'll never guess what's happened. My *son* has decided to be a fishing guide. Isn't *that* a kick in the pants. Uhhh, uhhh, uhhh"... You know he has that inward laugh.

LAINE *(shocked)*. He took the party from you?

GRIFFITH. I lost a week's work.

LAINE. How could he do that? *(GRIFFITH has now removed most of his gear and is standing with his waders pulled down to his ankles. His pants are wet from the crotch down, as if he has wet himself.)*

GRIFFITH *(shaking his head)*. I don't know, but he did. And I just... Pssh.

LAINE. What did you do?

GRIFFITH. I just stood there grinding my teeth while his L.A. pals were loading their stuff in the boat, and going on about whose four wheel drive is better and whether to get manual or automatic. Like they all need four-wheel drive in L.A.—for getting on and off the goddamn *ramps*, you know?

LAINE *(looking at his clothes)*. Grif, what happened? Did you fall in the river?

GRIFFITH. No. I was trying to get out of there before I belted Peter in the mouth, and the boat wouldn't plane. Something was caught in the jet. So I had to strip down to my underwear and dive under the back end. And while I'm half-naked pulling river grass out of the jet, I look back and these L.A., slick C.E.O.s are looking at me like, isn't this a riot! Ha ha!

LAINE *(protectively)*. Well, they're all jerks! *(She sweeps some cobwebs under the eaves.)*

GRIFFITH. Watch the rod-tip, Laine.

LAINE. Sorry.

GRIFFITH. So finally, after about an hour, I get the boat going, and I come up the river, and I go by where they're fishing, and Peter's son is *waving* at me, "Come here, Grif!" So I pull in, and I notice that nobody's fishing. They're all huddled around this one guy. I get on the side, and this C.E.O. has hooked himself through the earlobe with a fly!

LAINE. You're kidding? Right through the ear?

GRIFFITH. That's right. And none of them have the guts to cut the barb off. And they don't know what to do. So I take out a pair of pliers, and I cut off the barb, and I tell the guy, next time you want your ear pierced, go to a professional. And then I head out and leave them all thrashing the water like lion tamers. So they're all having one hell of an expedition. With my good friend Peter Dohrman's yo-yo son.

LAINE *(protectively)*. Well, he's crazy. After all the years you've been friends. He's practically been a father to you.

GRIFFITH *(dazed)*. I don't know. It's...I guess blood's thicker than water. *(He hangs his waders up on a hook and starts putting away his flies and leaders in a tackle box.)*

LAINE. Boy, that makes me mad! He's got a lot of nerve! What did you do about their down payment?

GRIFFITH. I never got it. I mean, they were friends of his. You know.

LAINE. Couldn't you have charged them for your time?

GRIFFITH *(defensively)*. What could I do? I had nothing in writing. I can't help it if they decide to jump ship. *(Changing his mind.)* Ah, maybe you're right, I should have demanded payment. If I said something to the troop leader, he would have had to cough it up to save face. *(Beat.)* Christ, just when I think I'm getting ahead... And now the jet on the boat is screwed up. I'm going to have to get the other one in the water.

LAINE. It's not your fault. At least now you can spend more time with us this weekend.

GRIFFITH *(guilty)*. Laine... I know we're using your money again, and I didn't want to let that happen.

LAINE. You can't expect to have a booming year so soon. Anyway, it was only supposed to be an experiment.

GRIFFITH. Laine, I know this river as well as anyone.

LAINE. I wasn't talking about your knowledge of the river.

GRIFFITH. Well, that's what people who go fishing are interested in. They're not interested in my... whatever.

LAINE. Well, I am.

GRIFFITH. Laine, all I'm saying is, it's not going to stay this way. And if it does, then...

LAINE. We'll think of something.

GRIFFITH. Goddamn Peter! Since when does his son know jack about fly fishing? Meanwhile, Jon knows every riffle from the mouth to the headwaters, and he can't get out of here fast enough! And Paul...

LAINE. Grif, you can't force them to stay here.

GRIFFITH. I know, I know, I'm not blaming them.

LAINE. Look, I haven't done much this summer either.

GRIFFITH. You've done plenty, Laine. You weeded the whole upper garden. You know you're supposed to take it easy.
LAINE. He said to stay active.
GRIFFITH. But not to overdo it. You still have that cough. Paul should be doing that work.
LAINE. He's been helping me, Grif. And he's put in a lot of time on Dina's project.
GRIFFITH. It's true, he's been real consistent with that. I'm proud of him. You know, the other day I came down and caught him singing nursery rhymes to the salmon eggs. He said they might respond to music. Anyway, he seems to be getting squared away. But he still goes off wandering around in the woods half the day talking to himself. I don't know where that's coming from. *(Beat.)* Where is he, anyway?
LAINE. He went running.
GRIFFITH. Again?
LAINE. Will you pick up this chair? *(GRIFFITH picks up the chair. LAINE sweeps under it.)*
GRIFFITH. Didn't he go this morning?
LAINE. Yes.
GRIFFITH. Look at this board, it's rotten. I'm going to have to replace it.
LAINE. He works out too much.
GRIFFITH. I told them to put a quarter inch between these boards. And now look what's happening.
LAINE. Did you hear what I said?
GRIFFITH *(distracted)*. Yeah, he works out too much.
LAINE. Maybe you should talk to him.
GRIFFITH. I will. I'll tell him if he has so much extra energy, he can put in a new septic tank.

LAINE. That's a good way to handle it. Okay, you can put it down now. *(GRIFFITH puts the chair back where it was.)* You know, I don't think it's good for his heart.

GRIFFITH. Dear, his heart's fine.

LAINE. He has a condition, Grif.

GRIFFITH. He had *mild* fibulations—

LAINE. Fib*rill*ations.

GRIFFITH. Whatever. They're gone now. He has a clean bill of health.

LAINE. Well, I don't trust those doctors.

GRIFFITH. Dear, are you putting in overtime in the worrying department? *(LAINE shrugs.)* Well, knock it off.

LAINE *(sighing)*. I just wish he weren't so down on himself.

GRIFFITH. Well, you indulge him. That doesn't help.

LAINE. He's depressed, Grif. He's not happy.

GRIFFITH. None of us are *happy*. That's natural.

LAINE. He was already in a fragile state before...

GRIFFITH. Well, then he shouldn't stay in the caretaker's cabin. All her things are in there...

LAINE. He says he likes that, he says it's comforting.

GRIFFITH *(disapproving)*. Hmm.

LAINE. What do you mean?

GRIFFITH. Nothing. Anyway, I wouldn't call him fragile. You don't go around spray-painting "Tree Killer" on lumber trucks because you're fragile.

LAINE. Well, I think something's wrong with him. I mean, he hardly even paints anymore. And when he does, it's these dark, strange self-portraits.

GRIFFITH. Maybe he's outgrowing it.

LAINE. Is that what you really think?

GRIFFITH. No. I don't know.

LAINE. Well, you might try talking to him, Grif. You might try asking him a few questions. Like why he's dropping the one thing he used to love doing and now he's exercising like he's training for the Olympics. I mean, why is it up to me to know what's going on with him?

GRIFFITH. It's not—

LAINE. He may only be here a couple more years, and then he'll be gone.

GRIFFITH. I got your point, Laine. Look, you want to know my opinion? I think he's growing up, and he's having to deal with some things, the same way we all are. But he and I are getting along better than we ever have. I mean, last night, we were out here, and he was trying to get me to teach him an osprey call. That never used to happen before. And we were talking about him raising salmon fry, like Dina did, and about how that big female's just about ready. It was good. By the way, didn't I say, mark my words she'd be ready this week?

LAINE. Yes, you did. *(Picking up something from the deck.)* Oh, look at this. A little bird's nest.

GRIFFITH *(taking a look)*. Must have fallen last night.

LAINE. There's an egg in it. Ah, it's cracked.

GRIFFITH. I thought I saw a robin flying around here this morning.

LAINE *(focused on the nest)*. Poor thing. And it's such a beautiful nest. Look at the way they made it. Stick by stick... All that effort...

GRIFFITH. What time's Jon arrive?

LAINE. Six.

GRIFFITH. And he's bringing his girlfriend?

LAINE. Her name's Lisa. She's a physical therapist. Jon met her at his health club.

GRIFFITH. Pssh! That's classic.

LAINE *(with innocent pride)*. Well, the deck looks nice, doesn't it?

GRIFFITH. Spic-and-span.

LAINE. I have a lasagna for tonight, and a twenty-five-pound turkey for Sunday.

GRIFFITH *(teasing her)*. You're doing a fine job, dear.

LAINE. It's nice, don't you think? Having us all here again after so long?

GRIFFITH. Yup. Now that my agenda's clear, I can take Jon out. I bet he'll be surprised to see how many fish are running.

LAINE *(innocently)*. Oh, it's going to be great! Taking a ride upriver... Picking blackberries...

GRIFFITH. They're something this year, aren't they?

LAINE *(beat)*. And just to have a nice dinner together, all of us, with the lamps flickering... *(Beat.)* She really loved that. She loved taking care of those old lamps, making sure the chimneys were clean and trimming the wicks, with her tongue sticking out. And setting the lamps around the room so well. She knew how to make the room glow.

GRIFFITH *(gently)*. Dear, don't...

LAINE *(controlling herself)*. I thought I'd put Jon and his girlfriend in the back room. Those beds are all right, don't you think?

GRIFFITH. Sure.

LAINE. Well, they're not the greatest, but what can you do. *(Suddenly.)* Oh my God!

GRIFFITH. What?

LAINE. Did you get toilet paper?

GRIFFITH. Yes.

LAINE. And it's dry?

GRIFFITH. Yeah. See? *(He pulls a ten-pack out of his duffel bag and waves it at her.)*

LAINE. Thank God. That would have been a nightmare. Anyway, everything's pretty much ready. I thought tomorrow we could take a ride in the boat.

GRIFFITH. Sounds good.

LAINE. And I thought on Sunday we might take a hike together—on the Ossegon trail. See the elks.

GRIFFITH. Roger the eight-pointed elm.

LAINE. Elm?

GRIFFITH. That's what Paul called him. Roger the eight-pointed elm. *Right* before he charged. God, he looked funny hiding under that car. *(Beat.)* Anyway, since you've got everything under control, I'm going to go up and work on the other boat for a while. I'd like to get it in the water by tomorrow.

LAINE *(shaking her head)*. Those boats...they're your real love in life.

GRIFFITH. That's not true, dear. You know, you're looking pretty cute since you've been out in the sun. Maybe I'll have to climb into your sleeping bag tonight. *(He kisses her.)*

LAINE. Only if you leave your snoring outside. Leave it in the orchard, it'll scare off the bears.

GRIFFITH. I thought I'd show them something else that'll scare them off. *(Imitating Peter Dohrman's inward laugh.)* Uh, uh, uh!

LAINE. Uh, uh, uh! *(Blackout.)*

# GAWK
## Gary Garrison

### CHARACTERS

WINNAPEG DUNN: 62, African-American. Gentle by nature. Hard-working, loving, compassionate. Has lived in the Chicago ghetto far too long.

JOYCE CRAINE: 55, a school teacher in the Chicago system for thirty years. Seen a lot of change. A "list" maker. Needs order. Hapless.

PLACE: Winnapeg's tenement apartment on the south side of Chicago.

TIME: Today.

SETTING: *The interior of Winnapeg's apartment represented by a door, a rocking chair, an ottoman and an area rug.*

AT RISE: *WINNAPEG sits in her old black-oak rocking chair, comforting herself with a slow rock forward, then back. A wall clock makes an unusually loud noise. She checks the time on her watch, holds the watch to her ear, shakes her wrist, then winds her watch. Her purse rests at her feet. We see JOYCE CRAINE clutching her tan-colored, patent-leather purse—the center of her being—enter the stage and check the imaginary apart-*

*ment door numbers against an address on an envelope, all the while incessantly dabbing at the perspiration on her face with an embroidered handkerchief. She makes her way to Winnapeg's door. JOYCE's knock brings WINNAPEG slowly to her feet She makes her way to the door, straightening her sweater and skirt as she walks. Three dead bolts later, she opens the door.*

JOYCE. Mrs. Dunn? Winnapeg Dunn?
WINNAPEG. Yes, ma'am. That would be me.
JOYCE *(extending her hand for a firm shake)*. I'm Joyce Craine.
WINNAPEG. Well, nice to meet ya, Miss Craine, and real nice of ya to come all this way, ma'am. Now, how 'bout comin' on in? *(JOYCE steps quickly through the door, dabbing furiously at the perspiration on her brow, then the corners of her mouth. A long beat.)* You had no trouble gettin' here, did ya? Did you drive, or come by the L? I don't drive anymore 'cause my old shoulder hurts me and— 's somethin' the matter, Miss Craine?
JOYCE *(blurting out, rapidly)*. Why do you ask? Because I'm pale—or am I flushed? Well, not to worry, Mrs. Dunn. I go back and forth—pale/flushed/pale/flushed—all day long.
WINNAPEG. Uhm-hmmm.
JOYCE. It's annoying, but I'm thin-skinned; practically translucent. It's from my father's side of the family. Certainly not from my mother's—they didn't have skin; they had hides. But that's neither here nor there, Mrs. Dunn. I'm not even sure why we're talking about this. What was your question?

WINNAPEG. I think the heat's workin' on you, sweetheart, I really do. Maybe you'd like to sit down?
JOYCE. Oh, no, thank you. Thank you, though. I've got to hurry on. I have a list of things that should have been done three days ago. But after what's happened, I don't seem to be able to get back in the routine of things.
WINNAPEG. Well, I certainly understand that. Myself, I've been sittin' here for days trying to—
JOYCE *(overlapping)*. —so yesterday's list is today's list which is actually a list from a week ago, and today's list will be moved till tomorrow and... *(A big gulp of air.)* ...you're gonna have to stop me, Mrs. Dunn, because I'm upset and I'm just babbling and I'll keep talking until you say something and maybe not even then, so...
WINNAPEG. Did you bring the letter, Miss Craine?
JOYCE. OH, YES! Of course, the letter. I'm so sorry. *(Opening her purse.)* Let me give you the letter. *(Closes purse.)* As I said on the phone, I knew you'd want this. I would've wanted it. And no one saw it but me. *(Opens purse.)* You know, I was surprisingly calm. I've never seen, well, street violence like that. And I assure you, it's not like in the movies. It's all very quick, and... quiet... very, very quiet.
WINNAPEG. 's that so?
JOYCE *(closes purse)*. That is, until the ambulance came. And the police cars. Then the noise was just short of deafening. People begin to gather and were pointing and talking and making it an event for horribly wrong reasons, and I just had to yell, "Don't gawk." They ignored me... *(Opens purse.)* ...as you might expect,

*Duets* 183

but I repeated it over and over: "Don't gawk!" Please know I never left Darren's side, and, Mrs. Dunn, you're gonna have to reach in my purse and take this letter out because all I seem to be able to do is to open and close my purse. *(WINNAPEG reaches for her purse. JOYCE closes it very quickly.)*

WINNAPEG. Now, Miss Craine, I'm gonna take that letter, but first, you're gonna have to let me have it, honey.

JOYCE *(losing the battle)*. I'm sorry. I...I just had this picture of how all of this was going to be, and nothing is falling into its rightful place. You're so calm.

WINNAPEG. Calm! I'm not calm, Miss Craine, I...

JOYCE. Then strong, maybe. That's it. I think maybe you're just strong, Mrs. Dunn. And I envy that because clearly I'm not. Not that I'm weak, per se. I can be a lion when provoked.

WINNAPEG. Can't we all, Miss Craine? I could wrestle a lion if I had to.

JOYCE. But on the day-to-day things, I...I... What I really mean to say is that I'm the kind of person that doesn't do well with things I haven't planned for. I'm not one for surprises. I like planned order. I'm a fourth-grade teacher and I chart, construct and plan everything from when my kids pick their pencils up to when they put them down. And I like that—that ability—so you can imagine with something like this...

WINNAPEG. Am I gonna get that letter, Miss Craine, or are you gonna talk a little more, sweetheart?

JOYCE *(opening purse)*. Mrs. Dunn, I brought the letter exactly the way I found it.

WINNAPEG. Well, I do appreciate it.

JOYCE. I had thought to clean it up, but, as you'll see, there was no way to do that.

WINNAPEG *(laughing)*. Miss Craine, I was used to Darren's filthy, trashy mouth. Lord, for a 10-year-old boy, he had more blue, loose language than a street drunk. So I'm sure there's nothing in that letter that would surprise me. Now, if you'll just...

JOYCE. Oh, I didn't mean "clean up" what was inside. No, I meant, the outside because... *(Her voice trails off. She carefully hands the blood-soaked letter to WINNAPEG, who stares long and hard at it. JOYCE sits quietly on the ottoman. Finally:)* I was walking behind him, on a sidewalk that is in such ill-repair, and we were both side-stepping and almost hopping over the cracks, and the car—the one I told you about—came by, and the next thing I knew, Darren was laying on the ground. But I thought he had tripped, see, on the sidewalk. But, of course, he hadn't. And when he didn't get up, or move, I called to him and... then I was right up on him, and saw that he'd been shot. *(A beat, quietly dabbing at her neck.)* The letter was in his hand, and I thought, well, when people come they'll question everything, and who knows what will happen to this letter. And since it was addressed to you... I thought it best to slip the letter out of his hand before anyone saw it. Just so you know, for the last week, I've had it pressed between the pages of my Bible. I thought that was proper.

WINNAPEG *(a beat)*. Has it been a week? Lord, I can barely make sense of time, now. *(Looking at letter.)* Uhm-hum, that's his handwriting, all right. The child *never* made his "p's" close all the way. Not that he didn't try. Lord, I drilled that boy one day from sunup to sundown just on his "p's". And look, it didn't change a thing, God rest his... *(Trailing off, looking at the letter.)* ...his sweet, little soul.

JOYCE *(consoling).* Most of the kids in my class don't close their "p's," Mrs. Dunn. But what can you do? We talk about completion, we talk about fulfilling a stroke, but the "p's", the capital "b's," and that ever-hateful "d" has always been a problem, especially to Darren, and he had a "d" in his name! But it's a challenge, and I do enjoy a good challenge. It's why I teach. I think it's fair to say I'm a born teacher, Mrs. Dunn.

WINNAPEG *(interrupting).* You taught Darren?

JOYCE. Excuse me?

WINNAPEG. You taught Darren. You didn't say on the phone that you taught Darren.

JOYCE. Didn't I? Oh, well, I...I certainly did. I must have just...not...thought about that when I called. Because I did teach him. I was his reading teacher.

WINNAPEG. So you knew my grandson. Hmmmmmm. I'm surprised you never said that, Miss Craine. Yes, ma'am, I have to say, I'm really surprised.

JOYCE. May I have a glass of water?

WINNAPEG. It's been turned off.

JOYCE. Turned off?

WINNAPEG. Well, as you can see, I'm moving.

JOYCE. You are? Oh... *(Looking around.)* Of course.

WINNAPEG. No reason an old woman my age should stay in this neighborhood any longer than she has to. I wouldn't have stayed this long, but Darren didn't want to change schools. That school was his anchor, Miss

Craine. Besides me, that's all that little boy had. Why, he couldn't wait to get up in the mornin' and get his clothes on so he could run, not walk, to that school. And I had a helluva time gettin' him home at the end of the day. He loved that school like nobody's money.

JOYCE. You must have been so proud—

WINNAPEG *(overlapping "proud")*. Now, I was always surprised that Darren cared anything about that school 'cause there were a few teachers who just wore his little butt out with meanness. Uh-hummm, just didn't like him, so they made life miserable for that little bean pole.

JOYCE. Are you sure, Mrs. Dunn? You know how children exag—

WINNAPEG *(overlapping)*. I knew my grandson, Miss Craine. Yes, ma'am, he never understood their meanness, and I have to say, neither did I. But I expect teachers are like everybody else: you have a bad time with someone and you tell the next person and they tell the next, and so on, and before you know it, there's a mob ready to string you up to the nearest tree.

JOYCE. Well, I can report that Darren and I had a good relationship. Tense sometimes, yes, but...

WINNAPEG. Well, whoever didn't like him, it upset him somethin' terrible. Some days I could hear that little tadpole crying all the way up the block 'fore he got home.

JOYCE. Well, he was an emotional boy...

WINNAPEG *(standing)*. With goddamn good reason to be, Miss Craine. Father dead—shot, like Darren was, senseless, in the streets; a good boy, too. *(Quietly.)* ...only child God give me. *(Harder now.)* With his father gone he only had a good-for-nothin' mother who was strung out on crack and every other mess those monsters sell. I don't know if you know, Miss Craine, but Darren was taken away from his mother by Social Services and for two solid years was shuffled around to fifteen—count 'em—*fifteen* foster families. Only THEN could they decide that maybe, just maybe, his own 62-year-old grandmother might be "physically able" of seein' after that child. So yes, he was emotional. But I guarantee you, nothing like this lady! *(Moving to her.)* ...So if that boy misbehaved in your class—and I'm thinking he did, Miss Craine, and you were one of the teachers who came down on him too hard—and I'm thinking you were—I would like to state for the record that I would have appreciated some understanding on his behalf. Not a insult in class, not a punishment he didn't understand, not a visit to the principal's office, or a note home that may or may not have reached me...

JOYCE. Which is exactly why I asked him to write the letter. *(A long beat WINNAPEG sits.)*

WINNAPEG. Would you repeat that, Miss Craine?

JOYCE. Well, I...I was going to tell you. I mean, that's why I...I came to tell you in person. I had...asked him to write this letter because... *(A deep breath.)* You seem upset, Mrs. Dunn, so maybe I should go now and come tomorrow when we've both had time...

WINNAPEG. Before you move your ass outta that chair, woman, you better tell me what's in that letter and why you really came here.

JOYCE. I will not let you badger me, Mrs. Dunn!

WINNAPEG. AND I WILL NOT LET YOU LIE TO ME AND LIVE TO TELL THE STORY, WOMAN! Now I have had it with you people. And I do mean, "you" people. Can't get a goddamn straight answer about nothin'. And never have been able to.

JOYCE. I should leave now.

WINNAPEG. Oh, no, honey. I want you to stay and listen to every charge I can level at you. Then I want you to run out of here like a chicken with its head cut off and tell everybody you know how this poor, old black woman mistreated you. Get 'em good and angry, Miss Craine, so's they start callin' people names, threatenin' big action and talkin' mean and Godless. Get 'em real charged up, Miss Craine, and have 'em storm down to this neighborhood, break through the doors of this building, race down that hallway and cave down this door. And have 'em finish me off, baby, 'cause that's the only thing that's gonna keep me from losin' my religion, huntin' you down and shooting you when you least expect it.

JOYCE *(standing)*. I AM NOT RESPONSIBLE FOR THE DEATH OF YOUR GRANDSON!

WINNAPEG *(also standing)*. THEN WHO THE HELL IS?

JOYCE *(cold as steel)*. Mrs. Dunn, I came here to offer my condolences...

WINNAPEG. You came here to cover your ass, Miss Craine!

JOYCE. From what, Mrs. Dunn?! I was not responsible for that heinous crime. I am only a fourth-grade teacher doing her damned best to work in a school system that is completely broken down, in a society that is not far behind. I did not make this world we live in any more than you did. *(Harder.)* I'm a damn fine teacher, Mrs. Dunn! I always do what I think best. So, yes, I insisted he write that letter, and yes, I walked him to the mailbox to ensure its delivery. But I cannot be responsible for the ills of this society. THAT'S for another pair of shoulders. Not mine.

WINNAPEG. Then whose? 'Cause somebody needs to shoulder the blame. Somebody's gotta own this and say "I'm sorry." Somebody needs to gather their courage, admit their wrong, look me right in the eye, honey, and try to put the fire out raging in my soul. 'Cause that's where real murder starts, Miss Craine. That's where wrong-sided ideas come from. See, all them mystics and what-have-you got the wrong idea. Darren's soul ain't floating around up there. My first son ain't floatin' around neither. They both came home—to my soul. They're both right here. In me. And they started a fire in there that screams out for somebody to get burned. Now knowing how life is, I'll probably go to my grave with their fire in me, but then I'll add my own fire, and we'll end up—the three of us—in somebody else's soul, and they in somebody else, and they in somebody else. Before you know it, you gonna have one poor man walkin' around like a powder keg, loaded up with everybody's fire. And he's gonna explode, honey, and he'll touch everything with his damnation. So you can put the fire out in me, or you can wait for him. But it don't just go away.

JOYCE. I'm not sure what we're talking about here, Mrs. Dunn.

WINNAPEG *(harder, louder)*. I want to know why, Miss Craine, that little boy had to live through all of the nastiness this life has to offer, and still get shot in the head. And I want to know why I've lost not *one* but *two* children to a bullet, and why people think I'll just fold up and be okay with that. I WANT—SOMEBODY—TO OWN THIS.

JOYCE *(tired, sad).* What would you have me do, Mrs. Dunn?

WINNAPEG. Well, thank you for asking. We're gonna start with that letter, Miss Craine.

JOYCE. The letter?

WINNAPEG. That's right. The letter you asked Darren to write to me. *(WINNAPEG hands her the blood-soaked letter. JOYCE hesitantly receives it.)* Now I want you to open that letter, and read it to me. And when you're done, I want you to tell me why you asked him to write that letter.

JOYCE *(repeating).* Why...I asked him...to write the letter...

WINNAPEG. That's right. And after all of that... *(WINNAPEG walks to her rocking chair, sits and sighs heavily.)* I'm gonna decide how much fire is still with me, and what I'm going to do with it. *(Sitting.)* Now take a seat, Miss Craine, and let's begin. *(JOYCE sits meekly in a chair, nervously tears open the envelope, slides the letter out, and unfolds it.)*

JOYCE *(reading).* "Dear Grandma, I already wrote one letter, but I threw it away. So now I have to write...another letter... *(Lights slowly fade.)*

# GRAY MATTER
*Jeanette D. Farr*

### CHARACTERS

MARGE: 66, a well dressed, middle class, white woman.

RUSSELL: 21, an African-American. Wears baggy clothes and a baseball cap.

PLACE: Any big city.
TIME: The present.

SETTING: *Small room in a police station. It resembles a doctor's office waiting room, but not as comfortable. There is a row of six chairs and a counter. On the counter is a clipboard with a pencil attached with string and a "front desk"-bell. Behind the counter is a piece of white poster board with black Magic Marker that reads: PLEASE SIGN IN.*

AT RISE: *MARGE is sitting in a middle seat in the row of chairs. She is reading, doing a crossword puzzle, knitting—something to occupy her time. She has her purse an the seat next to her. RUSSELL enters, looks around, notices sign, signs in, then moves to find a seat. MARGE, not looking up, moves her purse to the other side of her and tucks it close.*

RUSSELL. I saw that.

MARGE. Excuse me?
RUSSELL. I caught you.
MARGE. I don't know you.
RUSSELL. When I walked in, you moved your bag.
MARGE. Please. I don't want any trouble from you.
RUSSELL. I'm not—
MARGE. Because if you're causing trouble, I can notify someone.
RUSSELL. I wasn't—
MARGE. Okay, then. *(Pause.)*
RUSSELL. Do I make you nervous?
MARGE. I don't even know you.
RUSSELL. Doesn't matter. I can still make you nervous.
MARGE. Look, I was in the middle of something, if you don't mind.
RUSSELL. Why did you move your bag?
MARGE. I was getting some gum. *(She searches for a piece of gum.)*
RUSSELL. Can I have a piece?
MARGE. It's Juicy Fruit.
RUSSELL. My favorite.
MARGE. I only have a stick.
RUSSELL. Can I have half?
MARGE. You're bothering me.
RUSSELL. Okay. So I don't make you nervous, but I bother you?
MARGE. I'm just not in the mood for... conversation.
RUSSELL. When I walked through that door you *thought*: Rapist, murderer, purse-stealer.
MARGE. I thought no such thing.
RUSSELL. But you moved your purse.

MARGE. I was just being polite by making more room. I would do that for anyone.

RUSSELL. I don't buy it. You know why I don't buy it?

MARGE. It doesn't really concern me if you buy it or not. That's the reason.

RUSSELL. Because there are five empty chairs I could sit in.

MARGE. All right. *(As if to satisfy him.)* You caught me.

RUSSELL. Unless you wanted me to come sit next to you.

MARGE. You sit where you'd like. *(RUSSELL sits in the farthest chair away from her.)*

RUSSELL. This one's too hard. *(He moves to the third chair closest to her.)* Nope. Not right either. *(He gets two chairs away.)* Damn uncomfortable! *(He sits next to her.)* Do you mind if I try yours? This one isn't right either. How 'bout you let me sit on your lap. *(MARGE goes to counter and rings the bell.)* Wait, wait, lady! I was only joking. Sit back down!

MARGE. Will you leave me alone?

RUSSELL. I'll be nice. I'll even sit over here if it'll make you happy. *(MARGE sits far away from him.)* Why are you here?

MARGE. Why are *you* here?

RUSSELL. I came to see my parole officer.

MARGE. Nice.

RUSSELL. Does that bother you?

MARGE. And you wondered why I moved my purse.

RUSSELL. But when I walked in you didn't know I was coming to see my parole officer. You just saw me and assumed I was a criminal.

MARGE. I followed my instincts. We're so much like animals. When the fight or flight kicks in you should listen to that. What you just said about you being a criminal was exactly what my gut was telling me.

RUSSELL. So you moved your purse.

MARGE. Right.

RUSSELL. Wow. You knew. Right off the bat. I guess I can't go anywhere anymore. That must be why people cross the street when they see me comin'. It's just like B.O. Nobody ever tells you that you have B.O. until it's too late. Then you come home after realizing you forgot to put on deodorant and wonder why in the hell nobody has been talking to you. Thank you. Thank you for letting me know you can actually see or *feel* through your instinctual animal feelings that there is criminal written all over my face.

MARGE. I'm sure if you dressed a little better, that might help too.

RUSSELL. Maybe kick down a few bucks, get a nice suit or something...

MARGE. Clean yourself up a little.

RUSSELL. Sure. Thanks. You've really helped me, uh... What's your name?

MARGE. Why do you want to know my name?

RUSSELL. Well, I can't tell all my "convict" friends that some nice lady helped me. I'd like to tie a name to a face.

MARGE. I don't think you need to know my name.

RUSSELL. Come on.

MARGE. If I tell you, you'll...leave me alone?

RUSSELL. Cross my heart!

MARGE. Sheila.

RUSSELL. What?

MARGE. That's my name. Sheila.

RUSSELL. Okay. *(Pause.)* It's a sin to lie.
MARGE. I know that.
RUSSELL. You feel okay being a liar.
MARGE. Who said I was lying?
RUSSELL. You don't look like a Sheila. Sheila is a young, beautiful lady's name.
MARGE. Thank you.
RUSSELL. No, no, no, don't take this wrong. But you ain't a Sheila.
MARGE. You get a name at birth and you keep a name for life. Even beautiful young women named Sheila eventually grow older.
RUSSELL. Yeah, but they don't grow up to look like you.
MARGE. How can you tell what a person should be called or not?
RUSSELL. You said I looked like a criminal.
MARGE. I did not.
RUSSELL. Did you or did you not just admit to me that I looked like a criminal? That you had a gut instinct—and you were right, weren't you?
MARGE. Let's just let it go, okay?
RUSSELL. Sheila? *(She doesn't respond.)* Hey, Sheila. That is your name, isn't it?
MARGE. Yes.
RUSSELL. For a minute there, I thought you didn't know.
MARGE. What is it?
RUSSELL. I wasn't exactly truthful with you a minute ago.
MARGE. Really.
RUSSELL. I'm not here to see my parole officer.
MARGE. That's nice.
RUSSELL. I don't even have a police record.

MARGE. Fine.

RUSSELL. Yet I look like a criminal.

MARGE. Well, what else was I supposed to think?

RUSSELL. Why?

MARGE. Why what?

RUSSELL. Why did you assume that I was a criminal? Was it because of this? *(Points to the palm of his hand.)*

MARGE. Your hand?

RUSSELL. No. Closer. Look. Right here. See it? *(MARGE moves closer to his hand, she is curious. Just as she gets close enough he forms his hand into a fist.)*

MARGE. What?

RUSSELL. Simple as that. *(He points to his fist.)* Black *(He points to her face.)* and white. *(A long pause. Just as MARGE is about to speak, RUSSELL goes over to the counter, leans over, and looks around.)*

MARGE. I haven't seen anyone at that counter in a while. They told me to wait.

RUSSELL. Man. This is messed up. Always like the government. Keep you waiting as long as they can. Unless of course you've done something wrong, then they're up your ass with a microscope. I can't be waiting all day. *(Rings the bell.)* Hey! Anyone there?

MARGE. The best thing is probably to just sit quietly and wait.

RUSSELL. I'm here on my lunch hour, man! *(To himself.)* I can't come back to work late, they'll have my ass.

MARGE. Where do you work?

RUSSELL. Excuse me?

MARGE. Your job? Where do you have to go?

RUSSELL. I get it. *(Pause.)* I have a job, so it's okay to talk to me, now.

MARGE. I just wondered how far you had to walk.

RUSSELL. I drove my ass down here. Jesus, lady! We LIBERALS have cars too, you know. Maybe not nice ones like you folks but at least it gets me from point A to point B, and I bought it with hard-earned workin'-man's money.

MARGE. I didn't mean—

RUSSELL. You didn't mean. Don't tell me you didn't mean. I may be what, at least forty-five years younger than you, but I'm not stupid! I know what you meant.

MARGE. Please. Don't be so sensitive, I—

RUSSELL. What? Am I wrong? Did I jump to conclusions about what you just said? Am I misunderstanding you?

MARGE. Yes!

RUSSELL *(calm, direct, and to the point)*. Now you know how it feels.

MARGE. I don't know what you are trying to prove here.

RUSSELL. I assumed things about you just like you assumed things about me when I walked through that door. I'm not trying to change the way you think, I'm just telling you how it goes. You can't tell me that if an elderly white woman was sitting next to you instead of me that you wouldn't be exchanging recipes and complaining about your arthritis or whatever the hell you all do. You certainly wouldn't have jumped out of your skin like you did when I walked in here.

MARGE. Would it make you happy if I gave you my recipe for pot roast?

RUSSELL. Aw, man!

MARGE. I won't give anyone that recipe, you know. Not even my sister. The key is the marinade.

RUSSELL. Forget it.

MARGE. You say "that's what we do" so I'm following through with it.
RUSSELL. I'm just saying you wouldn't be so uptight if I was someone different.
MARGE. Uptight! The reason I'm uptight has nothing to do with who you are.
RUSSELL. Don't bother apologizing for who *you* are. You don't have to talk to me or trust that I'm not going to take something of yours. If that's what you believe—then—way it goes.
MARGE. I don't trust anyone at the moment! *(Pause, having trouble getting this out.)* Somewhere between here and 13th Street I've misplaced my wallet. The sad thing about it is it had a lot of money in it not to mention my driver's license and pictures of my grandchildren. I don't even care about the money, but the fact that someone out there knows my identity isn't too comforting to me. I came down here to file a report in hopes that someone would be honest enough to... what was I thinking? I've wasted half my day in here just for one chance that there is one honest person left in this world.
RUSSELL. I'm sorry. I'm sure someone will find it.
MARGE. Oh, I'm sure someone has found it by now and had a fine time maxing my Gold Card. I don't know why I'm wasting my time. *(She gets up to leave.)*
RUSSELL. Hey, Sheila. Why don't you wait a few more minutes. I'm sure if we make enough noise, someone will come out to help us. *(MARGE stops.)*
MARGE. May I tell you something?
RUSSELL. What is it?
MARGE. You did catch me.
RUSSELL. No sweat... I mean, I didn't know.

*Duets* 199

MARGE. My name... it isn't Sheila.
RUSSELL. Well, whaddaya know.
MARGE. Don't be funny. Actually it's...
RUSSELL. Marge.
MARGE. What— How?
RUSSELL. You just *look* like a Marge to me.
MARGE *(amazed)*. You're good at that.
RUSSELL. It says it on your license. *(He reaches into his pocket and pulls out a ladies' wallet.)* Here.
MARGE. You— Where?
RUSSELL. I tried phoning, but there was no answer. *(MARGE opens up her wallet.)* You can count it if you want. I didn't take nothin'.
MARGE. Come here.
RUSSELL. Aw, lady. I didn't take any of it! I just found it like that—
MARGE *(takes out a photo and shows it to him)*. This is my granddaughter. *This* is Sheila.
RUSSELL *(smiles)*. She's pretty. I can see the resemblance.
MARGE *(a beat, she stands)*. Well, no use staying around here if I don't have to and *you* need to get yourself back to work. You'd better cross your name off that list. Don't want some government employee working too hard calling your name.
RUSSELL. They have to do something. *(MARGE exits without her purse which she left on the chair.)* You forgot your— *(RUSSELL goes over to clipboard and crosses out his name. He turns around, runs over to the purse and picks it up. MARGE re-enters.)*
MARGE. I forgot my—
RUSSELL & MARGE *(simultaneously)*. Purse.
MARGE *(taking her bag)*. Thank you. *(Blackout.)*

# THE QUESTION
*Mayo Simon*

### CHARACTERS

NETTY: In her upper years.
DR. BRONSTEIN: A younger doctor.

PLACE: Dr. Bronstein's examination room.
TIME: The present.

AT RISE: *DR. BRONSTEIN is taking NETTY's blood pressure.*

NETTY. The man is crazy, that's all there is to it. I say, Julius, if you want to take a trip, we can go to Las Vegas. We can go to San Francisco. There's art museums, fine restaurants, beautiful shows. No, he wants to go to Mexico and see bullfights. *(NETTY shakes her head with exasperation.)*
BRONSTEIN. Heart—like a 20-year-old. *(He takes the wrapping off NETTY's arm and gets out his stethoscope.)*
NETTY. Well, I suppose if I had to I could endure it. I have nothing against Mexican people per se, but there's deserts to cross. There's bandits. And I hate that food, you never know what you're eating. He says, Netty, there's nothing to be afraid of when you're with me. I'll always protect you. With his emphysema and...and his ulcer and...and his heart murmur, he's going to protect me.

BRONSTEIN. Breathe... *(NETTY breathes, BRONSTEIN taps her back in various places.)* Again. Deep breaths...

NETTY. I say, Julius, what is so good, what is so valuable about bullfights? And you know what he says? *The possibility of death inspires the passions.* Do you understand this?

BRONSTEIN. Lungs—perfect.

NETTY. So what do you think, Doctor Bronstein? Should I go with him to Mexico to see the bulls killing each other?

BRONSTEIN. I see no reason why not.

NETTY *(with a sigh)*. I don't know. I feel I'm awful pale, ashen, like people look before they die. Of course, when I look in a mirror I see next to nothing. *(Laughs.)* Maybe that's a blessing.

BRONSTEIN. You've been taking the penicillin.

NETTY. That could be what's making me sick.

BRONSTEIN. Not very likely. You have a rash?

NETTY. No rash.

BRONSTEIN. Upset stomach?

NETTY. I'm just awful tired.

BRONSTEIN *(looks at her for a moment)*. So what do you think it is?

NETTY. I'll tell you what it is. The man is impossible. Last week he calls me. He calls me every morning, or I call him, just to make sure we're both still alive. Ah-ah, listen, honey. My cleaning girl is coming five-thirty, six o'clock. Would you mind going to an early dinner like three, three-thirty? I say, wasn't the cleaning girl there two days ago? Well, I made a big mess in the kitchen, I don't feel like washing the floor myself. Okay, it's fine with me. He comes to the door, he's all dressed up. A beautiful beige jacket and charcoal pants, and he's wearing a pink shirt with—I can't see it exactly but maybe palm trees and stars on the front. And he smells like a beauty shop. I say, Julius, you're certainly all dressed up for your cleaning girl. He laughs.

BRONSTEIN. Laughs?

NETTY. Ha-ha-ha! Like a comedian.

BRONSTEIN. I see. And you find that—

NETTY *(ignoring him).* And then he takes me out to a beautiful turkey dinner at the Marriott, with all the trimmings, and he's so charming, so kind, so courtly, it's a pleasure to be with him. But I'm thinking: Why is he being so nice to me?

BRONSTEIN. Well, maybe he enjoys your—

NETTY *(ignoring him).* Because when he tells me his cleaning girl is coming at five-thirty, six o'clock, I don't know if she is coming to spend the night with him or *what.* So he's trying to make it up to me in some way, that's why.

BRONSTEIN *(looking at her).* How old is the cleaning girl?

NETTY. Not a day over 60.

BRONSTEIN. Ah.

NETTY. They say she's good-looking. I say, to each his own. *(Lowering her voice.)* I hear she wears black net stockings and five-inch heels. And she's not that good a cleaner. Not that I care. I wouldn't lower myself... So I call him eight o'clock at night, there's no answer. Well, maybe he's had a stroke. Or maybe they're in bed together and he's not answering. I don't know which one I prefer. Later he told me he had to drive the cleaning girl home.

BRONSTEIN. Well, isn't that a possibility?

NETTY *(stares at him).* Any woman he meets is a possibility. I'll bet he's had so many marriages, he can't even count them. But he talks so nice, so pleasant, everyone wants to have dinner with him. *And he pays!* Where do you find such a man? *(Bitter sigh.)* Day and night they call him. The phone never stops ringing in his apartment. Those old dames, they're all so hungry for attention, they'll do anything for a meal. It's sad. *(NETTY reflects on this for a moment before she continues.)* This man has been absolutely wonderful to me. He takes me to the finest restaurants. He gives me beautiful gifts. Gold coins. Silver chains. Dresses. Hats. But if he didn't have a car, you think I'd give him a second look? He drives me everywhere, I don't need a white cane. He pushes my basket in the supermarket, he lifts my packages. He's a big help to me. So we get to the check-out counter, he says "This is my fianceé!" He calls me his fianceé. "She's 84 and she's blind but you'd never know it." I say, please, does the whole world have to know my age? Besides, I'm not 84, I'm a hundred and four. I say that for a little humor. What's the point of getting mad? Sometimes he takes me to look at places we might live together. He says, I like that building over there, let's get a suite of rooms. I say, what do you take me for? A common street woman? *(Laughs.)* Every five minutes he tells me how much he loves me. He takes me around and kisses me, he doesn't care where he is. Netty, I love you. I love you, Netty. You're the only one I love. A thousand times he tells me, you're so beautiful, you're so intelligent, I just love you. I say, what about these other women? He says, I have no other women. Such a liar. But if I say so myself, none of them can hold a candle to me... *(Pause.)* They say he's good-looking, but I can't see his face so what's the difference? Of course, I would never let him touch me without a blood test.

BRONSTEIN. Well, at his age, I'm not sure he really needs—

NETTY *(ignoring him)*. He claims he's going to take me on an ocean cruise, starting with Hawaii. He says he was at Pearl Harbor when the Japanese attacked, a young lieutenant of the Navy. When he retired, he retired a captain, if you can believe him. He never tells the same story twice. But how can he take a trip, he can barely walk? *(Laughs.)* I think what he needs is a traveling nurse. Well, I took care of my husband for three years before he died, my nursing days are over. Oh, if I had my eyes again, it would be goodbye Charlie. *(Lowering her voice.)* And now he's very busy with the cleaning girl. He's either picking her up, or... or he has to go home and open the door for her, or... or they're having lunch, or... or she's giving him special instructions, whatever that means. If anyone can stand this man they're welcome to him. *(NETTY shakes her head.)* So tell me, Doctor Bronstein. What do you think? Should I marry the son of a bitch? *(Blackout.)*

# HAVING A GOOD TIME
*Steve Allen*

### CHARACTERS

ROGER STILEGER: A scholar in his mid-50s, attractive, moderately urbane but bookish.

BETTY: Young, quite pretty, dark-skinned—perhaps part black, part Latino.

PLACE: A public park.
TIME: The present.

SETTING: *A secluded area of a public park, at night. Two lampposts are visible, greenery, a park bench, etc.*

AT RISE: *ROGER enters, sighs deeply, looks at his watch and places his old-fashioned briefcase on the bench. He sits, rubs his eyes tiredly. A few moments later, sounds of an argument between a man and a woman are heard. BETTY appears, still speaking angrily to someone offstage. She sees ROGER, her tone changes.*

BETTY. I said, how you doin'?
ROGER. Oh. Why, fine, thank you.
BETTY. You wanna have a good time?
ROGER *(considers the question briefly, then nods).* More than anything in the world.
BETTY. You got it.

ROGER. I beg your pardon.

BETTY. I asked you if you wanna have a good time.

ROGER. Yes. Everyone wants to have a good time. The American people, in fact, expend an inordinate amount of their energies in the attempt.

BETTY. What the hell you talkin' about?

ROGER. I was about to ask you the same thing.

BETTY. Let's get down to business. Twenty-five bucks.

ROGER. I have the impression I'm listening to a badly edited tape recording. What *about* twenty-five bucks?

BETTY. That's how much it'll cost ya.

ROGER. How much *what* will cost me?

BETTY. How much a good time will cost you.

ROGER. How can you possibly know that? A good time could conceivably cost nothing at all in financial terms, or it might rob me of my life's savings.

BETTY. You crazy?

ROGER. There were times when my late wife thought so—but, no, I'm not. How about yourself?

BETTY. Hey, Jack, do you know what I am?

ROGER. You would appear to be a young, pretty woman of Latino extraction, and perhaps black ancestry as well.

BETTY. Hey, what the hell are *you*, Ted Koppel? Listen, I asked you if you wanted to have a little action. If you do, just get up the scratch and we can get to it.

ROGER *(truth suddenly dawns on him)*. A-hh, I see. You're a prostitute.

BETTY *(sarcastically)*. Hey, man, don't ever go on *Let's Make a Deal.* You wouldn't win doodley-squat.

ROGER. I do not know what doodley-squat is, although I have never liked the sound of the term. Nor have I ever

*Duets*

watched *Let's Make a Deal*, which I take it is a television program. Nor, I'm sorry to say, am I interested in your sexual favors.

BETTY. Who said anything about doin' you any favors?

ROGER. Young lady—if I may use the term—I sat on this bench a moment ago because I was seized by a feeling of utter exhaustion.

BETTY. Then you ain't cruisin'?

ROGER. That is correct.

BETTY. Then you don't want to make it with me, no way at all?

ROGER. I'm afraid not.

BETTY. You gay?

ROGER. I have moments of gaiety. But I am not as it happens, homosexual.

BETTY. Well, you certainly are a wise-ass.

ROGER. It's not my intention to be.

BETTY. Ain't you got the scratch?

ROGER. The what?

BETTY. The money, the twenty-five.

ROGER. If you'll forgive me for saying so, I don't think it's any of your business how much money I have.

BETTY. What I meant was, if you ain't holdin' right now, we could go someplace where you could *get* the bread, you know?

ROGER. Why are you so persistent?

BETTY. Why are you so goddamn nosy? You sound like the law.

ROGER *(chuckling)*. No, I'm not a policeman.

BETTY. What *do* you do?

ROGER. I teach. But I find myself curious—why do you keep bringing up the subject of your, er, availability?

BETTY. Why the fuck do ya think? I happen to need twenty-five dollars right now.
ROGER. Why didn't you say so? If your need is that desperate, I'll be happy to *give* you twenty-five dollars.
BETTY. What do you want for it?
ROGER. Nothing.
BETTY. You puttin' me on?
ROGER. No.
BETTY. No schoolteacher I ever knew could afford to go around handin' out money. You teach at one of the schools around the neighborhood?
ROGER. No, I teach at the university.
BETTY. Lookin' at your shoes I'd say you do pretty good.
ROGER. What do you mean?
BETTY. I size up guys by their shoes. Guy's got a sharp pair of shoes, he usually does pretty well.
ROGER. To judge by *your* shoes, you're not doing very well. Why, may I ask, do you work as a prostitute?
BETTY. Because I'm too nervous to steal. *(Laughs.)* That's an old joke.
ROGER. Then there's honesty in you.
BETTY. What makes you say that?
ROGER. Because you told an old joke and then confessed. That shows your case isn't hopeless. But you still haven't answered my question. Why are you a prostitute?
BETTY. Because I have these funny habits I have to support—like eatin', drinkin', wearin' clothing, sleepin' with a roof over my head. All that stuff costs money, you know.
ROGER. Indeed it does. The whole human race has to worry about such things. But other people have regular jobs. Why did you choose this?

BETTY. I never did. It chose me. I got on junk, I needed money. I still need it.

ROGER. There are other ways of making it. Did you ever stop to think that there isn't much future in your present profession?

BETTY. Oh, yeah. I think of it all the time.

ROGER. I don't run into too many 50-year-old prostitutes. Do you?

BETTY. I don't think you run into too many prostitutes of any age.

ROGER. You're right about that.

BETTY. Don't I turn you on at all?

ROGER. Appeal to me sexually, you mean?

BETTY. Yeah.

ROGER. It's an interesting question. I've already described you as pretty. There's part of my consciousness that's quite prepared to concentrate on that prettiness. I might even entertain a momentary fantasy or two—about you, I mean. But I choose not to have sexual contact with you.

BETTY. Why not?

ROGER. Well, you might be carrying a venereal disease, for one thing.

BETTY. Yeah, I might. But I ain't. I'm clean.

ROGER. It's a relative term.

BETTY. So what you're saying is—you're chicken. If you *knew* I didn't have VD, you'd jump on my bones, right?

ROGER. No, I would not. I guess it's that I think you're wasting your life, and I see no reason why I should help you to do it.

BETTY. Give me the twenty-five bucks.

ROGER. Very well. *(He takes out his wallet, withdraws two tens and a five, and hands them to her.)*
BETTY. Thanks.
ROGER. My pleasure.
BETTY *(laughs)*. Well, I'm glad you're into *some* kinda pleasure. You sure you don't want somethin' for this?
ROGER. What would I want for it?
BETTY. I don't know, a hand job?
ROGER *(solemnly)*. A hand...job. That's sad.
BETTY. If you ain't tried it, don't knock it. You don't look to me like no guy who's got ten chicks hanging all over him.
ROGER. I'm not. One doesn't need ten, you know. One will do. In fact, one is much preferable.
BETTY. Unless you tried ten all at once you'll never know.
ROGER *(chuckles)*. Scientifically speaking, I suppose you're right.
BETTY *(stands and tucks the money safely away)*. Well, hey, thanks for the bread. You sure I can't give you nothin' for it?
ROGER. You already have.
BETTY. I didn't give you a damned thing.
ROGER. You gave me my life.
BETTY *(considers this peculiar observation briefly)*. I guess there can be well-dressed crazy people, too.
ROGER *(laughs)*. What I meant was, something about this peculiar conversation has made me change my mind.
BETTY. About what?
ROGER *(quite calmly)*. About killing myself.
BETTY *(stares at him, truly perplexed)*. Killin' yourself?
ROGER. Yes.

*Duets* 211

BETTY. Why would you do a stupid thing like that?

ROGER. I'm afraid it would take me quite a few hours to properly answer that question.

BETTY. Well, I ain't got no few hours.

ROGER. I, by way of contrast, now probably have another forty years or so, thanks to you.

BETTY *(with a shrewd look)*. Hey, Jack, if I gave you that much, how about layin' another twenty-five on me?

ROGER *(laughs)*. That would come to about fifty dollars an hour—not far below the professional rate for this sort of service. Oddly enough, I have only seven dollars left at the moment.

BETTY. Then why the fuck did you give me twenty-five bucks?

ROGER. For the soundest of reasons. I thought I wasn't going to be needing it anymore.

BETTY. Then why didn't you give me the other seven?

ROGER. Because you only asked for twenty-five.

BETTY. Shoot, if I knew you was gonna buy the farm I coulda asked for everything you got in the world... How were you gonna do it?

ROGER *(takes revolver out of briefcase)*. With this.

BETTY. But now you ain't gonna do it, right?

ROGER. That's right.

BETTY. Then you ain't gonna be needin' that piece.

ROGER. Right again.

BETTY. Then give it to me.

ROGER. Very well. *(He rises with gun in hand.)*

MAN'S VOICE *(offstage)*. All right, you son of a bitch, drop that gun! *(ROGER whirls, startled, and faces offstage, still holding the revolver.)* Get back, lady. *(BETTY jumps back a few feet, panicked.)*

MAN'S VOICE. Drop it!

ROGER. But I was just— *(He gestures with the gun toward BETTY. Two shots ring out. ROGER groans and crumples to the bench, then to the ground.)*

MAN'S VOICE. You okay, lady? *(BETTY, stricken, staggers to the bench, sits and begins to weep as the curtain slowly falls.)*

# TRIOS

# SCENES FROM THE PENITENTIARY
*Anne Harris*

### CHARACTERS

MARE: In her upper years.
JOE: In his upper years.
BISHOP O'BRIEN: In his upper years.

PLACE: The kitchen in Mare and Joe's Brooklyn apartment.
TIME: The present.

AT RISE: *JOE and MARE sit at the kitchen table eating dinner. JOE wears a pair of trousers and dirty T-shirt, MARE is in a tatty housecoat.*

MARE *(eyes remain fixed on the table).* So what'd ya tell 'im, Joe?
JOE. Whattaya mean, "What'd ya tell 'im, Joe"?
MARE. Just what I said.
JOE. What in the hell does that mean, "What'd ya tell 'im, Joe"?
MARE. It's English, ain't it?
JOE. Well, I don't know, Mare. I don't know what the hell it is.
MARE. Which part confused ya?
JOE *(pause).* I ain't happy, Mare.
MARE. Well join the friggin' club, Joe. You oughtta try menopause.
JOE. I mean it, Mare.

MARE *(throws down her fork, looks up for the first time).* Well, I ain't goddamned happy neither, Joe. How about that?

JOE. So what is it yer tryin' ta SAY?

MARE *(deep breath).* Remember your brother Peter?

JOE. So?

MARE. Remember his wife Pepper?

JOE. Yeah, so?

MARE. Remember she had a gallstone attack two months ago?

JOE. Yeah, so what?

MARE. Remember we happened to lend 'em two thousand bucks? Do you remember that?

JOE. You don't hafta go this slow, Mare.

MARE. When the hell are they gonna pay us back?

JOE. How should I know?

MARE. You said you was gonna talk to Peter this mornin'. *(Pause.)* What'd'ya tell 'im, Joe???

JOE *(pause).* Oh, jeez, I forgot to ask him. I'll hafta talk to 'im tomorra, Mare. Sorry.

MARE. You are pathetic, Joe.

JOE. Awright, Mare.

MARE. No, you are. That's the clinical term for it: pathetic. Trust me. I used to be a nurse's aide.

JOE. You was never a nurse's aide; you mopped floors is all. That is not a nurse's aide. *(Doorbell rings.)* Get the door, Mare.

MARE *(resumes eating).* You get the door.

JOE. It's probably Martha anyways; get the door. *(Pause. Doorbell rings again, longer.)* I ain't gonna say it again, Mare. *(Pause, JOE stares hard at MARE.)* IT'S OPEN!

MARE *(dropping her fork).* My eardrums just hit the back wall.

JOE *(resumes eating)*. I tole ya to get the door, Mare.
MARE. Thank you very much. I hope you visit me in the institute for the deaf and dumb.

*(BISHOP O'BRIEN pokes his head around the door. He carries his hat in his hand.)*

BISHOP. Hello?
JOE. Yeah? Who are you? *(JOE stands, as BISHOP enters further. MARE pulls her bathrobe around her more closely.)*
BISHOP. Good evening! I'm Bishop O'Brien.
JOE *(to MARE)*. What'd ya call the bishop fer?
MARE. Why in the hell would I call a bishop? Pardon my language, Bishop, it comes from living with a slob. *(BISHOP is at the table now; extends his hand.)*
BISHOP. Quite all right. I guess you don't remember me.
JOE. Sure, have a seat... I'd know you anywhere.
MARE. Yeah...
JOE. The, uh—
MARE. Right, the—
JOE. Coronation.
MARE. Emancipation.
JOE. Proclamation.
MARE. No, no, no. It was the—
JOE. Miniature golf tournament at Jones Beach.
MARE. Hold it. I got it right on the tip of my—
JOE. It wasn't the Statue of Liberty celebration, was it?
MARE. Will you let me think for a minute, please? Can you shut your trap for one minute and please let me think?
JOE. Sure. *(He resumes eating, BISHOP still stands, awkwardly. Neither JOE nor MARE offer him a seat.)*
MARE *(triumphant)*. It was Jack's ordination!

*Trios* 219

BISHOP. You're absolutely right! It's nice to see you again. How are you both?

JOE *(to MARE)*. Well done, Einstein.

BISHOP. I hope I'm not interrupting your dinner. May I sit down?

JOE. I'm flabbergasted, Mare. Absolutely flabbergasted.

MARE. Thank you, Joe.

JOE *(aside)*. You got a memory like an elephant.

BISHOP *(insistent)*. May I please sit down now??

MARE *(glares at JOE. To BISHOP)*. Sure. Take a load off.

BISHOP. Thanks. You've got a lovely house here. *(He sits.)*

JOE. So what brings you out to Bensonhurst, Bishop?

MARE. To what do we owe this honor?

JOE. I mean, we're simple folks.

MARE. We're not stupid. Don't get us wrong—

JOE. —We just like the simple things in life. That doesn't mean we don't love the church, though. I loved church when I was a boy.

MARE. We're very proud of our son. Sure, we've had our ups and downs, but Jack's a good kid—

JOE. I always thought he'd change his mind about bein' a priest. Not that I don't like priests... I was raised a Catholic, you know. Very religious. But sometimes people change their minds...

MARE. And now he's happy as a pig in mud.

JOE. Jeez, Mare—

MARE. He says he's found his "vocation." Do you know what that is, Bishop?

BISHOP. Yes I do, Mrs. Esposito. A vocation is God's call to a man, his one true path in life...

MARE. That sounds nice. Does it work for women?

JOE. Women all got the same vocation, Mare, so He don't have to call anymore. Your supposed to learn from your mother.

MARE. You're such a riot, Joe.

BISHOP. I'd like to talk to you both for a moment, if I may—

MARE. This is the first time you've been out to the house, ain't it? Would you like a tour? Joe, give him the grand tour.

JOE *(rising)*. Sure, Mare. Follow me, Bishop.

BISHOP. No, it's all right, I—

JOE *(sitting)*. He ain't interested, Mare.

BISHOP. Yes I am. I'd love to see your house, but we've got to talk about your son first. It seems—

MARE. Did you know he studied at Cambridge for a year?

BISHOP. No, actually, I didn't.

JOE. That's in England. Next door to Italy, almost. I was in Italy during the war.

MARE. He was an English major.

JOE. My son, that is. Not me. Certainly not me.

MARE. Shakespeare, I think it was. He knows every book by Shakespeare.

BISHOP. That's wonderful, Mrs. Esposito. I had no idea he'd studied abroad.

JOE. Shakespeare ain't a broad. He's a guy.

MARE *(to BISHOP)*. Please, call me Mare.

JOE. A man's gotta be able to do somethin' with his learnin', or what's it worth? Take me, fer instance. Before I retired, I was a—

BISHOP. May I interject? *(Pause, as JOE looks at MARE questioningly.)*

JOE. Sure, we don't mind intersecting.

BISHOP. I have some bad news.

MARE. Oh. Well, in that case, don't intersect after all. We've got enough bad news, don't we, Joe? *(Wagging her head at the door—apparently a code of theirs. JOE stands, wiping his mouth, and waits for the BISHOP to rise.)*

JOE. Sure, sure, every day. Well, anyway, thanks for comin' by. *(BISHOP doesn't move.)*

BISHOP. Joe, please sit down.

JOE *(sits)*. Sure.

MARE. I'm waitin'.

JOE *(to MARE)*. You always gotta have the last word, doncha? Let the bishop get it off his chest.

BISHOP. Please, this is difficult enough...

MARE. Well spit it out, Father.

BISHOP. It's about Joe—

JOE. I'm right here, Father.

BISHOP. No, I mean your son.

JOE. Oh, JACK...you must mean Jack.

MARE. He means Jacky.

JOE. We call him Jack. He's Joe junior, really, but he never liked bein' called Junior, so—

BISHOP. Well, I'm afraid there's—some bad news.

JOE *(whispering, to MARE)*. Mare, you didn't offer him a cuppa coffee or anythin'.

MARE. Sorry, Bishop, I'm forgettin' my manners—

BISHOP. No, I don't want anything. I have bad news. I came to tell you bad news. It's about Jack. Your son. He's dead. He died today. He's gone now. I came to tell you. I tried to tell you. Can you hear me? Do you understand what I'm saying? Are you deaf? Can you hear anything at all? *(Pause. All three freeze. After a beat, MARE rises.)*

MARE. I'll get that coffee. I don't know what I was thinkin'.

JOE. She ain't normally like this. She retired last month, and she's been in a funny mood ever since. She— She— *(He stops, looks up, confused. BISHOP rises, hat in hand, very formally.)*

BISHOP. If the diocese can be of any assistance, please don't hesitate to call. You know you have our deepest sympathy. *(BISHOP puts his hat on, pauses. MARE and JOE are still frozen in place.)*

JOE. Doncha want that grand tour now?

MARE. We're outta coffee. I'll have to go to the shop.

BISHOP. You'll need to make arrangements for the funeral.

JOE *(to MARE)*. You can't go out now. You'll have to go in the morning.

BISHOP. I'll check in on you later in the week, but you can reach me at the rectory for the next day or two. If you need anything. You should probably ask for me. Not everybody knows the...circumstances.

MARE *(crosses back to table)*. I'm sorry, Bishop. I'm all outta coffee.

BISHOP. That's all right.

MARE *(sitting, to JOE)*. What time do they open down at the Red Apple?

JOE. I don't know, Mare. Have I ever even been to that place? Ever?

BISHOP. I'll...uh...see myself out. Good night. *(He exits. Pause.)*

MARE. Do you remember seein' him at Jack's ordination?

JOE. Remember what?

MARE. Him.

JOE. Who?

MARE. Bishop somethin' or other. Do you remember him from Jack's ordination?

JOE. No. Was I drunk?

MARE. Hard to say.

JOE. You?

MARE. No, I don't drink.

JOE. Do you remember him, I mean?

MARE. Him?

JOE. Yeah.

MARE. Nah.

JOE. Me neither. *(Long pause. MARE stands and begins collecting plates. JOE stands and switches on radio.)*

MARE. Still, it was nice of him to drop by.

JOE. Not really. *(Lights down.)*

# THE TALKING BENCH
## Kent R. Brown

### CHARACTERS

TERRY LYNNE: In her late 40s-early 50s.
JOANNA: In her upper 70s, married to Marcus.
MARCUS: In his upper 70s.

PLACE: A park bench in Brooklyn, New York.
TIME: It is early summer, nearing sunset.

AT RISE: *TERRY LYNN is toweling off, drinking bottled water. Her bicycle is leaning against the back of the bench. Standing nearby is JOANNA, dressed for an airplane trip. A single suitcase and tote bag are near the bench. She looks perturbed, is picking up idle pieces of paper and debris and throwing them into a trash barrel.*

JOANNA. This used to be the place to come on an early summer's night. Stroll down the sidewalk, see a few friends. Stop for a chat.
TERRY LYNN (*softly under her breath as JOANNA continues*). Now it's nothing but joggers and gum wrappers.
JOANNA. Now it's nothing but joggers and gum wrappers.
TERRY LYNN. Mom? I don't think Dad meant a word of it, okay?
JOANNA. Do you live with your father? Do you hear the tone of his look?

TERRY LYNN. Mom, please.

JOANNA. He can just look at me and I can hear "Joanna, please, don't be so hysterical." I'm not hysterical. I'm intelligent. I'm in good health. I take good care of him!

TERRY LYNN. He knows that, Mom. He really does. Told me on the phone that he wouldn't know what to do without you.

JOANNA. Does he tell me? No. He tells my daughter.

TERRY LYNN. His daughter, too, Mom.

JOANNA *(beat)*. Do you think he'll come? Do you think he got the note?

TERRY LYNN. Where did you leave it?

JOANNA. Them. One in the bathroom. One in the refrigerator. One on top of the remote control.

TERRY LYNN. I think he got it.

JOANNA. Then why isn't he here?

TERRY LYNN. I don't know, Mom. All I know is that you called and told me you were going. I asked where and you said—

JOANNA. Italy! He said he'd take me to Italy three years ago and he hasn't done it. "Next year, Joanna. I promise. But not now, I got things to do now. Next year, I promise."

TERRY LYNN. And then I asked if Daddy knew you were going to Italy tonight—

JOANNA. And I said, "Hell, no, he doesn't know. Not yet, anyway!"

TERRY LYNN. Right again. And then I asked...

*(MARCUS enters hurriedly. He looks as if he has stepped into a battle zone.)*

TERRY LYNN. Hi, Daddy. Mom, it's Daddy. Daddy, do you see Mom standing over there?

MARCUS. I'm not blind, young lady, thank you. Hello.

TERRY LYNN. Hi. *(A long silence as everyone waits for the first land mine to explode.)*

MARCUS. When I got home from the dentist, I decided to have a bit of your excellent chocolate pie. My way of getting back at the inevitability of Fate. So I opened the refrigerator and found your note pushed down into the whipped cream. Thank you.

JOANNA. You're welcome. *(MARCUS hands the note to TERRY LYNN.)*

TERRY LYNN. "You shouldn't be looking in here until dinner time, but I know you will because you're a sneaky man." Mom! *(Continuing to read the note while MARCUS and JOANNA are staring at each other.)* "But after forty-six years of marriage you don't know me at all! If you want to know who I really am, meet me at the bench at four-thirty."

MARCUS. Then I felt one of nature's little tugs and went into the bathroom. As I reached for the toilet paper I noticed another note. Lucky me.

TERRY LYNN. Mom, you wrote it on toilet paper?

MARCUS. In red ink. "I'm going to Italy to have a very nice time without you. I will be at the bench at four-thirty if you want to say goodbye. P.S. Don't forget your medications." *(To JOANNA.)* Very thoughtful.

JOANNA. Thank you.

MARCUS. I checked the bedroom, the closet, your jewelry box. You were right. You weren't there.

JOANNA. I haven't been there for a long time, Marcus. And I'm not going to feel like this any—

TERRY LYNN. Mom, he showed up, didn't he? Give him a chance.

MARCUS. A chance to do what?

TERRY LYNN. Mom's a little put out with you, Dad.

MARCUS. Are you the translator? I don't speak English, or what?

TERRY LYNN. Dad, please. She wanted me here, that's all.

MARCUS. You calling out the troops, Joanna? We can't talk like civilized people, you and I?

JOANNA. Italy, you said. For ten years. Italy. I buy books on Italy. I fix Italian meals. We even take Italian lessons.

MARCUS. They are wonderful meals, Joanna. I eat every one of them, don't I? I love your cooking. It sends me to the dentist. But do I mind? Can't we talk about this?

JOANNA. You're going to take over again. I'll try to talk about this but you'll take over. When I wanted to get a new sofa and chair you just bought the first one we saw. You have to shop, look, think about it, take home a swatch or two.

MARCUS. You said you liked it. You sat in the sofa and said it felt great. So I called up the guy after we left and had it delivered. What's so bad about that?

JOANNA. Just because I said it felt great doesn't mean I want it in my house for the next twenty years.

TERRY LYNN. You're trying to control the situation, Dad.

MARCUS. And that's so bad? There's a problem somewhere, I solve it. That's what I do at work. Solve problems. Move paper from one side of the desk to the other side, another problem solved.

TERRY LYNN. You're the problem, Dad.

MARCUS. Me? *(To JOANNA.)* You said I was the solution. When we met you said you came alive. Those were your words. Here. *(He pulls out another note, a bit worn but clearly protected.)* "You make me feel so alive. I'll love you forever." See, you signed it. Joanna.

TERRY LYNN. That's very pretty. When was that?

JOANNA. Valentine's Day, 1957.

MARCUS. And every year since.

JOANNA. Not last year, or the year before, or the year before that.

TERRY LYNN. Oh.

JOANNA. These rips and tears don't just happen over night, Terry Lynn.

TERRY LYNN. I know, Mom.

JOANNA. Did you and Phil just go phht!...up in smoke overnight?

TERRY LYNN. We didn't go up in smoke, Mother. We just realized we were at the end of the movie, that's all.

MARCUS. So it's all about movies, now? When the movie's over you just call it quits? Is our movie over, Joanna? Is that what you're telling me? All that's left are the credits and that thing about the names being changed to protect the innocent?

JOANNA. That was *Dragnet*, Marcus. *Dragnet*'s been off the air for decades.

MARCUS. So we've been off the air, now? For decades? And you're just now finding a way to tell me?

TERRY LYNN *(moving as if she is a referee)*. Look, hey! No punches below the belt, okay? Let's take a break. Time out. Dad, you sit here at this end, and Mom—

MARCUS. Are you telling your father—

*Trios*

TERRY LYNN. Dad, just for a moment, okay, let me do this. Please. And Mom, you sit here. *(MARCUS and JOANNA are now seated on the bench. Both look like school children being punished during recess.)*

MARCUS. If I raise my hand, teacher, can I go to the bathroom?

TERRY LYNN *(laughing, breaking the tension)*. May I, not can I? And no, you can't. Not until the end of recess. *(A long silence.)* Mom says the two of you decided to conceive me here on the bench. Is that right, Dad?

JOANNA. Well, that's not exactly how we—

MARCUS. We talked about it here, Terry Lynn. We conceived you in the Hi-Ho Motel.

JOANNA. Marcus!

MARCUS. She's a big girl, Joanna.

TERRY LYNN. At the Hi-Ho, Dad? That's very romantic. I appreciate that.

MARCUS. We love you anyway.

JOANNA. It was after the fire in the bedroom. The wiring gave out and we had to spend two weeks at the Hi-Ho.

TERRY LYNN. But you decided here, right, Dad? Right here on this bench.

MARCUS. Yeah, we did. We wanted a child.

JOANNA. We wanted you.

TERRY LYNN. And here I am. See what a good decision that was? And the new job, Dad, when you wanted to go into business for yourself. You came here, remember? And you talked it out.

MARCUS. We needed more money for the house, your education. If your mother had said no, then I wouldn't have taken the chance. I would have stayed with Shoemaker's and Sons. That's what I told her.

JOANNA. Oh, please. When was I ever necessary to you.

TERRY LYNN. Mom!

MARCUS. It would have been hard out there for a new man. New people to meet, had to sell myself. I needed your mother's support. She was wonderful.

JOANNA *(to TERRY LYNN)*. We sat here and I listened. His boss was a dummy, no one appreciated your father at Shoemaker's, and how were we ever going to get enough money for your education if he didn't go out on his own and did he have anything to bring to the table or was he all washed up?

MARCUS. We didn't use that phrase in those days.

JOANNA. What, your boss was a dummy?

MARCUS. Bringing something to the table. Very Washington D.C.

JOANNA. So shoot me already, I'm on the cutting edge.

MARCUS. Why are you going to Italy without me? You're bluffing. *(JOANNA opens her purse and takes out her single ticket to Italy. She looks at it. MARCUS extends his hand as if asking to look at the ticket. JOANNA hesitates, then hands it to him. He reads it.)* You got a good price. Twenty-one day advance?

JOANNA. Three months.

MARCUS. Oh. That far in advance.

JOANNA. We were right here, Marcus. Sitting right here, don't you remember?

MARCUS. I must have had a lot of things on my mind. I'm a busy man—

TERRY LYNN. Dad, listen to her.

MARCUS *(beat)*. I remember you said you were going to get the tickets one of these days but I said no, that I had a lot of things on the desk, I couldn't get away, and you said I always have things on my desk because that way I'll be too busy to die.

JOANNA *(to TERRY LYNN)*. Your father has an excellent memory.

MARCUS. And you said there is no way to postpone dying, that it happens eventually but we can make reservations and think about the trip and do our Italian lessons and make our dream come true.

JOANNA. Yes, I did.

MARCUS. I don't dream. I *do*. Everyday, I *do*. *Do* this, *do* that. Tomorrow I'll *do* it all over again. I'm very good at *doing* things.

JOANNA. Dr. Schnable said you can travel, that travel will perk up your spirits.

MARCUS. I've got deadlines, no one can do what I can do, Joanna, you know that!

JOANNA. No one can do my husband as well as you do, Marcus! You! Not Regis Filbin or Peter Jennings or David Letterman. These are the other men in my life, Marcus. But they're real small and stuck inside a television set. I want you. *(A considerable silence.)*

MARCUS. I'm forgetting things! I'm in the middle of a telephone conversation with someone and I forget his name! And we're talking and I'm thinking "What's this man's name! I've known him for thirty years," and then I scream out his name. "Franklin!" And he says "Marcus, what are you yelling at me for?"

JOANNA. So what's new? You've been forgetting things for years.

MARCUS. So what do I do?

JOANNA. You come with me, that's what you do! I want to feel needed again, Marcus, and I'm going to Italy with or without you, and some wonderful man... you're my preference, Marcus, but if you're not there, then some nice Italian man will take me out to dinner in Positano and drink wine with me as the sun sets into the sea. Now I want to spend the rest of my life with you, you workaholic, but you're going to die on me if you don't stop... *(She is beginning to cry but fights against it.)* I promised myself I wouldn't do this! I'm finished. That's all. No more begging. *(She moves to her suitcase.)*

TERRY LYNN. Dad, she's leaving!

MARCUS. Are you leaving, Joanna?

JOANNA. No, I'm brushing my teeth!

TERRY LYNN *(coaching her father).* Don't go!

MARCUS. Don't go.

TERRY LYNN. The suitcase, Dad! *(MARCUS takes hold of JOANNA's suitcase and holds it behind his back. Softly:)* Please.

MARCUS *(to TERRY LYNN).* What?

TERRY LYNN. Please! Don't go, please.

MARCUS *(to JOANNA).* You heard her.

TERRY LYNN. Dad!

MARCUS. Take me with you! I can call the office from the airport. I can call each day from Italy.

TERRY LYNN. No, you can't!

MARCUS. No, I can't, I can... I can...

TERRY LYNN. Take long walks with you.

MARCUS. I can take long walks with you.

JOANNA. Anywhere I want to go?

MARCUS. Anywhere you want to go.

JOANNA. Antique shop? Art galleries? *(Beat.)* Renaissance cathedrals?

TERRY LYNN *(after a long beat).* Dad, that's your cue.
MARCUS. I don't want to be without you. And if that means old furniture and little cherubs flying in the sky then the answer is...yes. But, I'll eat all the cheese I want, I don't care what Dr. Schnable says. *(A long pause.)*
TERRY LYNN. So, what do you say, Mom? A deal, right? I've got to get going here. I've got my divorce support group at seven o'clock.
MARCUS. Do they have support groups for old codgers?
JOANNA *(to MARCUS).* I made two reservations. The other ticket is at the counter.
MARCUS. In my name?
TERRY LYNN. Dad, let it go, will you?
MARCUS. I'm not packed.
TERRY LYNN. You got credit cards, Dad. That's why you work so hard.
MARCUS. I got medications to take.
JOANNA. Dr. Schnable prescribed a second set. I've got them packed in here. *(She taps her purse.)*
TERRY LYNN. Dad? Just say yes. I'm really late.
MARCUS. Yes! But what if it rains every day?
JOANNA. Then we open an umbrella.
MARCUS *(beat).* That's a good thing to do when it rains.
JOANNA. I thought so, thank you.
TERRY LYNN. Hey, a great movie. Nip and tuck right up to the end. I gotta go. Love ya. *(She kisses them both.)* I'll get the mail, turn out all the lights. Don't you worry. Come back when you're ready. Gotta go. Hey, thanks for the Hi-Ho, folks. It's a great life. *(TERRY LYNN exits with her bike. MARCUS and JOANNA look at each other for a moment.)*

JOANNA. I read the other day they were going to replace the benches.
MARCUS. No.
JOANNA. They're going to widen the sidewalk for roller bladers.
MARCUS. Maybe we could buy it.
JOANNA. Maybe. *(Lights begin to fade.)*
MARCUS. Put it in the garden?
JOANNA. We don't have a garden.
MARCUS. You want a garden?
JOANNA. We'll see.
MARCUS. So, you would have picked up an Italian man?
JOANNA. He would have picked me up, Marcus. That's how it goes.
MARCUS. Well, fat chance of that happening. Right? *(He looks at JOANNA who smiles in reply.)* Right? Right. Hey, we better be going. *(He walks to the edge of the stage and looks off.)* How do you say taxi in Italian?
JOANNA. Taxi.
MARCUS. Really, I've been speaking Italian every day and never knew it. *(Calling off.)* Taxi! Taxi! *(Lights continue to fade. JOANNA shakes her head slowly while looking at MARCUS. But she has a warm and loving smile on her face.)*

# THE FAMILY TREE
*Karen Smith Vastola*

### CHARACTERS

JEAN: 30's, a genetic counselor.
ELIZABETH NICHOLS: 40's, a patient in hospital.
RUTH: 70's, a woman on park bench.

> PLACE: A hospital room. A park bench.
> TIME: The present, morning.

AT RISE: *At R there is a hospital bed. ELIZABETH sits on bed dressed in a hospital gown, an open suitcase next to her. Clothes are in the suitcase and more lay next to it ready to be packed. JEAN sits in a chair next to the bed. She wears a hospital coat and has a clipboard on her lap. At L is a park bench. RUTH sits on the bench and wears a jogging suit and sneakers. RUTH can be seen and heard only by ELIZABETH.*

JEAN. So you had your operation on...?
ELIZABETH. Six days ago.
RUTH. I was in the hospital for ten days. I don't understand how they do things nowadays, Rush you in. Rush you out... *(ELIZABETH turns and glares at RUTH. RUTH stops talking.)*
JEAN. And you're checking out...?

ELIZABETH. Today. I told the doctor I'd answer your questions, but I haven't much time. My husband's picking me up in a half hour. I need to change and pack.

JEAN. I'll try to do this as quickly as possible.

RUTH. Rush. Rush. Look at her. She's not ready to go home. Why, this is the first day she's had a full meal. She's barely able to walk... *(ELIZABETH turns sharply to RUTH and glares slightly longer than last time. RUTH stops talking.)*

JEAN. The doctor explained the genetic component of your type of disease?

ELIZABETH. He said they have identified a gene for this disease and there's a good possibility that I have the gene.

JEAN. Based on your family history?

ELIZABETH. Yes.

JEAN. You could be tested for the gene.

ELIZABETH. But I chose not to. What's the point? I know I have it. What's the difference where it comes from?

RUTH. Tests. They love to test you. I know all about that. I'm at the doctor every other week. And what do they find? Nothing. And when they do find something, it has to be as big as a football. How many times did I complain about that lump in my side. A hernia! Why, it must have been in there for years before they got it right.

ELIZABETH *(turns to RUTH)*. If you don't keep quiet I'm going to have to ask you to leave.

RUTH. Leave? Leave. But I'm not here.

ELIZABETH. Yes, you are.

RUTH. No, I'm not.

ELIZABETH. Mother, I see you. I hear you. You're here.

RUTH. Well, if I'm here, then ask her. Ask her if she sees me?

ELIZABETH. Don't be ridiculous. Of course she doesn't.

RUTH. Then how could I be here?

ELIZABETH. I see you, so you're at least half here.

RUTH. Well then, I'll half stay. You'll see me, but you won't hear me say another word.

ELIZABETH. Nothing?

RUTH. Not one. *(Makes zipper gesture across mouth.)* I was just going for my walk anyway. *(Gets up from bench and walks around it.)*

JEAN. You know there can be a difference in knowing if your disease is random or genetic. It could inform any future medical decisions you may need to make.

ELIZABETH. It could also inform my insurance company to drop my coverage, or inform a future employer not to hire me.

JEAN. There are ways to do it without your insurance company finding out. You can pay out of pocket for the test. Your results would be given another name. Only those working on the research will be able to link you with the results.

RUTH. What's the name of those guys that fiddle around with the computers? Hucksters? No. Hackers. That's it, hackers. One of those hackers could get your medical records. I saw on the news last night that a hacker had broken into a Secret Service computer. He found out the travel schedule and the route the President was taking the next day on his visit to the Liberty Bell in Philadelphia. If they can find out about the President, why not you?

ELIZABETH. Mother. Keep walking... *(To JEAN.)* I've already made my decision about the test. I've accepted this disease, I don't need a lifetime warranty to its authenticity... Now, you said you have some questions, please go ahead. *(Stands up gingerly.)*

JEAN & RUTH *(reach out hands)*. Can I help you?

ELIZABETH. No.

JEAN *(looks through papers on clipboard)*. I'm going to draw your family tree on this paper. Let's start with your mother's father. You can keep on packing. Your grandfather had... cancer, and he died from it at the age of 70...

ELIZABETH. ...2. He died on my first birthday. I never knew him...

RUTH. And he never knew you, not really. Every time he would come over for a visit you would be asleep. *(ELIZABETH silently mimics RUTH's repeating of her grandfather's words.)* "Doesn't that baby ever do anything but sleep," he used to say. I don't think he even got a chance to hold her, not once.

JEAN. And his cancer occurred in the same place as yours...?

ELIZABETH. Somewhere. In his abdomen. It's not clear exactly where. When they found it, it had spread.

RUTH. That's wrong. Tell her about his heart. He had a weak heart. The doctor said he could have taken out yards of his intestine and he still would survive, but his heart just couldn't take it. They opened him up to repair a hernia, and he was full of it, full of it. He died two days after the operation.

ELIZABETH. Mother, please. How can your abdomen be full of cancer and the cause of death be a weak heart?

RUTH. I'm telling you what he died of. He died of heart failure. She's putting on that paper what our family died of. His was heart failure. What good is that tree if it's not the truth.

ELIZABETH. I can't find my comb.

JEAN. I'll put down intestinal cancer. Did your grandfather have siblings?

ELIZABETH. Two sisters. One died in her 50s. Mother, did you take my comb?

JEAN. Of?

ELIZABETH. Breast cancer,

RUTH. There was nothing to be done. Her husband had all the money in the world and he still couldn't save her. It had spread. *(Makes gesture with hand all over chest and abdomen.)* Do you remember her? How she'd pick us up in her Packard and bring us to her house. Ramsey, her husband, would go to the basement and bring up his French champagne. He'd wind and wind the old gramophone and she and him would waltz...

ELIZABETH. How can I remember her? If she died before Grandpa and he died when I was one, how can I remember her? *(Looks in hand mirror on table.)* How am I supposed to walk out of this place with my hair like—

RUTH. Well, you remember the stories, don't you?

ELIZABETH. Yes, Mother. I remember the stories.

JEAN. Mrs. Nichols? Your comb's in your hand. You said your grandfather had two sisters.

ELIZABETH *(looks down at hand)*. What?

JEAN. You said your grandfather had two sisters.

RUTH. No comparison.

ELIZABETH. She's not asking for comparison. She's asking what she died of?

RUTH. Old age.

ELIZABETH. Old age? I thought there was something else? *(Props up hand mirror on suitcase, winces as she tries to bend down to look in mirror. Throws it and comb in suitcase.)*

RUTH. Well, no one came out and said it, but it might have been, it probably was cancer, but she was so old. Eighty-two.

JEAN. How old was she?

ELIZABETH. Eighty-two. And I think there was cancer when she died. She might have had an earlier operation for...

JEAN. For what?

ELIZABETH. For what, mother?

RUTH. Oh, that was nothing, I heard about that through the grapevine. She'd never tell you. Cancer. Here. *(Points to abdomen.)* But it was just a little thing. They took it out. She lived for twenty years after that.

ELIZABETH. A little thing?

RUTH. You have to die of something. Your generation thinks that with the right health club and enough fiber you'll live forever, but you're not the one who decides. God chooses the day you're born and the day you'll die, and no one else.

JEAN. Mrs. Nichols? Mrs. Nichols? Do you know if your aunt's operation had any relevance to your family tree? What was it for?

ELIZABETH. I think it may have been cancer. *(Opens cabinet next to bed. Throws open box of tissues in trash can.)*

JEAN. Where?

ELIZABETH *(touches abdomen)*. Here, but she lived for many years after...

RUTH. Twenty, at least. Tell her that, she should put that down. That's part of the family tree, too. She lived for twenty years... Why are you throwing away those tissues?
ELIZABETH. I don't want them.
RUTH. What's wrong with them. The box is half-full.
ELIZABETH. I have tissues at home.
RUTH. But these are perfectly good and they're free. That's wasteful. Just wasteful.
ELIZABETH. I have my own tissues in my own house and that's what I'm going to use. I don't need their tissues.
JEAN. What about your grandmother?
RUTH. Leave her alone. She was a saint.
ELIZABETH. Now that's a mystery. She died when my mother was young. The only unconfirmed piece of information that I have about her is that she was a living saint.
RUTH. Don't be smart. If there are saints walking this earth, then my mother was one of them.
JEAN. Should I put down that she died of an overabundance of grace? *(ELIZABETH laughs.)*
RUTH. Don't let her do that. She's got a lot of nerve making fun of my mother. What's she anyway, a genealogist? I'm surprised she hasn't asked their horoscope signs.
ELIZABETH. She's a geneticist. She studies genes in families that may carry and pass along certain diseases, like our family with cancer.
RUTH. Well I think it's a lot of baloney. They can't figure out a cure so they waste our time with nonsense like this. Why doesn't she go back to her laboratory and figure out how to fix it instead of worrying families to death.

ELIZABETH. I think our family has died of something other than being worried to death.

JEAN. So I'll put down cause of death unknown. Let's go on. I suppose if you don't know your grandmother's cause of death you wouldn't know anything about her siblings?

ELIZABETH. No.

RUTH. She never spoke about brothers or sisters. She was one of those who escaped. Came over on her mother's lap. In steerage. No place to sleep or even sit but her lap. Very little food. They were desperate. All of the rest of her family had died in the famine. Don't worry about those family genes. They're all six feet under.

JEAN. What about your father's parents, those grandparents. Did you know them?

RUTH. That old bitch. There's another one that died of old age. Why is it the miserable ones live forever?

ELIZABETH. My grandmother...god rest her soul...died of old age, as they used to say. My grandfather on the other hand, had bone cancer.

RUTH. She killed him.

ELIZABETH. Mother, Grandma did not kill Grandpa. He died of bone cancer.

RUTH. She never gave the man a peaceful moment. Always complaining, always yelling at him. "What's the matter with you, Ambrose? You're falling asleep. Sit up." He could hardly hold his head up. He was sick then and no one knew it. If she wasn't such a bitch she might have noticed. He was eating his guts out. That's what gave him cancer. The poor man. He was such a nice man. Do you remember him?

ELIZABETH. Only his wake. *(Blackout.)*

# THE GRAND MOMMY
## *Adam Kraar*

### CHARACTERS

LISA: 33, feels under pressure to have a baby.
GRANNY: Lisa's husband's grandmother.
ANNIE: Lisa's sister-in-law.

PLACE: The patio of a suburban house, anywhere, U.S.A.
TIME: The present.

AT RISE: *GRANNY sits in a chair, showing her charm bracelet to LISA. Offstage, we hear a baby wailing for several seconds.*

GRANNY. I just added this golden flute for Marissa. With the way she wails and carries on, I feel certain that she's going to be a musician. Don't you just think she's the most adorable child you ever saw?
LISA. She's got a good set of pipes.
GRANNY. Now you see these little hooks here? One two three. These are spaces I'm reserving for *your* children.
LISA. Three?
GRANNY. I can always find room on this bracelet for more, so don't you let that stop you. But if you're thinkin' of havin' more than three—
LISA. I'm not—
GRANNY. Hadn't you better get started right away?
LISA. How's your arthritis, Granny?

GRANNY. What are you waitin' for, anyway? I want to be around to enjoy my great-grandchildren.

LISA. You've already got four. That's more than most.

GRANNY. Are you two havin' problems in the bedroom?

LISA. No, Granny.

GRANNY. You sure? You know, you can tell Granny anything.

LISA. Your grandson is great in bed.

GRANNY. Well! Then what's the problem?

LISA. Granny, there is no problem. We're just not ready.

GRANNY. But *I'm* ready.

LISA. I'm still building my practice and you know how much Richard makes on his sculptures.

GRANNY. You don't need money to have a baby.

LISA. Of course you do.

GRANNY. God will provide. Hell, I'll provide. Y'all can come live here. That's what Rhonda and Sam did until they got on their feet. It worked out just fine until Rhonda put a plastic potty in my dishwasher and it broke. That's what brought on this awful arthritis. But when I see those three kids of hers and their children, why, I hardly feel the sharp, shooting pains at all. *(Clutching her hand.)* Ow.

LISA. Want me to get you some—?

GRANNY. Could you just rub it a little? *(LISA rubs GRANNY's hand.)* That's better. I hope I live to see your children. Ow, that's a little too hard, honey. Look out on the patio. Annie has just blossomed since she became a mommy. We all thought she was gonna end up in the loony ward till she got pregnant and then married Milton. Now she's the best mommy I ever saw.

Don't you think, since she became a Mommy, she's just the most wonderful person you ever met?

LISA. She's okay.

GRANNY. Just okay?

LISA. Her interests are a bit limited.

GRANNY. Are you jealous?

LISA. No.

GRANNY. That could be you out there changing that Pamper.

LISA. I think people should use cloth diapers.

GRANNY *(new subject)*. What kind of underwear do you have Richard wearing? I read somewhere that some kinds of underpants interfere with the proper processing of—

LISA. There is nothing wrong with Richard's sperm.

GRANNY. Are you makin' him wear jockey shorts? Oh no, don't tell me you've got him wearing a bikini! No wonder he's been looking so frail.

LISA. We simply do not want to have babies right now. Is that okay with you?

GRANNY. Why not?

LISA. We are happy without them.

GRANNY. You *think* you all are happy—but you're not. I can tell.

*(Enter ANNIE, Richard's sister, who is very pregnant and carries a bundled infant. Sound of baby crying.)*

ANNIE. Oh, hi, Lisa.

LISA *(gives ANNIE a perfunctory hug)*. Hi, Annie.

ANNIE *(to the infant)*. Marissa, say hi to Aunt Lisa. Hi. Hi. Hi. That's a good girl.

GRANNY. Isn't she *precious*?

ANNIE *(to LISA).* You can kiss her if you want. It's okay, that's just baby food on her chin. She hasn't thrown up for over an hour.

LISA. That's okay.

ANNIE. Go ahead, I want her to bond to all her aunties.

LISA. I've actually got a bit of bubonic plague. Wouldn't want to spread the germs.

ANNIE. You're just like Richard. You don't like children, do you? *(Shouting to someone offstage.)* JASON! We do not play shooting people. Why don't you pretend the hose is Mr. Snake? Sorry. What were you saying?

LISA. I love children. I really do.

GRANNY. Let her hold her little niece.

ANNIE. Oops. I think she just made a poopie. Would you like to change her?

GRANNY. Just hold her. Try her on for size. *(She takes the infant from ANNIE and hands her to LISA.)* There. Isn't that nice? Kinda makes you feel all peaceful inside, doesn't it? *(For a moment, we see LISA enjoying the infant. Then we hear the infant scream piercingly at LISA.)*

ANNIE. Oh boy. That Pamper is filling up fast. *(LISA starts to hand the infant back to ANNIE, but ANNIE crosses to the side of the stage.)* JASON! Mr. Snake is not a boa constrictor! He's a garden snake... What do garden snakes do? They make baby snakes. *(Coming back in.)* Sorry. What were you saying?

GRANNY *(to LISA).* Just hold her. She won't bite. Will you? Will you bite? Nooo. Isn't she *darlin'*? *(Renewed screams from the infant.)*

ANNIE. Granny, will you be going to the mall? Marissa needs another gross of Pampers.

GRANNY. I do need to go the mall. Richard needs some boxer shorts.
ANNIE. Would you mind picking up a couple gross? I'll pay you back.
GRANNY. Oh, honey, don't worry about it. I just love to buy Pampers for my great-granddaughter. That's right, I love to pamper you. Yes I do. Yes I do. Isn't she—?
LISA. Adorable. Annie—
GRANNY. I'll take her.
ANNIE. Granny, I better.
GRANNY. No. I'll take her.
ANNIE. Granny, she wants Mommy.
LISA. Well, someone take her; she's about to burst.
ANNIE *(takes the infant)*. Sorry, Lisa. It's not like grown-up poopie, it's a lot easier to get out. Jason, what are you doing?! Snakes don't need condoms. Where did you get that? *(ANNIE exits with the infant.)*
GRANNY *(to LISA)*. Well. It looks like little Jason has been in your room again. *(Blackout.)*

# THE OPEN WINDOW
## *Kent R. Brown*

### CHARACTERS

AMY LOUISE GUNTER: In her middle years.
DIANE EASTMAN: In her middle years.
CLORIS PINGSTON: In her middle years.

PLACE: The interior of a hotel room in Europe.
TIME: The present.

AT RISE: *It is the end of an exhausting three-week tour of the highlights of Europe. AMY LOUISE and DIANE are packing their suitcases for the return trip. CLORIS is staring out an open window. Occasionally we hear sounds of street activity. CLORIS has not yet begun to pack.*

AMY LOUISE. What was the name of it.? You remember? Diane? The one with the huge dome inside—
DIANE. They all have domes inside. That's why they're called cathedrals.
AMY LOUISE. This had all the paintings of the apostles standing and looking very wise? *(Takes the classic "Apostle in the Fresco" stance.)*
DIANE. Just keep packing. I can see Oprah beckoning to me.
AMY LOUISE. I just loved it, loved it all. Everything's so...well, old.

DIANE. That's not our favorite word, Amy Louise. Charming, worldly, these are friendly words, happy words. Old is not a happy word. I've seen enough old buildings to last my entire life, heard languages I couldn't understand and ridden so many miles on that bus that my butt will never recover.

AMY LOUISE. You are such a wet blanket! Cloris?

CLORIS. What's that?

AMY LOUISE. Isn't Diane a wet blanket? Isn't she? *(CLORIS continues to look out the window.)* Cloris, start packing, it's time to go! We've got to be on the bus in thirty minutes.

DIANE. And I need a Wal-Mart that goes on for miles. How do they live over here!

AMY LOUISE. You liked the food, didn't you?

DIANE. It stayed down.

AMY LOUISE. You know you did. Just look at you. *(Pointing to DIANE's midsection.)* See that pooch there? That's all the pasta and bratwurst and paté and pastry and—

DIANE *(laughing)*. Cloris, Amy Louise is pickin' on me. *(DIANE sees CLORIS still at the window.)* Cloris, for fifteen dollars and your window seat, I'll pack your bags for you. What do you say?

CLORIS *(smiles quietly)*. Thanks, but I'll do it. I don't need much. *(Begins to pack, selecting a few items from the closet.)* Anybody want these?

DIANE. For what?

CLORIS. To wear.

AMY LOUISE. It's not my color.

DIANE. It's not your size.

CLORIS *(selecting another item, a blouse or shawl perhaps)*. What about these?
AMY LOUISE. Cloris, what are you talking about?
DIANE. Robert bought you that shawl for this trip.
CLORIS. I know.
DIANE. Gave it to you at the airport.
CLORIS. I know, Diane. I was there.
DIANE. Claude gave me a kiss on the cheek between calls on his cell phone. "Jack, I told that asshole to put six thousand down on Chicago"—kiss, kiss—"and three grand on Seattle."
AMY LOUISE *(to CLORIS)*. Did you have any breakfast? Want me to get you an apple or something? I'm sure they've got an apple downstairs.
CLORIS *(folding two sweaters and placing them on the chest of drawers)*. Maybe the cleaning lady can do something with these.
AMY LOUISE. You're not taking them back?
CLORIS. No.
AMY LOUISE. Why? What's wrong with those sweaters? Robert bought them at Nieman Marcus. My William hasn't bought me anything in years.
DIANE. Claude buys me sweatshirts at trade show conventions. John Deere, Budweiser, Snap On the Wonder Tool! He likes that one a lot. But, Claude's all mine. Lucky me.
CLORIS *(handing out a piece of paper each to AMY LOUISE and DIANE)*. In about a month or so, Amy Louise, you can write me a letter if you want. Send it to this address. Tell me how you're doing. I should be there around then.
AMY LOUISE *(reading her note)*. Istanbul?

CLORIS. And Diane, you can reach me at this address. They'll keep it for me until I pick it up.

DIANE *(reading her note)*. Singapore?

CLORIS. I'm not going home. It's all set up. American Express has been very helpful. All I need is one bag and my toothbrush.

AMY LOUISE. Not going home? Today? With us?

DIANE *(realizing the implications of what CLORIS has been saying)*. She's not going home at all, are you, Cloris?

CLORIS. Not for a while.

AMY LOUISE. When?

CLORIS. I don't know.

AMY LOUISE. Does Robert know?

DIANE. He will when she doesn't get off the plane.

AMY LOUISE. But you have to go home.

CLORIS. Why?

AMY LOUISE. You have so much to do. There's Robert, and you and I go to the club every Thursday...what will you do?

CLORIS. Nothing I don't want to do.

DIANE. Good lord, you're serious.

CLORIS. We didn't really see anything on this trip. Nineteen big, crowded cities in eight countries in twenty-one days. Nothing but cathedrals, castles, rivers, mountains and more cathedrals. But I never met the people.

AMY LOUISE. We know Ramon.

DIANE. Ramon's our bus driver, Amy Louise. We know his wife's name and the name of his six children. That's about all.

CLORIS. I want to know more. I want to ride a bus or a train to a town no one ever goes to. And get off, and look for a hotel on my own, and walk up three flights of stairs to my room and just sit there and wonder what happened to my life. Then, if I have the courage, I'll go back down the stairs and walk into the street. And listen to the people. To the sounds. Look at their faces, go to their dances. Anything that is not my safe, cautious, reasonable, protected life.

AMY LOUISE. Oh, honey, you're just tired.

DIANE. Shell-shocked is more like it.

AMY LOUISE. It's a real common feeling. I read about it. You see all the colors and the sounds and can't understand a word anyone speaks for three weeks and you go a little ga-ga. It'll all be better when you get back to the bridge club and Sunday brunches.

DIANE. You'll be all alone.

CLORIS. Yes, I know.

DIANE. Is that what you want?

CLORIS. For now, yes.

DIANE. I don't know what I'd do with only my own thoughts to keep me company. I have to complain or moan about something, poke my nose into everyone's business. Makes me feel special. If I just had myself and that's it, I don't know what I'd—

AMY LOUISE. That's garbage talk, Diane, and you know it. We weren't meant to be alone.

DIANE. That's why you have William and I have Claude, Amy Louise.

AMY LOUISE. And Cloris has Robert. There. Everybody's covered. *(To CLORIS.)* Is it Robert? Is he an awful man? You would have told us if he was an awful man, wouldn't you?

DIANE. They're all awful men. That's why we love 'em.

CLORIS. No, Robert isn't awful. It has nothing to do with Robert. It's my decision. I have never been on my own since I was born. After high school I went to college, joined the sorority, met Robert and married.
AMY LOUISE. You must have been alone when Robert went on business trips.
CLORIS. I was at the club or volunteering, or taking classes. Always with someone I knew. I want to approach someone in a restaurant and ask if I may join them for dinner.
AMY LOUISE. But you won't know them.
DIANE. That's the point, Amy Louise.
CLORIS. You better get moving.
AMY LOUISE *(finishing up her packing)*. This is all very disturbing. I can't imagine what you're thinking. Leaving Robert all by himself. And us. Leaving us behind.
DIANE. Will you send us a postcard now and then?
CLORIS. I don't know. Maybe.
AMY LOUISE. Oh, my lord! Your medications. What will you do about your medications?
CLORIS. I'll be all right. I'll have them sent to me.
DIANE. Are you frightened?
CLORIS. Yes.
DIANE. Well, you've got my vote, honey. Good for you. Let's go, Amy Louise.
AMY LOUISE *(begins to cry, appears disoriented)*. I just don't know...will you be all right... I mean, what if something happens to you?
CLORIS. I hope it does. That's why I'm staying. To let something happen, make something happen.
AMY LOUISE. Oh, I don't like this at all. I'll miss you.

DIANE. She's not going to the moon, Amy Louise. Come on.
AMY LOUISE *(to DIANE)*. Claude always tries to kiss me in the kitchen whenever we're over at your house.
DIANE. Hell, don't feel special. Claude tries to kiss me in the kitchen, too. He's harmless. Forty-nine years of marriage will make anyone harmless. *(DIANE and AMY LOUISE kiss CLORIS, then exit. For a moment CLORIS is motionless. Then she looks around the room, moves to the window and looks out. As the lights fade we see a smile move across her face.)*

# PAIN AND PAINT
*Nicholas Zagone*

## CHARACTERS

JACK: Early 70s.
DORIS: Late 60s, Jack's ex-wife.
JERRY: Late 20s, admirer of Doris.

PLACE: An art gallery.
TIME: Today or recent past.

SETTING: *An art gallery. We see only indications of the actual paintings, just the frames maybe or possibly spots of light or maybe nothing at all. The only thing we must see is a video camera above the scene.*

AT RISE: *Enter JACK. His movements are accompanied by the down-home music of a country fiddler. He wears a red and black checkerboard hunting shirt, blue jeans and red bandolier suspenders. He carries a rather dog-eared postcard/invitation. As he walks to each painting and stops to study them, the accompaniment of a classic violinist takes over "painting" each picture. Some paintings are wildly orchestrated while others are very sad. The final one, positioned where JACK can look out at the audience, is accompanied by a great high-pitched wailing melody. A bit screechy and grotesque, but beautifully so. It is the same one on JACK's postcard. JACK looks confused, frightened, and a bit heartbro-*

*ken. JERRY, in a nice suit, enters about half-way through JACK's visit. He slithers up beside JACK and also looks at the painting. Silence.*

JERRY. This one hurts me.
JACK. Huhn?
JERRY. Absolutely tears my guts out.
JACK. Maybe you shouldn't look at it.
JERRY. Exactly! I still want more! Why?
JACK. It's a bunch of smeared paint.
JERRY. It's not just smeared. It's *layered*. The woman has so much feeling. It's there. And there, I bet you there's tears in there—with all that pain and paint. Oh it just hurts.
JACK. You want a Tums?
JERRY. Oh thank you. *(He takes one.)*
JACK. Maybe you got an appendicitis,
JERRY. No-no. It's her brilliance. *(A beat.)* So...you know the artist?
JACK. You know how much—say this one here would cost me?
JERRY. Ten-thousand-eight-hundred-seventy-nine-dollars and eighty-eight cents.
JACK. That much, huh?
JERRY. Actually, that's relatively inexpensive. If you have, say, any of her *early* work...or the paintings during her year of rehab? They're priceless.
JACK. Why?
JERRY. All that pain costs. The hurt I feel—oh stop, stop...stop! Can we change the subject?
JACK. What's the cheapest one here?
JERRY. The portrait of her ex-husband down the hall. But it's not very good.

JACK. Why not?
JERRY. I don't hurt.
JACK. If you don't hurt, it's not good?
JERRY. Exactly!
JACK. Maybe it would hurt me.
JERRY. One person's pain does not necessarily make for good art.
JACK. Why?
JERRY. Because we both know, my friend, that truly good art is reflected in the price. So—would you like me to wrap up "Disgusted Woman Hanging Herself With Her Own Apron Strings—#9 on Canvas"?
JACK. I don't think so.
JERRY. Maybe the ex-husband portrait then. Let me show you—
JACK. Is she here?
JERRY *(looking at the video camera)*. Ms. MacDermott? No! She's on the lecture circuit right now, I'm afraid. She is one of the only people I know who loves what she does.
JACK. Will you go tell her Jack is here, please.
JERRY. The ex-husband. In the portrait. You know Doris.
JACK *(looking at the painting)*. Not anymore.

*(DORIS, wearing a long, red, flowing Asian gown, floats in smiling. Grand sweeping violin melodies.)*

JERRY *(taking out a notepad. To JACK)*. Perhaps I can ask you a few questions...
DORIS. It's all right, Jerry, honey, I'll take it from here.
JERRY. Doris! Back so soon?!

DORIS. Hello, Jack. What a surprise. *(A beat as DORIS and JACK take each other in.)* Uh—please forgive my personal assistant, Jerry. Jerry, why don't you get us something to drink, I'll have a spritzer, Jack always has coffee.

JACK. Juice. Cranberry if you got it.

DORIS. I tried to warn you—

JERRY. So, Mr. Conti—

DORIS. You got the order now, Jerry—shoo. Shoo!

JERRY. Mr. Conti, we'll talk again later I'm sure. *(Exits.)*

DORIS *(sotto voce)*. Jerry's writing a book about me. But I'm not supposed to know.

JACK. Were you scared?

DORIS. Oh, Jerry? No. I was watching the monitors from the, um, video cameras here and, frankly, it's been such a long time, Jack, I wasn't quite sure it was you!

JACK. You were scared,

DORIS *(changing tone)*. You were looking at my paintings, I was afraid you'd conjure this up again. *(They look at the painting. A great high-pitched wailing melody from the violin, a bit screechy and grotesque, but beautifully so. An awkward moment.)*

JACK. Tums?

DORIS. Thank you. *(She takes one. They munch their Tums.)*

JACK. I guess I missed something. In you. I didn't see any of this.

DORIS. Neither did I.

JACK. I'm sorry.

DORIS. For what?

JACK. Suppressing you. Suppressing this.

DORIS *(bursts out a laugh)*. Oh, Jack. I don't think there was much time for suppressing anything, We were a

little busy, don't you think? After losing Billy it's not surprising what happened to me. What happened to us. That was a lot of life. *That* was art. This—this—
JACK. I'm still sorry.
DORIS. Billy was my responsibility, there's nothing for you to be—
JACK. Not—not for that.
DORIS. If it's a sorry because you left me, I forgave you a very long time ago. *(A beat.)*
JACK. Remember Clyde? *(DORIS makes a noise, JACK laughs.)* You hated Clyde.
DORIS. He encased rotting crab meat into the framing of our Buick.
JACK. It was a practical joke.
DORIS. It wasn't funny.
JACK. He's dead. Prostate cancer. *(After a silence.)* Season opened in Jackson this morning and for the first time I was going to go hunting alone. So I got ready, got my red and blacks on, opened the front door... and there on the lawn is a buck. Right there in my yard. Eight pointer. And he looked at me. We stared at each other—then I'll be damned if ever so slowly it came walking towards me. I got a gun in my hand and he's walking towards me. It got so close I could almost feel his breath.
DORIS. What did you do?
JACK. I came here. *(A beat.)* Virginia died last spring.
DORIS. Oh my, Jack.
JACK. Twenty years. *(JACK pulls out Tums and offers one to DORIS. She shakes her head. He is about to have another one and can't. DORIS slowly embraces him.)*

DORIS. She was a good woman. To you. Eleven more years she would have beaten my record. *(A beat as they separate.)* Why are you here, Jack?

JACK. I miss you.

DORIS. You miss *somebody*.

JACK *(putting an arm around her waist)*. Do you miss me?

DORIS. Every day. And I get over it every day. *(JACK takes his arm away.)* You should be going, Jack.

JACK. I don't have anything, I don't know what's in me. Seventy-three years. Seventy-three years— Seventy-three years! *(He looks at painting.)* And I don't know what I'd paint.

DORIS. Come on, we're going out.

JACK. Where?

DORIS *(taking his arm)*. We're going out, having a good time—have a drink and chat—then we're going to come back here...

JACK. And then?

DORIS. And then you're going to say goodbye.

JACK. Not again.

DORIS. That's what you're going to do. *(She stands looking at her painting.)* It's what you need to do.

JACK. And what do you need?! I want to paint!

DORIS. I don't need you.

JACK. I don't care.

DORIS *(after a long beat, crossing to the video camera)*. Jerry? Jerry, honey, answer me— I know you're there—Jerry!

*(JERRY enters with drinks.)*

JERRY. Yes, Doris?

DORIS. Let's take a rain check on those drinks. Jack and I are going to go out...

JERRY. You're leaving? Where? Where to?

DORIS. Out! Please—say good night, Jerry.

JERRY. Doris...

JACK. Nice to meet you there, Jerry. Oh. And thanks for the invitation. *(He attempts to pass the postcard to JERRY, but DORIS intercepts. She reads the card and gives JERRY a look.)*

JERRY. Really! Me? Nonsense, Doris! I'm appalled.

DORIS. Jerry.

JERRY. You told me you always wondered what he'd think.

DORIS. Well now we know, don't we. *(She crosses to JACK.)* My very first job was an usherette down the street at Capital Cinema. *(To JERRY.)* Well don't just stand there—what are you waiting for? You want an authorized or unauthorized bio?

JERRY *(putting down drinks and grabbing his notepad)*. Go on! Please!

DORIS. And many, many years ago I ushered this man— he was in a Navy uniform back then—I ushered this man to his seat— *(To JACK.)* You were by yourself—

JACK. Of course.

DORIS. Why?

JACK. There was an usherette there that I found particularly attractive.

DORIS. We'll continue this later, Jerry. *(To JACK.)* Come on. Let's have a drink. I'm going to teach you how to paint. *(They leave as JACK makes a frightened look at the painting and at JERRY. DORIS must give him a little pull. The violin and fiddle music rise and combine harmoniously. JERRY watches them go and looks after them. He excitedly jots some notes in his notepad but then stops and puts the pad away. He grabs the spritzer, but before drinking he toasts where JACK and DORIS have exited. He looks closely at the painting and slowly toasts it as well, as the music crescendos. Lights fade to black.)*

# LAST LAUGHS
*Rachel Feldbin Urist*

### CHARACTERS

ROSE: Recently moved out of her home to stay with SALLY in the Hospice of the Assumption of the Holy Virgin. Rose has terminal brain cancer.

GEORGE: Rose's husband who would greatly prefer to care for Rose in their home.

SALLY: Rose's long-time friend who also has terminal brain cancer.

PLACE: The Hospice of the Assumption of the Holy Virgin.
TIME: The present.

ROSE. I can't stay home anymore, George. I've decided I want to be here, with Sally.
GEORGE. At the Assumption of the Holy Virgin?
ROSE. Yes.
GEORGE. But we're Jewish.
ROSE. It's just a name.
GEORGE. I won't have my wife becoming a virgin.
ROSE. Why not?
GEORGE. I won't have you in any such place.
ROSE. George, you won't have me anywhere. *(Beat.)* I'm going of my own free will.
GEORGE. You're being rash.

ROSE. I'm being practical.
GEORGE. You're crazy.
ROSE. I'm *sick*. And old.
GEORGE. That doesn't mean we give up!
ROSE. Exactly! I want to have a bit of fun before I go. Don't think of it as a hospice. Think of it as a preemptive paradise. They'll take care of me. I'd be with Sally, and I think I'll like it.
GEORGE. Well I won't.
ROSE. Then it's settled. *You* will not go.
GEORGE. Sally and Rose. How is it that the two of you are friends? You're so different.
ROSE. Opposites attract. You know that.
GEORGE. But she's Catholic.
ROSE. I'm not marrying her. I just want her company—in my final days.
GEORGE. I'm not good enough?
ROSE. Oh, George, you're wonderful! I don't know what I'd do without you.
GEORGE. So?
ROSE. I need a friend.
GEORGE. Not a husband? I'm not your friend?
ROSE. You don't like clowns. Or bingo. Oh, George, of course I need you. But I need a...
GEORGE. A mother.
ROSE. Yes.
GEORGE. Ah.
ROSE. You're everything I could ever possibly want in a husband. You're warm, and tender, and nurturant, and loving.
GEORGE. But I'm not female.

ROSE *(agreeing)*. No. I don't want to spend the last days of my life watching you grieve. I want to hear jokes, and laugh, and— Oh, George. *(Gently.)* You can't do that.

GEORGE. Maybe I can. Maybe I'll take a vacation. I'll go on a cruise. I'd like to laugh, too.

ROSE. You're wife's dying and you'd go on a cruise?

GEORGE. You can experience it vicariously.

ROSE. Over my dead body.

GEORGE *(chuckling)*. I'll go water-skiing! They say it's fun.

ROSE. You can't.

GEORGE. Why not?

ROSE. 'Cause I *want* you to be sad.

*(A knock at the door, SALLY enters.)*

SALLY. Am I interrupting?

ROSE. Sally!

SALLY. Listen, I know what you're going through, and I just want to make sure you know that it's just her *living* quarters that will change. That's all. She's still the same Rose, and you are still her husband, and you love each other as much as ever. You and Rose have to look at this as your final adventure. It's all in the way you look at it.

GEORGE. We've been together forty-seven years.

SALLY. Oh, George. Don't start blubbering. If Rose stays here, the two of you will be free to enjoy each other's company. Otherwise she'll be a burden. You'll grow tired of her. You wouldn't want that. Listen, before Joe went off to Sunny Horizons, I took care of him for two years. By the time they took him, I was ready for divorce. Now, I'm happier than I've ever been in my life. I'm relieved of my burdens. I have visitors! People bring me flowers! Godiva chocolates! And I can eat as much as I please.

ROSE. But you can't. You don't. You don't taste anything anymore.

SALLY. That's beside the point.

ROSE. Ah.

GEORGE. Sally, didn't you have an activity scheduled? Basket weaving? An egg toss?

ROSE. Don't send her out, George.

SALLY. He can't send me out, sweetheart. It's my room. *(Awkward moment.)* But I'm sure there is something going on for me. I'll check. *(She leaves.)*

GEORGE. Is Sally good company for you?

ROSE. Oh, yes. She really is. What is it with you two? Why is it always fireworks when you're together?

GEORGE. Doesn't matter.

ROSE. It does to me. *(Pause.)*

GEORGE. I counted up the cards. A hundred and twenty. A great many people are going to miss you. Nobody'd write to me if I were sick, Rosie. They write to *you*.

ROSE. Oh, please. If you had something dramatic, a brain tumor, you can bet your boopie they'd write to *you*.

GEORGE. It's not the drama of it, Rose. It's you.

ROSE. Well, professors shouldn't get love letters from their students, my sweet.

GEORGE. *You* were my student.

ROSE. I'm different.

GEORGE. Yes, you are. *(Fighting tears.)* I miss you already, Rose. I want to tell you these things now, while

we can still look at each other, and hold hands, and talk together. And if there's anything, Rose, anything at all that you want to say to me while we still have time, please, please say it. *(Pause.)*
ROSE. You've just talked with them, haven't you?
GEORGE. Who?
ROSE. The doctors.
GEORGE. What makes you say that?
ROSE. What's the prognosis?
GEORGE *(dismissing her worries)*. Oh, Rose. *(Hangs his head.)* They won't say.
ROSE. Which means they did.

*(SALLY re-enters.)*

SALLY. I'm back! Nothing scheduled for me!
GEORGE. Surely they can find something.
SALLY. Why don't you like me, George?
GEORGE. Who said I didn't like you?
SALLY *(blows him raspberries)*. You're not convincing.
GEORGE. Sally, I like that you appreciate my Rose.
SALLY. But?
GEORGE. But for as long as I can remember, you've acted as though I was the worst thing that could happen to her.
SALLY. Well, you're a man, aren't you?
ROSE. Sally!
SALLY. Joke! That was a joke!
GEORGE. It wasn't funny.
SALLY. I'm sorry.
ROSE. George just spoke with the doctors, Sally.
SALLY. Really? Don't listen to them.

GEORGE. Why not?
SALLY. Gloom and doom. That's all they know.
GEORGE. They tell the truth.
SALLY. As they see it.
GEORGE. I need to know.
SALLY. What they call truth? Why? Why does their truth have to be your truth? Why can't you and Rose just cuddle and giggle for a few days? Why turn to doctors when you can have a little fun? I *will* leave you two alone. *(She heads out, then turns back.)* I know that Rose knows this about me, George, but maybe you don't. I was the...head...I was valla...the valenectarine...of my high school class. Just so you know. I'm a...cummerbund. I'm not stupid. *(She leaves.)*
GEORGE. Sad.
ROSE. I'm going to sound like that, too.
GEORGE. I wasn't referring to her speech.
ROSE. I love you, George.
GEORGE. I know. I've always known that, Rosie.
ROSE. I was wondering, George, whether we could ask the doctor about this sudden need for sleep. I do get so sleepy.
GEORGE. I'll ask tomorrow.
ROSE. Yes. Ask the cloney one. You know, the dapper one with suspenders. And those handsome...those... liney jackets.
GEORGE. Herringbone.
ROSE. Yes. Dr. Herringbone. I knew you'd know who I meant.
GEORGE. You can count on me.
ROSE. And there's something else, George.
GEORGE. What is it, sweetheart?

ROSE. I want you to make sure that the food is strictly kosher. They served something yesterday that made me wonder—a kind of fish... *(Remembering its name.)* Quail. It didn't look right.

GEORGE. You want kosher food?

ROSE. Of course I do, George. I wouldn't be here if I thought it wasn't strictly kosher. You know that.

GEORGE. I'll check with the kitchen.

ROSE. Thank you, George. Will you ask Rabbi Herringbone for me?

GEORGE. Of course I will.

ROSE. You're always here for me, aren't you?

GEORGE. I try, Rose. *(Silence. He holds her hand, kisses it, fondles her fingers.)*

ROSE. Benny?

GEORGE. It's George.

ROSE. There's this noise. A clicking. Clippety-clop. Like horses. I don't like it. It's clamorous, embarrassing, like cleverless clowns. Clickety-clack. Clappety-cloop. Maybe John can explain it. If we only knew the basis of it we could stop this clarified clucking, this clinging and cleaving to one another. It's downright clannish! And they give classes in it! If they were classy, or clairvoyant, they could learn from one another instead of giving these clumsy, cloudy opinions. And such claims! They clash! Acclaim is clandestine. It's nothing. And people are so very talkative; it's C L this and C L that. They don't *need* to clap. They cloak themselves in all this C L knowledge, and it just makes people feel bad. It's not nice to make so many people feel C L ignorant. It's clammy! And some of the C L meanings may not even be known. *That* makes people feel bad, let me tell you. We should get a C L dictionary. Because the lack of C L knowledge should *never* be used to humiliate people. That's clowning. And we're *not* clowns. *(Pause.)* I have to send out New Year's cards. It's almost time. *(She falls asleep. GEORGE strokes her hair.)*

GEORGE. You're leaving me, aren't you, Rose? I don't want you to leave me. *(With sudden assurance.)* You know what? You can't leave me. You've become part of me, Rose. Like a phantom limb. I feel you with me even when you're not there. I woke up this morning and I felt you beside me. I went down to make coffee, and I heard you singing. I set the breakfast table for two, Rose. And somehow, you were there. You'll always be there. You're part of me, Rose. You'll never leave me. Never. Never. Never. *(Sound of ROSE snoring. Lights fade.)*

# THE PICKUP
## Kent R. Brown

### CHARACTERS

WILLIAM: In his upper years, dressed nicely in vest, coat and good slacks.

BARTENDER: Man or woman, mid-40s.

JEAN: In her upper years, dressed quite nicely.

> PLACE: A bar in Seattle.
> TIME: The present.

SETTING: *The bar is slightly rundown, but there was some class here at one time. Two tables, chairs, counter.*

AT RISE: *Eight-thirty in the evening. It is raining outside. WILLIAM is sitting at a table sipping a drink and making some notes in a ledger. A black briefcase is open on the table. The BARTENDER is cleaning behind the bar, etc.*

BARTENDER. I'll be closing up pretty soon.
WILLIAM. Yeah, okay. Thanks. Just a bit longer, okay?

*(WILLIAM continues working and glances at his watch. JEAN enters and moves to a second table. WILLIAM*

*continues working. The BARTENDER approaches JEAN.)*

BARTENDER. Hi, how are you tonight? Pretty wet out, eh?
JEAN. Fine, thank you. And yes, it is. Raining cats and dogs.
BARTENDER *(helps JEAN with her coat and umbrella).* Here, I'll take these, put them over here. *(Hangs the coat on a coat rack, opens up the umbrella so it can dry.)*
JEAN. That's very kind, thank you.
BARTENDER. I won't be staying open much longer.
JEAN. Well, I won't take long. A glass of white wine, Chablis if you have it.
BARTENDER. Sure. *(Returns to the bar.)*
WILLIAM *(who has been overhearing the conversation).* They have rotten wine here.
JEAN. Is that so?
WILLIAM *(to BARTENDER).* Bring her a glass of—
JEAN. Thank you, but I can order for myself.
WILLIAM. Sorry. But they buy their wine by the gallon, that's all.
JEAN. Nothing wrong with jug wine.
WILLIAM. You're right. My mistake.
BARTENDER *(returns with a glass of Chablis).* Here you are.
JEAN. Thank you.
BARTENDER *(leaning in confidentially, but WILLIAM is still able to hear).* His name is William. Don't know his last name. Comes in here twice a week. Traveling salesman. Keep your guard up. *(BARTENDER returns to the bar. JEAN takes a sip of her wine. She winces.)*
JEAN. Oh, dear.

WILLIAM. So what do you think? Smooth, mellow?

JEAN. The bartender told me to keep my guard up, that you are a traveling salesman and come in here two nights a week. He said your first name is William.

WILLIAM. And the last name is Franklin.

JEAN *(toasting WILLIAM).* To your health, Mr. Franklin. *(JEAN shifts her elbows slightly and the table wobbles. She barely saves her wine from spilling.)* Oh, dear.

WILLIAM *(overlapping as he rises and moves to JEAN's table).* Oh, oh. I'll get it. Just need a little something to level the table—let's see... *(He returns to his table and finds something in his briefcase, tears it in half, and returns to JEAN's table. He kneels down and jiggers the paper under one of the table legs.)* Yep, this'll do it. There we are. No problem at all. Done.

JEAN. Lortell. Jean Lortell. *(They shake hands.)* Thank you. I appreciate your effort. Very much.

WILLIAM. Well, I didn't like how those sales figures were turning out anyway. May I join you, Ms. Lortell? My table's way over there and this chair is right here.

JEAN *(laughs; to BARTENDER).* You warned me. He is very smooth.

BARTENDER. He has a soft spot for classy women.

WILLIAM. Babes. Classy babes.

JEAN. That's not politically correct, Mr. Frank.

WILLIAM. Bill.

JEAN. Does this approach do pretty well for you, Bill? It seems a bit forward.

WILLIAM. I'm sitting here, aren't I?

JEAN. For now, yes.

WILLIAM. So what brings you here? This isn't exactly the Ritz.

JEAN. I'm visiting my sister. She's the manager of the movie theatre at the end of the block.

WILLIAM. The Majestic. Great balconies.

JEAN. And you would know, wouldn't you...

WILLIAM. Bill.

JEAN. Bill. And she told me to meet her here. That I'd be safe.

WILLIAM. Little did she know. I'm an engineering consultant. Building materials. I have clients all around the country.

JEAN *(beat)*. I'll be staying three weeks. Then I'll return to Wyoming. And you?

WILLIAM. Wyoming! What a surprise. I have two clients in Laramie.

JEAN. You'll say anything, won't you?

WILLIAM. Would you go out with me this Friday? Dinner at six, maybe a movie?

JEAN. And I suppose you'll want my sister to get us in free.

WILLIAM. What a good idea. *(To BARTENDER.)* Anywhere around here to take a lady to dinner?

JEAN. I require fine food and good wine and excellent service.

BARTENDER. We have a Denny's out on the highway and a Howard Johnson's on the interstate.

JEAN *(smiles at WILLIAM)*. They've got good ice cream at Howard Johnson's.

WILLIAM. And good pancakes at Denny's.

JEAN. We'll see.

WILLIAM. See? Why, I can see everything. Here, let me read your palm.

JEAN *(to BARTENDER)*. Does he ever get tired of hearing his own voice?

BARTENDER. Where's a good case of laryngitis when you need it?

JEAN *(extending her hand to WILLIAM)*. Read on, old Swami.

WILLIAM *(making "Swami" gestures before he reads her palm)*. I can see it all now. Yes, you will meet me for dinner this Friday. It will be raining.

BARTENDER. It always rains in Seattle.

WILLIAM. We'll go to Denny's. The best seat in the house. I'll have the turkey club and you'll have—

JEAN. The chicken salad.

WILLIAM. Then we'll go to Howard Johnson's for dessert.

BARTENDER. The man is definitely a charmer.

JEAN. A legend.

WILLIAM. A vanilla ice cream soda for me and—

JEAN. Nope.

WILLIAM. Nope?

JEAN. Chocolate.

WILLIAM. Really? A chocolate soda?

JEAN. Really.

WILLIAM. And a strawberry sundae for you?

JEAN. Banana split.

WILLIAM. No!

JEAN. True.

WILLIAM. I'm certain it was a strawberry sundae.

BARTENDER *(to JEAN)*. I bet he doesn't ask for directions either.

WILLIAM. Hold on now. Here comes the best part.

BARTENDER. Hang on tight.

WILLIAM. I'll go on business for several weeks.

JEAN. Will you call?

WILLIAM. Every night. Then, quite suddenly, I'll return for three days. It'll still be raining.
JEAN. My sister will be sick and I'll volunteer to help out at the movie theatre. I'll let you in free.
WILLIAM. We'll get to see *It Happened One Night* with—
BARTENDER. Clark Gable and Claudette Colbert.
WILLIAM. Hey, whose story is this?
BARTENDER. Sorry.
WILLIAM. And we'll sneak up to the balcony.
BARTENDER. You won't.
JEAN. We will.
BARTENDER. Making out at the movies! At your age?
WILLIAM. At any age.
JEAN *(to WILLIAM)*. Then you'll call me when you get to Laramie.
WILLIAM. I'll stay at the old Brownstone Hotel.
JEAN. And that's where we'll get married. And it will be a lovely day, flowers everywhere, clear blue sky—
WILLIAM. The minister will have this terrible cold. "Dearly beloved..." *(BARTENDER sneezes.)* "We are gathered together to..." *(BARTENDER sneezes.)* And you will make me so very happy. *(He leans in and kisses JEAN.)*
BARTENDER *(pause)*. So, this is really how it happened?
WILLIAM. Yep. And this is where we met. *(WILLIAM moves to the location.)* Over here were several booths.
BARTENDER. Dad loved those booths. Said it gave a cozy feel to the place.
WILLIAM. And I was seated about here and Jean came in, looked around, and sat right about—
JEAN. Where I am now. My sister was ill. Her husband had died quite young and she was left to run the movie

*Trios* 277

theatre. I had come to help out. Just finished college. William was a traveling salesman.

WILLIAM. And I knew she was the one for me. Didn't even know her name. Never even heard her voice. But the way she stood. So open and honest.

JEAN. I invited him into my life.

WILLIAM. And I accepted the invitation.

BARTENDER. Dad had just opened the bar a few months before.

JEAN. This became our place. We'd meet here, rain or shine. He proposed while we were dancing. And Bill asked your father to be his best man.

WILLIAM. He flew out to Laramie and got so smashed he couldn't find the ring in his pocket.

JEAN. Kept fumbling around so bad the minister took his own wedding ring off and gave it to Bill.

BARTENDER. Then what?

JEAN. Just as he was kissing me at the end of the service your father found the ring, held it up in the air and yelled Eureka! So Bill put that one on, too. It was like I got married twice.

WILLIAM. I got another territory after that. Haven't been back to Seattle in years. Then your Dad and I lost touch over time.

BARTENDER. After Dad died, I went through his old address books. Notified everyone I could find.

WILLIAM. Thanks for tracking us down. We're sorry about his death. He was a wonderful man.

JEAN. Thanks for playing along with us tonight.

BARTENDER. Hey, after all the years of hearing the stories about you two, this was great, believe me. Well,

I'm going to close her up now, but no rush. Take your time. *(Begins to close the bar.)*

JEAN *(to WILLIAM)*. That was very clever the way you joined me at the table.

WILLIAM. I'm still sharp as a tack.

JEAN. What did you tear up, by the way? Not the tickets, I hope.

WILLIAM. Anniversary card.

BARTENDER. Oops.

WILLIAM. Here, I'll get it. *(Reaches under and retrieves the anniversary card from under the table leg. He hands it to JEAN.)*

JEAN. My, how lovely. Now show me the tickets. *(WILLIAM crosses to his table and rummages through his briefcase, having difficulty finding the tickets. He frantically checks his suit pockets, his trouser pockets. JEAN and the BARTENDER are looking worried.)*

WILLIAM. I have them right here... I'm sure I put them in... I wouldn't have left the house without... *(JEAN reaches into her purse and pulls out the tickets and holds them high above her head.)*

JEAN. Eureka! You left them on the bed, after you packed.

BARTENDER. I wouldn't let her out of my sight if I were you.

WILLIAM. I try not to. *(Music is heard quietly. WILLIAM extends his hand to JEAN and they begin dancing. They are dancing the waltz and move confidently as the lights begin to fade.)*

BARTENDER. Next time you're in the neighborhood, I'll have some new paint on the walls. Maybe put in a few booths, change the curtains maybe. So where are you going for your anniversary? Bermuda? Paris? Hey, so where are you going on your—? Well, wherever you're going, I think you're there already. Happy Anniversary. *(He picks up WILLIAM's beer, toasts the dancing couple and drinks to their good health.)*

# THE BOOKMOBILE DOESN'T COME BY ANYMORE
*Billy Pullen*

### CHARACTERS

MARTHA: 70s.
JOSEPHINE: 70s.
LAURA FAY: Early 40s.

PLACE: Living room of a home in a small Mississippi town, a good two hours from anywhere important.

TIME: The present.

MARTHA *(doing leg lifts).* Twenty...nineteen...eighteen ...seventeen... Shoot! This hurts! Sixteen...fifteen... fourteen... Josephine! Josephine! Thirteen... twelve... eleven... JOSEPHINE! I thought *Guiding Light* had done gone off. Six...five... LORD! JOSEPHINE! Three...two... JOSEPHINE!
JOSEPHINE *(offstage).* WHAT?
MARTHA. REACH IN MY PURSE AND SEE IF YOU CAN FIND THAT EXTRA-STRENGTH TYLENOL—
JOSEPHINE. YOU SURE YOU DOING THOSE LEG LIFTS RIGHT?
MARTHA. YES! *(To herself.)* She's gonna start about the VCR—
JOSEPHINE. YOU KNOW IF YOU BOUGHT A VCR YOU COULD DO YOUR EXERCISES WHILE—

MARTHA *(overlapping).* WHILE YOU WATCHED! CAN YOU NOT FIND—

*(JOSEPHINE enters with Tylenol and water.)*

JOSEPHINE. You know, you really ought to get one of those—
MARTHA. I'm not getting one of those purse-wallet things.
JOSEPHINE. Wal-Mart's got 'em on sale for nine, ninety-six—
MARTHA. I'm not studying Wal-Mart. Besides, Laura Fay macramed that purse for me when she was at that clinic in Memphis.
JOSEPHINE. You could probably do more leg lifts if you—
MARTHA. I'm not buying a VCR!
JOSEPHINE. I don't understand you, Martha. You don't even have a microwave!
MARTHA. I'm just not modern... besides, I saw that exercise tape at your house. Old women showing off wearing that wild-colored spandex just like they got something to show.
JOSEPHINE. When's Laura Fay supposed to be here?
MARTHA. You can't tell about Laura Fay. She said after lunch time. One thing about these leg lifts, it makes you clean all the dust balls out from under everything. Laura Fay used to laugh at me for going barefooted all the time.
JOSEPHINE. Martha, I've never seen you go barefooted!
MARTHA. I used to mop the kitchen floor about every hour. I just couldn't stand my bare feet touching a nasty floor.

JOSEPHINE. I'll swear, Martha, you spend half your life cleaning. You know you could afford help—
MARTHA. Josephine, I'm 77 years old, and you've known me long enough to know—
JOSEPHINE. —you're not gonna change!
MARTHA. Seventy-seven! I still can't believe I'm 77!
JOSEPHINE. Honey, I'll be 71 next month!
MARTHA. Baby Girl's in her 70s!
JOSEPHINE. I haven't been called Baby Girl in years. What was Mama and Daddy thinking?
MARTHA. Did they really not name you?
JOSEPHINE. Called me Baby Girl till I was 6...the school wouldn't accept nicknames. Daddy called me Baby Girl till the day he died.
MARTHA. How old was Mr. Waycaster?
JOSEPHINE. Seventy-seven...sorry.
MARTHA. It's all right. I'm not afraid...
JOSEPHINE. Martha Fuqua!
MARTHA. Not too much. I accepted Jesus Christ as my personal Savior when I was in the sixth grade and I was baptized, totally immersed, not sprinkled.
JOSEPHINE. You don't believe in once-saved-always-saved?
MARTHA. Oh no! Faith without works is dead—
JOSEPHINE. Let's leave this kinda talk for the preacher—
MARTHA. I know for sure you can fall from Grace. Just look at Laura Fay...never mind... I'm doing the best I can on my personal salvation. Seventy seven!
JOSEPHINE. What?
MARTHA. Neither one of my parents lived this long.
JOSEPHINE. Oh, Martha, people are living a lot longer now.

MARTHA. Is that so good?

JOSEPHINE. MARTHA!

MARTHA. My brother died at 75! He withered away into nothing. Seventy-seven!

JOSEPHINE. If you put some Miss Clairol number four—

MARTHA. Josephine!

JOSEPHINE. It's not a permanent rinse—

MARTHA. Did you come over here to talk about my hair?

JOSEPHINE. It'll take ten years off, honey—

MARTHA. It's not vanity!

JOSEPHINE. Martha Fuqua!

MARTHA. I quit putting that rinse in my hair not long after Houston got electrocuted—

JOSEPHINE. That was ten years ago—

MARTHA. I used to beg Laura Fay to fix my hair. She spent a year up at Vaughn's Beauty School and still hadn't earned a dime doing hair. I offered to pay her good money to fix my hair, and it was twelve years ago not ten.

JOSEPHINE. What?

MARTHA. It was twelve years ago when Houston... I told Houston not to waste our money on that beauty school for Laura Fay, but he wouldn't have it no other way. Big hearted. That's what killed him. I told him those sharecroppers didn't need him to help put those copper pipes in the well...all those old pipes. Houston was pulling those old pipes from the well and they touched the electric wires. I heard the screams all the way to the house. Suddenly I ran out all the way through the soybean fields. "Oh my God! It's Mr. Fuqua!" I heard them scream over and over as I ran and ran. They begged me not to look. His fingerprints

were burned on the pipe. Monroe County Power and Light was at fault. The wire was too close to that house! Our house and all of five hundred acres of farm land was paid for, and Houston took out a two hundred and fifty thousand dollar life insurance policy I didn't even know about. No, I chose not to take legal action. I just want...wanted Houston back. Well, I wish to goodness Laura Fay would come on. I don't know whether to put that casserole in or not—
JOSEPHINE. Go ahead and cook it. You can always heat it back up. I haven't seen Laura Fay in over a year.
MARTHA. It's just as well. That clinic didn't even want me up there.
JOSEPHINE *(delicately)*. Was it alcohol this time?

*(LAURA FAY enters.)*

LAURA FAY. ALCOHOL, VALIUM, FOOD, DIET PILLS, YOU NAME IT! If it's addictive, Laura Fay "Fuck Way" does it!
MARTHA. Laura Fay! I thought you were gonna call me when you got to Memphis!
LAURA FAY. Surprise! Surprise!
MARTHA. But how did you get—
LAURA FAY. I rented a car, Mother!
MARTHA. But, your driver's license—
JOSEPHINE. You're looking good, Laura Fay!
LAURA FAY. Twenty-five pounds. First time in fifteen years, I been a size eight—
MARTHA. I wish you wouldn't say "Fuqua" like that—
JOSEPHINE. I can handle it, Martha, I'm Episcopalian!
MARTHA. What makes you pronounce it like that?

LAURA FAY. Hello, Mother, don't you look nice? *(They finally hug.)*
MARTHA. That's a cute outfit, honey, you mighta lost too much weight—
LAURA FAY. Too fat. Too thin. Never could please a "Fuck Way." You're looking good, Miss Josie.
JOSEPHINE. This hair just won't do right.
LAURA FAY. A little trim in the right places, and maybe a dark auburn rinse—let "Fuck Way" do your hair!
JOSEPHINE. I don't know.
MARTHA. Laura Fay! Why on earth do you keep—
LAURA FAY. When I first checked in, I got pissed off 'cause nobody knew how to pronounce it.
MARTHA. It rhymes with You Pay.
LAURA FAY. My first time in group therapy, they had this Dr. Wilma—just like on the Flintstones—Dr. Wilma Thompson, she had this god-awful, whiny Yankee voice. Had one of these phony smiles, I think she's a lesbian and don't know it—
MARTHA. I'm not even gonna answer to that.
JOSEPHINE. How could you not know that?
MARTHA. Don't bait her, Josephine.
LAURA FAY. You ARE a titty-baby, Josie!
JOSEPHINE. That is NOT why they called me Baby Girl!
LAURA FAY. Huh?
MARTHA. This is worse than television.
LAURA FAY. Anyhow, when Dr. Thompson was calling the roll—God, it was SO eighth grade—she said in that pitiful Yankee voice, "Laura Fay F... How do you pronounce that?" I couldn't resist. I just stared at her and said in my best Kathleen Turner voice with a Southern Baptist smile, "Fuck way."

MARTHA. How much more trouble did THAT get you into?

LAURA FAY. I got to be real popular after that—you know me, Laughing Laura—but they did have to lock Dumb Brother back in his room. He wouldn't shut up laughing.

JOSEPHINE. Who?

LAURA FAY. This fucking fool, I don't even know his real—

MARTHA. Laura Fay!

LAURA FAY. Sorry about the f-word, Mother—

MARTHA. I know you have a better vocabulary than that.

LAURA FAY. Three years of Latin...exempt on every exam.

MARTHA. Are you hungry? I got a casserole ready to put in the oven.

LAURA FAY. Who else but Mother would not even brag about her 45-year-old loser daughter dropping down to a size eight, giving up booze and dope for a year, and say nothing except. "Are you hungry?"

MARTHA. You look real nice, Laura Fay.

LAURA FAY. Just doin' the best I can.

JOSEPHINE. Did that lesbian doctor lock up Dumb Brother?

LAURA FAY. Honey, she had two butch assistants to do that—

MARTHA. Oh please! Why did you call him Dumb Brother?

LAURA FAY. Oh, he was all the time cutting loose singing gospel songs, you know "Amazing Grace," I nearly shit when he started singing "Will You Come?" to the lesbian doctor—

JOSEPHINE. Did she have real short hair?

LAURA FAY. But he would sing over and over, "Are you sowing the seed of the King, dumb brother," and laugh out loud about the dumb brother sowing the king's seed.

JOSEPHINE. Did that lesbian have real short hair?

MARTHA. JOSEPHINE!

JOSEPHINE. The one in Memphis that does that TV commercial for Auto Zone—

MARTHA. That's a man, Josephine!

JOSEPHINE. How can you tell?

LAURA FAY. Robin is androgynous.

JOSEPHINE. What's that?

LAURA FAY. It's from Latin, meaning—

MARTHA. I don't want to know.

LAURA FAY *(winking at JOSEPHINE)*. You can look it up in the dictionary.

JOSEPHINE. What?

MARTHA. ANDROGYNOUS!

JOSEPHINE. Oh.

LAURA FAY. Don't be embarrassed, Josie. If it weren't for the dictionary, Mother wouldn'ta made it through my teenage obsession with rock music—

MARTHA. At least I took an interest in what you listened to.

LAURA FAY. Mother didn't know they were nasty words till she looked them up in the dictionary—

MARTHA. That's enough, Laura Fay!

LAURA FAY. I was hell as a teenager, huh?

JOSEPHINE. Sometimes ignorance is bliss.

LAURA FAY. Ignorance just gets you fucked up.

MARTHA. Laura Fay!

LAURA FAY. Sorry, Mother. I'm just a bull in a china shop. What I don't step on, I shit on!
MARTHA. I can't believe you drove down here—
JOSEPHINE. I'll go put the casserole in the oven.
LAURA FAY. It was real easy, Mother, I can drive a stick shift.
MARTHA. I'm talking about a driver's license, Laura Fay!
JOSEPHINE. We're just glad to see you, Laura Fay. Let's go make a pot of coffee.
LAURA FAY. Good idea! Decaf for me!
MARTHA. Since when did you start drinking decaf?
LAURA FAY. It's been a year, Mother. Lot you don't know about me.
MARTHA. I know enough.
LAURA FAY. Do you, Mother? *(Blackout.)*

# FOOD IS LOVE
*Sandra Fenichel Asher*


### CHARACTERS

MRS. EDELSOHN: About 70, neatly dressed, very self-assured.

HERBIE COHN: Late 20s, shy and nervous.

WAITRESS (or WAITER): Any age.

PLACE: A hospital coffee shop.
TIME: The present.


SETTING: *A table for two is at center stage.*

AT RISE: *It is the lunch hour. WAITRESS, harried by noon rush, is clearing off dirty dishes. MRS. EDELSOHN enters, wearing a hospital volunteer's smock, mimes squeezing past crowded tables.*

WAITRESS *(as MRS. EDELSOHN sits).* Mrs. Edelsohn! You're early today.
MRS. EDELSOHN. My daughter-in-law had a business appointment. Fancy-schmancy. I told her I would take the bus, but she insisted on dropping me off first.
WAITRESS *(smiling, but not really listening; as exits with dishes).* Well, isn't that nice?

MRS. EDELSOHN *(to no one in particular, and without pleasure)*. Yes, she treats me like her own mother.

*(HERBIE enters, gestures to the empty chair at her table.)*

HERBIE. Excuse me, do you mind if I sit here? There—uh—doesn't seem to be any other—
MRS. EDELSOHN *(indicates he is welcome)*. Of course.
HERBIE *(sits)*. Thank you very much.
MRS. EDELSOHN. You're in a rush?
HERBIE. Yes, actually, I am.
MRS. EDELSOHN. You should never rush your meals. Terrible for the digestive system.
HERBIE. I know, but this is—

*(WAITRESS enters, pad and pencil in hand, and interrupts.)*

WAITRESS. Okey-dokey, Mrs. E., what can I get you?
MRS. EDELSOHN. The usual, please.
WAITRESS. A cup of tea? No lunch? You're sure?
MRS. EDELSOHN *(shudders at the thought)*. No, thank you. I ate already at home.
WAITRESS. One of these days, Mrs. E., you're going to break down and eat a lunch here. It ain't that bad, y'know? And, what the heck, the emergency room's right down the hall. *(She laughs, pleased with her own joke. HERBIE smiles. MRS. EDELSOHN's look could freeze alcohol.)* Okey-dokey. One cup of tea. With lemon. *(Finishes writing, then to HERBIE.)* You two together?

*Trios* 291

HERBIE. I beg your pardon? Oh! No. I just—um, you know—sat down.

WAITRESS *(annoyed)*. Separate checks, then?

HERBIE. Yes, please. *(WAITRESS sighs and flips her pad to a new page.)* Although I suppose we could—I mean, one cup of tea—

MRS. EDELSOHN. Don't even think of it! Please! We're total strangers.

HERBIE. Right. It's just that—well, you know—

WAITRESS. Are you ready to order?

HERBIE. What? Oh, sure. Ah—I'll have a hot dog, fries, and a large Coke.

WAITRESS *(as MRS. EDELSOHN eyes HERBIE with concern)*. Okey-dokey. *(Snaps menu out of his hand and exits.)*

MRS. EDELSOHN. Ralph Nader's mother would never serve him a hot dog. Never.

HERBIE. I beg your pardon?

MRS. EDELSOHN. I read it once in an article. You never know what they put into those things. I *read* that.

HERBIE. Oh, well, I guess what I don't know won't hurt me.

MRS. EDELSOHN. What you don't know—God forbid—could kill you.

HERBIE. Yeah, well—that, too.

*(An awkward pause, then WAITRESS enters with tray; sets food in front of them.)*

WAITRESS. One cup of tea, with lemon. Hot dog, fries, and Coke. Enjoy! *(She exits. MRS. EDELSOHN frowns at HERBIE's food. He looks from her to his food anx-*

*iously a time or two, then takes a deep breath and pops a fry into his mouth.)*

MRS. EDELSOHN. I take a bite of fried food, you know what happens? *(HERBIE stops chewing; she clutches a fist to her chest.)* It stops right here. For hours. I could just die. *(HERBIE swallows, gags, reaches for his Coke.)* Coca Cola, I don't even want to talk about. You read about the experiment where they put the human tooth into a glass of Coca Cola and it eats the enamel? *(HERBIE nods, hopelessly.)* Tell it to my granddaughter. Please. The junk they let her eat and drink, you would not believe! I tell them until I'm blue in the face, but do they listen? Ha! What do I know? *(A pause.)* You have children?

HERBIE *(perking up).* Well—um—actually, yes. My uh—we just had a—you know—a little girl.

MRS. EDELSOHN. You just had a baby?

HERBIE. Well—uh—my wife, actually. She—um—yes, she did. A little girl.

MRS. EDELSOHN. *Mazel tov* to you both! You should have nothing but *naches* from her.

HERBIE. Uh—thank you. That's very kind of you.

MRS. EDELSOHN. You know Yiddish?

HERBIE. A little. A *bissel.* You know. My—um—my grandparents—

MRS. EDELSOHN. You're Jewish! How about that! What congregation?

HERBIE. Well, actually, we—uh—we don't belong to any—

MRS. EDELSOHN. Shame on you. It's nice to be with your people. You'll come to Temple Israel Friday night. I'll introduce you to the rabbi myself. Rabbi Samuels, a wonderful man. Brilliant. The best. His wife—eh, never mind. *(Confidentially.)* You'll come.

HERBIE. Well, ah, I'll have to see—

MRS. EDELSOHN. It's settled. You'll come. Now, what room is your wife in? I'll pay her a little visit. *(HERBIE starts to protest.)* That's my job. Every Monday, Wednesday and Friday, rain or shine. I take up flowers, messages, I sit, I listen. I tell you, the things I hear. You sit long enough, they spill out their whole life story. Especially if they're alone, you know, a widow, a widower. They have no one else to talk to. It's a crazy thing, you can feel closer to a total stranger sometimes than to your own— *(Gesturing, she knocks her spoon off the table.)*

HERBIE. Oh! I'll—ah—get you a clean one. *(As he stands up, he knocks over her tea.)*

MRS. EDELSOHN. *Oi Vey!*

HERBIE *(pulls all the napkins out of the holder trying to mop up)*. Oh, I am so sorry!

*(WAITRESS hurries in.)*

WAITRESS. Will you look at that! Will this day never end? *(Mops table vigorously with her rag.)* Did you get any on your smock, Mrs. E.?

MRS. EDELSOHN. Well, yes, a few spots here and there—

WAITRESS *(neither looking at her nor listening; finishes mopping)*. That's good. That's all right, then.

HERBIE. Could you please bring—um—

MRS. EDELSOHN. Mrs. Edelsohn.

HERBIE. Mrs.—ah—Edelsohn—another tea? Please. Put it on my check.

WAITRESS. One more cup of tea? Why not? *(Takes away cup as she exits.)*
MRS. EDELSOHN. That's very kind. You're a good boy.
HERBIE. Are you sure you're all right?
MRS. EDELSOHN. I'm fine. I'm drip-dry. Now, what was I saying? It was something important. Oh, yes, you can get closer to a stranger sometimes than to your own flesh and blood.
HERBIE. I think that's terrific, what you do. Visiting the sick and all. I mean, I spent a lot of time with my grandmother, but—well, you know, she was my grandmother. What you do takes a—a very special kind of person.
MRS. EDELSOHN *(pleased with him and herself)*. Yes. It does.

*(WAITRESS enters, sets tea in front of MRS. EDELSOHN.)*

WAITRESS. There you go, Mrs. E. Better luck this time. *(She shoots HERBIE a withering look as she exits.)*
HERBIE & MRS. EDELSOHN. Thank you. *(As MRS. EDELSOHN fiddles with her tea, HERBIE picks up his hot dog and takes a bite.)*
MRS. EDELSOHN. Heart attacks, cancer—oh, yes, I've seen it all. Such misery. *Such misery.* *(HERBIE puts down his hot dog miserably. MRS. EDELSOHN notices.)* When they get cold, they're really awful, aren't they?
HERBIE. I guess so.
MRS. EDELSOHN. You're a slow eater.
HERBIE. Well—sometimes.
MRS. EDELSOHN. That's good. You must chew your food carefully.

HERBIE. I try.

MRS. EDELSOHN. That's very good. *(Takes a sip of her tea, looks at her watch, begins preparations to leave.)* Well, it's time to begin my rounds. What is your wife's room number, did you tell me already?

HERBIE. Uh—no, I—um—well, it's—uh—407, I think. It's right across from the nurse's station—

MRS. EDELSOHN. And the name?

HERBIE. Herbie.

MRS. EDELSOHN. Mrs. Herbie?

HERBIE. Oh! Oh—ah—no. I thought you meant me. That's my name. Herbie Cohen.

MRS. EDELSOHN. *Chaim?* In Hebrew, my son Henry is also a *Chaim.* It means "life," did you know that? *L'chaim,* to life.

HERBIE. Yes, I knew that.

MRS. EDELSOHN. And your wife's name?

HERBIE. She's—uh—Mrs. Cohen. *(A pause; then, muttering.)* Mary Theresa.

MRS. EDELSOHN. Mary Theresa—Cohen?

HERBIE. Well—uh—yes, actually, Mary Theresa McCartney Cohen.

MRS. EDELSOHN *(nods knowingly and in disapproval).* I see. *(HERBIE pushes his plate away, slumps, and sighs.)* Your parents are living?

HERBIE. No—ah—no, they're not.

MRS. EDELSOHN *(nods, as before).* It killed them.

HERBIE. What?

MRS. EDELSOHN. You know what. It killed them.

HERBIE. No! They were dead anyway. I—I mean, they died before. Long before. My grandmother raised me. But she died long before, too.

MRS. EDELSOHN. Well, I am sorry for your losses. May they rest in peace. Did she convert?

HERBIE. My grandmother? No, she was born Jewish.

MRS. EDELSOHN. I meant your wife.

HERBIE. Oh. No.

MRS. EDELSOHN. You signed away the children?

HERBIE. What?

MRS. EDELSOHN. They make you sign away the children. To be Catholics.

HERBIE. Oh. No. Um—actually, she's not—um—a practicing Catholic. She's—ah—well, I guess I'd have to say agnostic.

MRS. EDELSOHN. That's a relief, anyway.

HERBIE. I—I think I better be getting back. My wife was—you know—having her lunch and I thought I—

MRS. EDELSOHN. You hardly ate a bite. A bird couldn't live on what you ate.

HERBIE. Probably not. I guess I really wasn't very hungry. *(He starts to rise. MRS. EDELSOHN lays a hand on his arm. He sits.)*

MRS. EDELSOHN. Your grandmother never told you about the starving children in Europe? *(HERBIE nods, a doomed man.) My* grandmother, of course, *was* a starving child in Europe. My mother, also. Well, so was I, for the first couple years. Anyway, my mama used to tell me a story about my *bubba*, my grandmother. You called your grandmother Bubba? *(HERBIE nods.)* My mama used to tell me that Bubba would say to her, "Faygela"—that was my mama's name, Faygela, little bird. And that's how she ate, like a little bird. Like you. "Faygela," my *bubba* used to say, "we have very little here and a mother wants to give so much to her child.

*Trios* 297

A good education, I can't give you. A nice house, I can't give you. Beautiful clothing, I can't give you. Safety, security, I can't even give you those." *(A pause.)* You know about the pogroms? *(HERBIE nods.)* You know? What do you know, a boy raised by his loving grandmother in the U.S. of A.? For days, weeks, whatever the Tsar decided, anybody could do anything they wanted to the Jews. *Anything.* So—my *bubba* used to say to my mama, "Faygela, there is one thing I can give you. Good food. As long as there is one fresh egg in this world, that I can do for you, because, Faygela, I cook it with all my love." And then, my mama, may she rest in peace, would say to me, "So eat, sweetheart. Food is love. Eat for your *bubba*, in the *shtetl*, in Russia." *(MRS. EDELSOHN glows with the memory. A long pause. HERBIE clears his throat, shifts in his chair, sits up straight, and begins to eat his cold hot dog. MRS. EDELSOHN beams at him for a moment, pats his arm, rises, and moves away, then stops and turns back, her face darkening.)* Of course, Ralph Nader's mother loved him, too, and she would never serve him a hot dog.

*(HERBIE freezes in mid-choke. WAITRESS bustles in.)*

WAITRESS. Listen, I hate to bother you, but I go on break the minute I clear your table. Are you finished here? *(HERBIE looks up at her, raises his hot dog slightly, then looks over at MRS. EDELSOHN and lowers his hot dog slightly. He looks at the audience, emits a tiny squeal of despair. All freeze. Lights fade.)*

# CARRY ME HOME
*Angela Counts*

### CHARACTERS

MOTHER: African American, 72.
NICOLE: African American, 19.
LENA: African American, 20.

PLACE: Urban America.
TIME: The present.

AT RISE: *MOTHER, a large and formidable woman, is in the living room seated in an overstuffed easy chair. She is wearing black mourning clothes and speaks with a warm North Carolina accent.*

MOTHER *(calling).* Lena, Nicole!? *(No response.)* I tell you... The funeral people gonna be here any minute now, and that child is doing God knows what... playing violin music all day. *(She reaches into her purse and begins reading from a pile of mail.)* Sear's... Montgomery Ward's... phone company. Child, I don't even want to look at that one. *(She looks at it anyway.)* Eighty-nine dollars! *(Looking off toward LENA and NICOLE.)* Who's been calling Baton Rouge on my phone? My phone bill ain't never been over thirty-dollars. *(She puts away the phone bill, and picks out another letter.)* This one here is for Lena. Peabody Conservatory... Lena!! Now come on child we ain't got all day.

*(Lights up on LENA and NICOLE's bedroom.)*

NICOLE. I've never been to a funeral before.
LENA. Neither have I. But Mama's in a good place.
NICOLE. I don't care about her being in a good place, I want her to be with us.
LENA. Me too. *(Gives NICOLE a hug. To NICOLE who has turned away from her.)* Are you going to be okay?
NICOLE. You're going away, aren't you?
LENA. What are you talking about?
NICOLE. I saw the letter. You got accepted into that conservatory.
LENA. Peabody's a half hour away, Nicole.
NICOLE. And I'm going to be here all by myself?
LENA. I'm not starting until the spring. It's a long ways off.
NICOLE. What about your job at the answering service?
LENA. I'm keeping it. Nothing's going to change except that I'll be studying violin.
NICOLE. You'll probably get a place on campus—
LENA. I can't afford to stay on campus—
NICOLE. Start talking and walking funny... Probably won't even recognize me when you pass me by on the street.
LENA. Nicole, I'm 21. I'm not a little kid who's going to go away to school, and come home a different person. You know me. Have I ever let you down?
NICOLE. No.

LENA. You ought to enroll in a community college in the spring.
NICOLE. School's your thing. Anyway, I'm still dealing with Mama... Are you happy about going to Peabody?
LENA. Not as happy as I would be if Mama were here.
NICOLE. I can't be happy about anything.
LENA. That'll change.
NICOLE. I'm not like you, Lena. It's going to take me forever to get over Mama.
LENA. We might never get over it. But she wants us to be happy. You know it's true, Nicole. *(No response.)* Are you going to be okay? *(NICOLE nods her head.)* Nicole, we have each other. And you can come to me for anything. Anything. I don't want you getting into any trouble.
NICOLE. I'm fine.
LENA. Not if you keep talking like that.
NICOLE. I'm just sad. Okay? Mama's dead and everybody's acting like nothing happened. Well, the world is standing still for me, okay? I don't have Peabody. I don't have anything.
LENA. You have me.
NICOLE. I know that.
LENA. So, you're going to be okay?
NICOLE. I haven't used in six months, Lena. No alcohol, no coke, no cigarettes. No nothing. I promised Mama. You know that.
LENA. I know. I just love you, that's all.
NICOLE. Where's Mother Cobb?
LENA. Mother Cobb?
NICOLE. Or just "Mother," if you prefer.

LENA. She doesn't move so fast on that cane. We'd better go help her.

NICOLE *(as they start to exit)*. Congratulations on Peabody.

LENA. Actually, the letter just says I have an audition.

NICOLE. You'll get in.

MOTHER *(rapping her cane on the ground for emphasis)*. You come stand right here, Nicole Renee Cobb. I said right here.

*(NICOLE enters and reluctantly stands before her grandmother. LENA remains in the bedroom.)*

MOTHER. If you didn't ever learn some manners, you gonna learn some now. And you look at me when I speak to you. *(NICOLE looks at her.)* Don't you ever sass past me like you just did.

NICOLE. Yes, ma'am.

MOTHER. What's taking that sister of yours so long?

NICOLE. She was playing the violin.

MOTHER. I can hear that. It's your mother's service today, and look at the two of you acting as if you don't have any sense. You ought to be ashamed.

NICOLE. Yes, ma'am.

MOTHER. The funeral people gonna be here any minute. Is she dressed?

NICOLE *(smiling)*. Yes, ma'am.

MOTHER. What's so funny?

NICOLE *(trying to hide her amusement)*. Nothing, ma'am.

MOTHER. And you don't have to call me "ma'am." Is that what you call your other grandmother?

NICOLE. Yes...

MOTHER. Then you can call me "Mother Cobb."
NICOLE *(as if she were trying out a new language).* Mother Cobb.
MOTHER. Or just Mother, if you prefer. *(Looking offstage.)* What kind of way is that to say goodbye to your mama? Playing the violin all morning as if she's gonna audition tomorrow. She ought to be thinking about your mama. The two of you are working my nerves. *(Affectionately.)* I have a mind to put you up for adoption.
NICOLE *(more for her own benefit).* I'm old enough to get married.
MOTHER. Old enough to get married? How old are you?
NICOLE. Nineteen.
MOTHER. You're old enough to follow directions. You got yourself a boyfriend, I suppose.
NICOLE. Tyrone.
MOTHER. You engaged?
NICOLE *(amused).* No.
MOTHER. Your mama did the best she could raising you two girls alone. *(Approaching the subject carefully.)* Your father ever come around?
NICOLE. Sometimes.
MOTHER. That figures. I haven't seen your daddy in over a year now. You know that? *(No response.)* So don't you feel bad about it. That's just the way he is. I left my husband in North Carolina—when your daddy was a little boy—and we moved to Baltimore. That was my mistake. A boy needs his father, even if he isn't much of one.
NICOLE. Do you think we'll get to see him now that we're living with you?

*(LENA enters unnoticed.)*

MOTHER. There's no telling. Your daddy only comes around when he needs something. And I guess he's been doing okay for some time now.

LENA *(to NICOLE)*. We've managed just fine without him.

NICOLE. I just asked.

MOTHER *(to LENA)*. Now where do you think you're going dressed like that?

LENA. Ma'am?

NICOLE. Don't say "ma'am," Lena. You sound so country.

MOTHER. It's the dead of winter, and—

LENA. It's October.

MOTHER. I don't care if it's June. You don't wear white to a funeral. Now go and change before Stinson's gets here.

LENA. Grandmother...I don't mean any disrespect, but my mother wasn't big on traditional funerals—

NICOLE. Go on, Lena.

LENA *(to NICOLE)*. Since when do you tell me what to do?

NICOLE. Okay, I'm out of this.

MOTHER. You and Nicole are in my care now.

LENA. How come we've never seen you before? You talk about how Daddy needed a father and all that, but we've never seen you either.

MOTHER. That's not true, Lena.

NICOLE. Lena, just drop it.

LENA. You know it's true, Nicole.

NICOLE. We're here now. You just want to hold a grudge.

MOTHER. Lena, you don't remember, but I used to keep you girls when your mama had to work late. Or sometimes your daddy would bring you by for a visit.
LENA. So what happened?
MOTHER. Your mama moved, went to live with her mother. I called, but as time went by, we didn't keep in touch like we should've. I know that. *(A car horn blows.)*
NICOLE *(looking out the window)*. They're here.
LENA. We'd better get going.
MOTHER. I'll get you a heavy coat, Lena. You'll catch pneumonia in that dress. *(MOTHER exits. Lights fade.)*

# MR. WONDERFUL
*Olga Humphrey*

### CHARACTERS

RABINOWITZ: 75 years old. Cantankerous.

NURSE: 60s.

MR. WONDERFUL: A clown. Late 60s, though you can't tell under the makeup. Sweet-natured and naive.

PLACE: A semi-private room in a hospital oncology ward.
TIME: The present.

SETTING: *There are two beds separated by a nightstand. The curtains, which offer privacy, are drawn back. RABINOWITZ sleeps in one of the beds. The other bed is made. On the wall near Rabinowitz's bed are pictures of old movie stars like Lana Turner and Hedy Lamarr, along with some newer faces like Demi Moore and Michelle Pfeiffer. There are a few personal effects on the night table.*

AT RISE: *NURSE enters with a tray of medication.*

NURSE. Mr. Rabinowitz, time for your medication. *(She unsuccessfully tries to rouse the old man, who is muttering unintelligibly to himself. She keeps trying.)* Mr. Rabinowitz!

RABINOWITZ *(finally wakes with a start).* What?! What, already? You people don't believe in sleep?

NURSE. Time for your happy pills. You do want to feel happy today, don't you?

RABINOWITZ. Why would I want to do that?

NURSE *(gives him the pills and cup of water).* I have some good news for you. You're going to have a new neighbor.

RABINOWITZ. Thank God! So that blue-rinse bitch and her two psycho schnauzers finally moved out?

NURSE. No. Here.

RABINOWITZ. What do you mean here? I was told I would have this room to myself.

NURSE. You were told we wouldn't put anyone in here with you *if* it was practical—which it no longer is.

RABINOWITZ. What do I care about practical? I'm supposed to have a private room!

NURSE. I can arrange for you to talk to Administration if you'd like, but I can tell you now, you're not going to get your way.

RABINOWITZ. You tell Administration Rabinowitz is not putting up with this. Not for a second.

NURSE. Okay, but you're still going to have to share the room until it's straightened out. Your new roommate's on his way over. You might want to be prepared...

RABINOWITZ. Prepared for what? Just make sure he doesn't disturb me.

*(The NURSE pulls the curtain as RABINOWITZ settles back down to continue his nap. She then exits. A few minutes later, a CLOWN, fully made up, and wearing a hospital gown and large clown shoes, enters pushing an IV stand with a balloon and horn attached to it. The*

*NURSE follows with his personal effects and a small suitcase.)*

NURSE. Here you are. Need any help unpacking? *(The CLOWN shakes his head.)* Now we're moving you here as a last resort, do you understand? *(The CLOWN nods.)* This is it. Your last chance. If you keep up the shenanigans, we're going to have to ask you to go elsewhere. Okay?

*(He nods. The NURSE exits and he goes about the business of settling into his room. He moves with a jaunty air, whistling a tune. RABINOWITZ wakes up, tears back the curtain and gapes at him. Most of WONDERFUL's luggage consists of toys. RABINOWITZ rings frantically for the NURSE. She enters.)*

NURSE. Yes, Mr. Rabinowitz?
RABINOWITZ. Nurse, there's a clown in my room.
NURSE. Where? *(She gets a kick out of her bad joke.)*
RABINOWITZ. What are you, a comedian? What's the matter with you people? Cancer not good enough for you? You have to give me a coronary on top of that?
NURSE. Have you met? This is Mr. Wonderful.
MR. WONDERFUL *(smiles broadly).* And what's your name, young man?
RABINOWITZ *(glares at him).* Why is he dressed that way? What if he had come at night and I had to go to the bathroom? Can you imagine seeing this thing at night?
NURSE. Mr. Rabinowitz, I really have to agree with you. We've been trying to get Mr. Wonderful out of his clown makeup for weeks, but he refuses.

MR. WONDERFUL. Nurse, if Elizabeth Taylor were staying here would you say: Look, Liz, I'm sorry, but the diamonds have got to go?

RABINOWITZ *(to WONDERFUL)*. Look, you, this matter's been placed in the hands of Administration. Until this situation is cleared up, you'd better stay out of my way.

NURSE. Try to be nice, Mr. Rabinowitz. *(She exits. RABINOWITZ is about to close the curtains again.)*

MR. WONDERFUL. Mr. Rabinowitz, since we're going to be roomies, I think that living with hostility just won't do.

RABINOWITZ. Shove it, clown.

MR. WONDERFUL. Now was that nice?

RABINOWITZ. Listen, Wonderful, or Chuck, which is probably your real name, a temporary mistake has been made. This is supposed to be my private room. But since you're here *temporarily*, you keep on your side and I'll keep on mine. It's a simple system developed after years of trial and error. Your side, my side. You don't disturb me, I don't disturb you. If you cannot adhere to these time-honored rules, then I will kick you flat on your ass out the door. Got it, bozo?

MR. WONDERFUL. Mr. Rabinowitz, may I confide in you for a moment?

RABINOWITZ. Yeah?

MR. WONDERFUL. I've been ejected from every other room in this place. This is my last chance. Otherwise, they're going to expel me from the hospital.

RABINOWITZ. They threw you out of the other rooms? What for?

MR. WONDERFUL. They made a big deal out of such minor things.

RABINOWITZ. Like?

MR. WONDERFUL. Riding my tricycle. Can you believe that?

RABINOWITZ. Aren't you supposed to be ill?

MR. WONDERFUL. Well, obviously, I have some health issues, but my spirit's doing better than ever. And that's the most important thing. I just don't understand why they're so excitable. It's hard to break old habits.

RABINOWITZ. Old habits, huh? What old habits, if I may ask?

MR. WONDERFUL. Juggling.

RABINOWITZ. Oh, boy.

MR. WONDERFUL. ... at night.

RABINOWITZ. Really?

MR. WONDERFUL. Flames.

RABINOWITZ. Of course.

MR. WONDERFUL. They got all bent out of shape when I set my roommate's bed on fire.

RABINOWITZ *(sudden realization)*. You're the one! We were evacuated from the building... in the cold... in the sleet... on the hill... in the wind... under hurricane conditions... in the middle of the night... under a full moon... in one of the worst neighborhoods in town! NURSE!!! NURSE!!!

*(RABINOWITZ frantically rings for the NURSE. She enters impatient and exasperated.)*

NURSE. What is it this time, Mr. Rabinowitz?

RABINOWITZ *(pointing a finger at WONDERFUL)*. FIRE BUG!!!

NURSE. We're all trying to give Mr. Wonderful one last chance. I'd like you to do the same.

RABINOWITZ. Get him out!

NURSE. Mr. Rabinowitz, I personally promise you that your bed will not go up in flames, okay? *(RABINOWITZ doesn't believe it for a second.)* Mr. Wonderful has his little eccentricities, but don't we all? I bet you've both got a lot in common. Now I don't want you ringing that buzzer unless it's absolutely necessary. Why don't you just relax and get to know him.

RABINOWITZ. But...

NURSE. I'm sorry, Mr. Rabinowitz. *(She exits and RABINOWITZ is left alone with WONDERFUL.)*

RABINOWITZ. Why haven't you tried another hospital?

MR. WONDERFUL. I've been banned from all of them. This one's the most liberal.

RABINOWITZ. You have anyone? Maybe they could take you in if you become too obnoxious here.

MR. WONDERFUL. It's just me.

RABINOWITZ. No kidding? Same here. A man like you with no children. Who are you leaving it all to?

MR. WONDERFUL. The clown college in Florida.

RABINOWITZ. Your people. Right. Look, Wonderful, I don't want to be the one to send you home alone. Maybe we can, you know, come to an understanding. If you want to stay until the room situation is straightened out, you're going to have to follow the law according to Rabinowitz.

MR. WONDERFUL. I'll try real hard.

RABINOWITZ. This is *my* room. I was here first. Nobody else wants you. That doesn't put you in a good position.

MR. WONDERFUL. I know.

RABINOWITZ. First of all, you need some guidance and I'm going to give it to you.
MR. WONDERFUL. Thank you, Mr. Rabinowitz.
RABINOWITZ. No tricycle and no juggling of flames.
MR. WONDERFUL. I swear. And for good measure I won't set up my high wire. I wouldn't want to fall on you by accident.
RABINOWITZ. That's the spirit. You've got to realize you've got a bad rep and I'm doing you a big, big favor. If that Pee Wee guy had someone to give him a break, I'm sure he wouldn't have been busted and he'd still be acting like a jackass on TV. But I'm going to give you a break. All right?
MR. WONDERFUL. I really appreciate this. *(RABINOWITZ pulls back the curtain and tries to catch up on that nap. WONDERFUL puts all his things away and then lies on the bed, bored. After a few minutes, he takes a pitch pipe and blows it. Then he starts to sing to himself.)*

"Pickle sweet,
Pickle sour.
I like a pickle every hour.
Pickle sour,
Pickle sweet.
Pickles are very good things to eat."

*(WONDERFUL blows on his pitch pipe and starts another ditty.)*

"There really is a person
under all that hair.

Don't think it's just
a common mutt 'cause
that's not all that's there..."

*(The curtains part.)*

RABINOWITZ. WILL YOU STOP IT!!! *(He glares menacingly at WONDERFUL, who stops mid-song.)*
MR. WONDERFUL. I wasn't disturbing you, was I? *(RABINOWITZ takes the pitch pipe and throws it in the wastebasket. He leaves the curtain open and gets back into bed. WONDERFUL puts some more things away. He leaves something on the bed and then accidentally sits on it. It makes another noise.)* I'm sorry. I'm sorry. It was an accident.
RABINOWITZ. THAT'S IT! GET OUT!
MR. WONDERFUL. You can't throw me out.
RABINOWITZ. Out. Now. Out!
MR. WONDERFUL. If I'm correct, you don't really have the authority...
RABINOWITZ. I'm going to count to three...
MR. WONDERFUL. But...
RABINOWITZ. One... *(WONDERFUL gets up and exits the room. He loiters in the hall as RABINOWITZ climbs into bed. WONDERFUL peers into the room. He's at a loss as to what to do. As people obviously pass by in the hall, he greets them.)*
MR. WONDERFUL. Hi. How are you? Good, good. Much better, actually. I know, wasn't that cherry Jello sublime? *(RABINOWITZ's eyes snap open. He leaps out of the bed again. He goes to the door and slams it shut. Lights fade.)*

# MEMORIZING TIPS AND TECHNIQUES

If you have stood onstage, ready to perform your scene or monologue and suddenly forgotten your lines, then you are not alone. Actors of all ages have, at one time or another, forgotten a line, and this type of panic situation can occur even if you have practiced your lines ad nauseam. Bear in mind that memorizing is a skill that will usually improve with practice. The following tips and techniques used by countless actors may be useful.

• Studies indicate that the number one block to memorization is anxiety. Thus, it is helpful to breathe deeply and concentrate on relaxing as you learn your lines. Visualize standing onstage in front of an audience and performing your lines without hesitation. A strong, positive attitude toward the task of memorizing will go a long way in helping you achieve your goal.
• Depending on the size of your role, try reading the script several times a day for five consecutive days. Read each time with a sense of freshness and commitment. The act of repetition will aid you considerably.
• Avoid memorizing lines as if they are simply lines. They aren't. They are blocks of thoughts and ideas aimed at achieving an objective. Be sure you understand the energy and intention behind the lines and memorize the lines in character.
• Memorize your lines out loud. You'll find yourself stepping into the energy and emotion of the lines which will make them easier to memorize. You will also find yourself investing your lines with more natural bodily ges-

tures. If you memorize in silence, you may be thrown off when you hear yourself onstage in rehearsals.

- Rehearse your lines with another person who is holding your script. You should stand ten to fifteen feet away from that person. If you need assistance on one of your lines, do not refer to your script. Simply say "line" when you need assistance.

- Use your blocking to help anchor your lines: a certain section when sitting on the sofa, another while standing in the doorway, and so on. Since the final blocking of a scene may shift from the initial blocking at the very beginning of rehearsals, don't lock yourself too securely to specific areas of the stage. Know your lines well enough that you can make some adjustments in blocking and still create an exciting character.

- About an hour before falling asleep, review the dialogue and repeat the process within an hour after awakening in the morning. Some older adults have found it useful to tape-record all of the dialogue in their scene or monologue and then play the tape repeatedly.

- Do not reinforce negative attitudes by saying things such as "Oh, darn, I knew that line this morning," or "I always have trouble with this section." Your mind will hear your self-doubts and be reluctant to feel confident about the memorizing process. Positive self-talk with such statements as "I can memorize," or "It's OK to forget a line; I can work around it," may help alleviate anxiety that would interfere with memorizing.

# OTHER TIPS FOR PERFORMANCE AND AUDITIONING

## The Audience

A word or two about your audience. They want you to succeed. Respect their understanding of life. They know good work when they see it.

- Audiences do not come to the theatre to watch actors talk and walk across the stage. They come to the theatre to renew their energy by emotionally involving themselves in the struggles of others who are attempting to deal with life's difficulties.
- Audiences expect actors to believe in the reality of the plot and the seriousness of the stakes involved in the drama. And they will know when you are holding back. Toss yourself fully into the fascinating world of make believe, but remember that the make-believe world on the stage will be judged by the real-life standards of the audience.

## During Rehearsal

- Come to rehearsals prepared to work. Be sure you have studied your part thoroughly and incorporated any changes you, your partner and/or the director have agreed will improve the scene.
- Do not rehearse on the telephone with your partner(s). Don't make a commitment to a scene if you cannot rehearse in person with the other actors. Consider doing a monologue instead.

- Do not rehearse in front of a mirror. It tends to create self-consciousness and truncate the creation of an inner life for your character.
- Don't expect special treatment because you are an older adult. Expend your energy properly and the rewards will be highly satisfying.
- Be candid about important health information that may seriously affect the rehearsal and performance process.
- Avoid the tendency to direct your partner(s). Always discuss the scene with your fellow actors. Don't assume you have come up with the most effective interpretation. Agreement about where the scene should go will help everyone create a fine ensemble performance.

**Auditioning**

Few procedures strike terror into the hearts of actors the way auditioning does. The following tips have been gleaned from numerous observations made by mature actors who have auditioned for hundreds of plays.

- While it is instructive to portray a younger character in an acting class, it is usually most effective in an audition to select a character that is close to your own age. If you perform a character in an audition that is markedly different from your age, then it may stretch the credibility of your performance.
- It is best not to write your own monologue for an audition. Monologues are complex dramatic contrivances that take the skill of a trained dramatist. Often, when actors write and perform their own audition material, they are blind to the dramatic blemishes and inconsistencies

that may exist in the piece. Your purpose in an audition is to impress them with your acting skills and insights.

- Do not select a poem, a piece from a novel or a speech from a film script. Each of these venues requires a special acting approach. (Theatrical casting directors prefer to hear how well you handle material written expressly for the stage.)
- Be sure to time your audition so it meets the time requirements requested by the director, stage manager or producer casting the production. It can be embarrassing to be asked to stop during your piece because it is running too long. Conversely, if your piece is too short, it may not give the auditors sufficient time to seriously evaluate your abilities.
- Arrive about thirty to forty-five minutes in advance of your audition appointment so that you can become acclimated to the audition environment. Arriving early also gives you time to warm-up physically and vocally.
- Wear clothing that is comfortable and enables you to breathe properly. If you are avidly pursuing a particular part, then consider wearing clothing that quietly suggests the role rather than costuming yourself fully as that character. Bear in mind, however, that the auditors may wish to consider you for another role other than the role of your choice. Dressing in a more neutral fashion, therefore, may afford you more opportunities to be cast in the play.
- The introduction to your piece should simply include your name, the title of the work and the playwright. If the auditors desire more information, they will ask for it.

Well, you're ready. Good luck and have fun! Stand tall and wear your years of experience proudly.

# ABOUT THE PLAYWRIGHTS...

**Steve Allen** has written over 7,000 songs, including "This Could Be the Start of Something," "Picnic," "Impossible," "Gravy Waltz," "Pretend You Don't See Her," and "South Rampart Street Parade." He has authored over 53 books, starred on Broadway, in motion pictures and on television. He created and hosted the *Tonight* show, and created, wrote and hosted the Emmy award-winning PBS-TV series *Meeting of Minds*.

**Sandra Fenichel Asher**'s plays have been produced nationwide and in Canada and Australia. Of those available from Dramatic Publishing, *The Wise Men of Chelm* and *Little Old Ladies in Tennis Shoes* feature challenging roles for mature actors. *A Woman Called Truth* received the AATE Distinguished Play Award, the IUPUI/Bonderman Award, and the Joseph Campbell Memorial Award. *Across The Plains: The Journey of the Palace Wagon Family* was featured at the Kennedy Center's New Visions/New Voices Forum. Most recently, Asher adapted Jane Austen's *Emma* for the stage. Writer-in-residence at Drury College and a member of The Dramatists Guild, she is also co-founder and literary manager of Good Company Theater.

**Leslie (Hoban) Blake**, a playwright/director member of the Cherry Lane Alternative at New York's Landmark Theater, was formerly part of Circle Rep Lab and the Actors Studio Playwright/Directors Unit. She has written, directed and/or performed at the Alabama Shakespeare Festival, San Francisco's Zephyr, New York City's Riverside Shakespeare Company as well as The Public, The Roudabout Theatre and La Mama ETC. *N.I.M.B.Y.* is part of her *Sideshow* series—an ongoing survey of the American scene. An arts and entertainment journalist, she is currently co-secretary of the Drama Desk and a member of Actors Equity, The Dramatists Guild and the Society of Stage Directors and Choreographers.

**Louis Broome** was born in Dallas, raised in Tulsa, and graduated with a BFA from Webster University, St. Louis. He returned to Tulsa and co-founded Red Meat Substitutes Terrorist Theatre. Broome attended the 1996 Mt. Sequoyah New Play Retreat where he developed his full-length play, *Texarkana Waltz*. In 1998 it was produced at Circle X Theatre in Los Angeles.

**Joan Calof** has written a one-act play, *Sitting Shiva*, and several monologues-performance pieces: *Antique Furs, The Facts of Life, Game, Maiden Voyage* and *Sisters* which she has performed at the Minnesota History Center, the Red Eye Collaboration, the Minnesota Fringe Festival, Patrick's Cabaret and the Minneapolis Playwrights' Center. She received a Jones Commission in 1996 and was chosen as an associate playwright in 1997.

**Roger Cornish**'s many produced plays, including *Open Twenty-Four Hours, Off-Shore Signals*, and *Rocky and Diego*, have been presented off-Broadway and on such major regional stages as The Alley Theatre in Houston, Atlanta's Alliance Theatre, the Actors Theatre of Louisville, and St. Louis Rep. The widely produced *A Class "C" Trial in Yokohama* will have its Tokyo debut in 1999. His prizes include a Kennedy Center Award, a National Archives Prize, and a Samuel French Award. He teaches playwriting at Rutgers University.

**Angela Counts** is the author of the award-winning play, *Hedy Understands Anxiety*, which won the 1994 Kennedy Center Lorraine Hansberry Playwriting Award and was published by Dramatic Publishing. The screenplay adaptation of *Hedy* was a semi-finalist in the 1998 Sundance Institute's Filmmakers Lab. Her plays have received readings at La Mama ETC and the National Black Theatre Network. Her screenplay, *The Appointment*, is scheduled to be directed by the script's co-author, Cristina A. Kotz Cornejo. Counts is a 1997-98 Van Lier Playwriting Fellow, in residence at the New York Theatre Workshop.

**Sheryle Criswell** is a middle-school drama teacher in Chapel Hill, N.C. *Where Late the Sweet Birds Sang*, from which *Blackout* was taken, has won several awards: the 1997-1998 Southeastern Theatre Conference Charles M. Getchell New Play Award, selection by the N.C. Triangle Network of Theatres as one of the best new plays of 1998, selection as the New Play for 1998 by the Greensboro Playwright's Forum, and chosen as a finalist in the N.C. State Thompson Theatre's New Play Competition for 1998. It premiered at the Theatre in the Park in Raleigh, N.C.

**Jeffery Scott Elwell** is professor and chair of the Department of Theatre at Marshall University in Huntington, W.V. A member of The Dramatists Guild, his plays have been produced by theatres in Chicago, Los Angeles, Memphis, New Orleans, St. Louis, Charlottesville, Roanoke, Va., and in Lund, Sweden. From 1995-1998, 17 of his plays were produced off-off Broadway. *Escape from Bondage, Being Frank, Dead Fish* and *Stepping Out* have been published by Palmetto Play Service; *The Art of Dating*, a winner in the 1995 Off-Off-Broadway Original Short Play Festival, is published by Samuel French. Two of his monologues are included in *Baseball Monologues* published by Heinemann.

**Jeanette Farr** is an actress-playwright and co-founder of the Fertile Theatre Project in Modesto, Calif. She received a bachelor's degree in theatre from California State University, Stanislaus, and is currently completing the MFA playwriting program at the University of Nevada, Las Vegas. Her works include *The Burning of White Trash, Accidentally on Purpose, Cut It Out!* and *Afraid of the Dark*. Her most recent work, *Human Wonders*, was developed as part of PlayWorks Festival at the University of Texas-El Paso.

**Gary Garrison** is on the full-time faculty of the dramatic writing program at NYU's Tisch School of the Arts. His plays include *Scream with Laughter, When a Diva Dreams, We Make a Wall* and *The Big, Fat Naked Truth*. His work has been produced at the Miranda Theatre, Expanded Arts, Pulse Ensemble Theatre, Circle Rep Lab, Turnip Theatre Company, African Globe Theatre Company, New York Rep, Spectrum and Metro Stage. He is a member of The Dramatists Guild.

**Linsey Hamilton** spent a number of years working in the entertainment industry and the corporate sector in southern California before earning her MFA in playwriting from the University of Nevada, Las Vegas. In 1997, *A Strange Growing Season* and *Running from Nineveh* enjoyed concurrent world premieres in Washington and Nevada. Her short play, *A Little Support*, and her monologue, *Dilemmas*, have been published by Dramatic Publishing. *Numb as a Hake* has been published by PPT Press.

**Anne Harris** has garnered many awards including Young Playwrights' Festival, Marc A. Klein Award, Legacy Foundation Uncommon Women Award, Harry Kondoleon Playwriting Award, Deep South Writers Conference finalist, and a 1997-98 Jerome Fellowship at the Playwrights' Center. Her plays have been seen at Perishable Theater (Providence), Cleveland Public Theatre, and have been done as readings in theatres such as SoHo Rep, Tribeca Lab, and Primary Stages. Her first play, *In the Garden*, was produced at the Joseph Papp Public Theater. *A Dyke Is Not a Dam* was presented by Vitalstatistix in Adelaide, Australia, in November 1997 as part of their international playwright exchange program. Harris earned her MFA in 1995 from New York University.

**Olga Humphrey**'s play, *The Exception*, was given its world premiere production by the University of Arkansas in 1996. It was chosen as one of the 1996 finalists for the Jane Chambers Playwriting Award, and as a finalist in the 1997 Chesterfield Writers Film Project (Amblin Pictures). In 1998 it was nominated by the George Street Playhouse for the Susan Smith Blackburn Award. Her play *Svetlana's New Flame* was named winner of the Perishable Theater's 1998 One-Act Play Competition and was produced at the theatre in Providence, R.I. Her work is included in *The Best Stage Scenes of 1997* and *The Best Women's Monologues of 1997*, Published by Smith and Kraus.

**Carleen Jaspers** is the 1991 winner of the Henrico Theatre Company's One-Act Play Competition. She is currently completing her MFA in playwriting from the University of Las Vegas, Nevada. Her play, *Snowing*, was featured at the 1998 New Development Workshop sponsored by American College Theatre Festival's Region VIII. *Impurities* was chosen for PlayWorks '98, sponsored by the University of Texas-El Paso.

**Julie Jensen** is a recent recipient of the Joseph Jefferson Playwriting Award, and her play *Stray Dogs* won the CBS/Dramatists Guild Prize. One of her most recent plays, *The Lost Vegas Series*, is part of the New Work Festival at the Mark Taper Forum. Dr. Jensen directs the graduate playwriting program at the University of Nevada, Las Vegas.

**Mark Steven Jensen** is a former farmer, youth camp director, theatre instructor and computer game designer. A graduate of the MFA playwriting program at the University of Nevada, Las Vegas, Jensen collaborated on several projects with the university's senior adult theatre program, including an adaptation of *Under the Gaslight* and an oral history review entitled *Seasons*. He currently is a freelance writer in Minneapolis where he is writing everything from software manuals to dramatic pieces.

**Adam Kraar** has had plays produced in New York by Alice's Fourth Floor, Abingdon Theatre, Metropolitan Playhouse, Theatreworks/U.S.A., Pulse Ensemble, and the Quaigh Theatre; and regionally at the Mississippi State Festival of New Works, New York State Theatre Institute, Theatre Americana (Calif.), Raleigh Ensemble (N.C.), and the Drama Center (Fla.). He has won awards from the Southeastern Theatre Conference and the Aspen Playwrights' Competition, has had plays published by Palmetto Play Service and Sundance Publishers. Kraar has received fellowships from the Shenandoah International Playwrights' Retreat, the Sewanee Writers' Conference and the Mt. Sequoyah New Play Retreat. He earned an MFA from Columbia University.

**Carol Wright Krause** holds a Ph.D. in theatre from the University of Missouri. Frequently produced by colleges and universities in her home region, her full-length plays include *Charlotte Cushman, The Car* and *Jonell Johnson and Ruthie Mapes*, all of which were developed at the Shenandoah International Playwrights' Retreat in Staunton, Va.

**Davey Marlin-Jones** is a winner of the Margo Jones Award for Advancing American Playwrights and the Theatre-Educator Medallion from the American College Theatre Festival. He was recently inducted into the College of American Theatre Fellows. Currently, he teaches playwriting and directing at the University of Nevada, Las Vegas, and works with The Asylum, a new company devoted to emerging American playwrights.

**Innes-Fergus McDade** has had plays produced in New York, Washington, Massachusetts, Florida, Oklahoma, Arkansas and Lithuania. She was awarded the 1994 Steinberg Playwriting Prize for *A Treasury of Useful Information*. McDade holds an MFA in playwriting from Brandeis University, an MFA in acting from Pennsylvania State University and a BA in philosophy from the University of Pennsylvania. She has trained dolphins in Hawaii, excavated Roman ruins in Carthage and made a living as an actor in New York City for 15 years before taking up the pen.

**Vin Morreale, Jr.,** currently has 17 plays in print, and is the author of *Burning up the Stage: Monologues, Audition Pieces and Short Scenes for Actors from Six to Seventy*, also published by Dramatic Publishing. Founder of the Senseless Bickering Comedy Theatre, his comedy has appeared in newspapers and magazines, and has been broadcast on radio stations nationwide. He has also written, directed or produced numerous theatrical performances, educational videos, museum exhibits and video documentaries. As a screenwriter, he has sold material to network television and the film industry. His current fiction titles include *Diagnosis* and *Exquisite Anxieties*.

**Loretta Novick** worked for several years as an advertising copywriter, as a contributor to consumer magazines and as a writer-editor with her husband's public relations firm. An ongoing interest in drama led to writing short plays and, recently, a movie script. *The Gallery* was first produced by Fleetwood Stage at the Wildcliff Center for the Arts in New Rochelle, N.Y.

**Steven Packard** is a native of Texas who lives in New York City where he acts, directs and writes for the theatre. *Prime Time Ago* became the first of Packard's Buntvill plays, reflections of life in rural America. The collection includes *In With Alma* (published by Samuel French), *The Fettered Rose, Aloha,* and *The Saturday Shoes,* among others. He is also the author of the multiple-award-winning British comedy *The Will of George*. Packard is a member of The Dramatists Guild.

**Hudson Plumb** is a resident of New York City. He writes poems, short stories and screenplays and has been in residence at the Sewanee Writers' Conference and The Mt. Sequoyah New Play Retreat. In 1996, the Plays-in-Progress World Premiere Theatre produced *Salmon Return*, which was also a finalist in the 1996 SWTA Annual New Play Contest.

**Bruce Post** is the executive director of the Maxwell Anderson Playwrights Series and the literary manager of Fleetwood Stage in New Rochelle, N.Y. His work has been produced in New York, Kansas City, Washington, D.C., Connecticut and Martha's Vineyard. His play, *Sloth*, is published by Broadway Play Publishers. Post teaches playwriting and drama at schools and colleges in the New York area and at Fleetwood Stage.

**Philip Potak**, a member of The Dramatists Guild, received his BFA and MA in theater from Adelphi University. His work has been produced at Circle Repertory Theatre, Polaris Theater North, Adelphi University, Producers Club, SUNY Cobleskill, Colonial Little Theater, The Open Eye Theater and other regional theaters. He has received a number of commissions and grants to write and direct. His plays include *Pops, Safe Harbor, Hedges, Thinness of Blood, No One's Home, Fern & Oldie, The Back Room* and *Strangers We Know.*

**Shelly Pruit-Wykes** has a BA in theatre from Texas Wesleyan University. She has appeared in numerous stage productions and regional commercials and is featured in the computer game, "Harvester."

**Billy M. Pullen**'s first play, *Fallen Short of the Glory,* won the Paul T. Nolan Prize from the University of Southwestern Louisiana and the Festival Grand Prize from Love Creek Productions in New York City. His plays include *Snake, The Prodigal Son* and *Cymbals and Sounding Brass* which received honors from the Moving Arts Theatre Company in Los Angeles and the Southern Appalachian Repertory Theatre in North Carolina. Pullen has been a Tennessee Williams Scholar at the Sewanee Writers' Conference and has twice attended the Mt. Sequoyah New Play Retreat.

**Kenneth Robbins** is the author of two published novels, 15 published plays and the recipient of such honors as the Toni Morrison Prize for fiction, the SETC New Play Award, the Associated Writing Programs Novel Award, a Japan Foundation Artists Fellowship, a South Dakota Artists Fellowship, and others. He is the director of the School of Performing Arts at Louisiana Tech University, and is presently working on a new stage play and a screenplay based on his novel, *The Baptism of Howie Cobb.*

**Joseph Robinette** is professor of theatre at Rowan University, Glassboro, N.J. He is the author or co-author of 39 published plays and musicals, and has received numerous playwriting awards including the 1976 Charlotte Chorpenning Cup. Robinette's works have been produced in all 50 states and in several foreign countries including England, Spain, Germany, Australia and South Africa.

**Mayo Simon**'s plays have been produced in New York and in many regional theaters, including the Mark Taper Forum, the Los Angeles Theatre Center, the Magic Theatre of San Francisco, the Actors Theatre of Louisville and the Pittsburgh Public Theater. He has also had productions at the Bush Theatre, London; the Lyric Theatre of Belfast; and in Oslo, Stockholm, Copenhagen and Rome. Simon lives in New York City.

**Kate Snodgrass** is producing director of the Derek Walcott's Boston Playwrights' Theatre and lectures on playwriting at the Boston University Graduate School. She has also taught at Brandeis University and the Institute for Advanced Theatre Training at Harvard (A.R.T.). Snodgrass is the author of *Haiku*, which won the Actors Theatre of Louisville's Heiderman Award, and is published in *The Best Short Plays of 1989* and in a Samuel French edition. Her film adaptation premiered at the 1995 Boston Film Festival. She is a former member of the Circle Repertory Theatre, and is a founding member of the Lab in New York City, which premiered *L'air des Alpes* and *Que Sera, Sera*. She has studied acting at Kansas University and the London Academy of Music & Dramatic Art, and has appeared in productions at Lincoln Center, in regional theatres and on national television. She is a member of A.E.A., A.F.T.R.A. and The Dramatists Guild.

**Staci Swedeen**'s comedy *Three Forks* had its world premiere in 1997 at Florida Stage in West Palm Beach, where it was nominated for a Carbonell for Best New

Work. Her work has been produced at the City Theatre in Miami, and at the Westbeth, Nat Home Synchronicity Space, Terry Schrieber Studio and Hunter College Theatre in New York City. She has received numerous fellowships for her writing, and her work is published by Broadway Play Publishing and Broadway Press. She is currently teaching playwriting in Westchester, N.Y.

**Jules Tasca** has taught playwriting at Oxford University in England and has performed with a *commedia dell'arte* group in Italy. He is the author of over 100 published plays that have been produced in national theaters from the Mark Taper Forum and the Kennedy Center to the Bucks County Play House, as well as in London and New York. He has adapted the stories of Oscar Wilde, Guy DeMaupassant, Mark Twain, Saki, and Robert Louis Stevenson. His work has also been broadcast on National Public Radio. His awards include a Thespie Award for Best New Play and a Los Angeles Drama Critics Award. Tasca is a member of The Dramatists Guild.

**Mike Thomas** holds a degree in theatre from the University of Arkansas. He has performed in over 50 plays and has directed productions in California, Oklahoma and Arkansas. He was a member of the core acting company at the Mt. Sequoyah New Play Retreat for eight years. He currently resides in the Ozark Mountains of Arkansas where he teaches elementary school. Most of his time is spent in "hammock therapy," reading, writing and working in theatre.

**Rachel Feldbin Urist** is the winner of four national playwriting competitions, and is a three-time recipient of the Individual Creative Artist Award from the Michigan Council for the Arts. She's a staff writer for the Washtenaw Jewish News, a frequent contributor to *Hadassah* magazine, and freelances elsewhere. She spends several months a year as writer-in-residence in Michigan schools. Her play, *Shtetl Tales*, written on a grant from the Michigan Council for the Humanities, was published in the 1986 *Playwrights' Companion* and later premiered in New York. Her most recent productions include *Luck of the Draw*, at the Attic Theatre Centre in L.A., and *The Sentimental Father* and *The Talking Cure*, both at the Performance Network in Ann Arbor, Mich.

**Karen Smith Vastola**'s plays, including *Home Brew, 1-800-Baby, Dog-Eat Dog, John Doe #2, Dead or Alive* and *The Family Tree*, have been widely workshopped and produced. Selections from her plays appear in *The Best Men's Stage Monologues of 1995* and *The Best Men's Stage Monologues of 1996*, Published by Smith and Kraus.

**Michael Wright** is head of playwriting and directing at the University of Texas-El Paso, and director of the PlayWorks Festival. Other affiliations include the WordBRIDGE Playwrights Laboratory, the Kennedy Center/American College Theatre Festival, and the Southwest Theatre Association. His plays include *Blood Relations, Heart's Desires, Shooting Stars* and *Payments and Debts*, published by Palmetto Play Service. *Shocking Secrets About Elvis Revealed in Agonizing True-Life Confessions of Long-Term Fan* is published in Heinemann's *The Elvis Monologues*. His books include *The Student's Guide to Playwriting Opportunities* (2nd Ed.) published by Theatre Directories, and *Playwriting in Process*, published by Heinemann.

**Saul Zachary** has extensive credits in film, TV, and theatre. He is co-founder of Manhattan Playwrights Unit and Grand Mal Theatre and is former artistic director of Playwrights' Platform. His work is published in *The Best*

*Short Plays of 1983*; his awards include fellowships from the NEA, CBS and Creative Artists in Public Service. He is a 1993 NYFA artist-in-residence, and a Sundance Institute finalist for his screenplay, *Nothing to Lose*. *The Color of Heat* was recently produced at the University of Ottawa.

**Nicholas Zagone** is the resident playwright at Open Circle Theater Co. in Seattle where his plays *A Fiend's Friendly Council, Ohio, The Shadow*, and most recently the hit *ETA: Phoenix* have been produced. He is a two-time winner of the Northwest's Playwrights Series, the International One-Page Play Competition at La Mama in New York and the Katherine Award. Zagone received a bachelor's degree in theatre from Willamette University where he is a visiting artist, and is currently earning an MFA in playwriting at the University of Nevada, Las Vegas. His work has also been produced at Cal State Fullerton, The American College Theatre Festival and the Association for Theater in Higher Education Conference.

# PERMISSION ACKNOWLEDGMENTS

BERTIE THE BEAUTY QUEEN by Shelly Pruitt-Wykes. Copyright 1996 by Shelly Pruitt-Wykes. Reprinted by permission of the author. All inquiries should be addressed to Shelly Pruitt-Wykes, Rt. 3, Box 54D, Jacksboro, TX 76458.

BLACKOUT by Sheryl Criswell. Copyright 1998 by Sheryl Criswell. Reprinted by permission of the author. Excerpted from WHERE LATE THE SWEET BIRDS SANG by Sheryl Criswell, copyright 1998. All inquiries should be addressed to Sheryl Criswell, 107 Shady Springs Pl., Durham, NC 27713.

THE BONFIRES by Kenneth Robbins. Copyright 1996 by Kenneth Robbins. Reprinted by permission of the author. Excerpted from ATOMIC FIELD by Kenneth Robbins, copyright 1996. All inquiries should be addressed to Lettie Lee, Ann Elmo Agency, Inc., 60 E. 42nd St., New York, NY 10165.

THE BOOKMOBILE DOESN'T COME BY ANYMORE by Billy M. Pullen. Copyright 1998 by Billy M. Pullen. Reprinted by permission of the author. Excerpted from THE BOOKMOBILE DOESN'T COME BY ANYMORE by Billy M. Pullen, copyright 1998. All inquiries should be addressed to Billy M. Pullen, 3681 Nottingham Rd., Memphis, TN 38111.

THE CACTUS PIRATE: RELATIVE VALUE by Davey Marlin-Jones. Copyright 1998 by Davey Marlin-Jones. Reprinted by permission of the author. Excerpted from LIES IN THE LOOKING GLASS by Davey Marlin-Jones, copyright 1997. All inquiries should be addressed to Davey Marlin-Jones, University of Nevada, Las Vegas, 4505 S. Maryland Pkwy., Las Vegas, NV 89154-5036.

CARRY ME HOME by Angela Counts. Copyright 1998 by Angela Counts. Reprinted by permission of the author. Excerpted from *To Thine Self* by Angela Counts, copyright 1998. All inquiries should be addressed to Angela Counts, 340 Haven Ave., #3H, New York, NY 10033.

CHILDREN by Innes-Fergus McDade. Copyright 1992 by Innes-Fergus McDade. Reprinted by permission of the author. All inquiries should be addressed to Innes-Fergus McDade, 55 Carver Rd., Watertown, MA 02172.

THE COLOR OF HEAT by Saul Zachary. Copyright 1983 by Saul Zachary. Reprinted by permission of the author. All inquiries should be addressed to Saul Zachary, 338 West 19th St., 46B, New York, NY 10011-3982.

DEATH ON THE DOORSTEP by Jeffery Scott Elwell. Copyright 1997 by Jeffery Scott Elwell. Reprinted by permission of the author. All inquiries should be addressed to Tonda Marton, Elizabeth Marton Agency, 1 Union Square, Suite 612, New York, NY 10003-3303.

ESTHER'S LAST STAND by Adam Kraar. Copyright 1998 by Adam Kraar. Reprinted by permission of the author. All inquiries should be addressed to Adam Kraar, 507 Henry St., Brooklyn, NY 11231.

FAITH by Louis Broome. Copyright 1998 by Louis Broome. Reprinted by permission of the author. All inquiries should be addressed to Louis Broome, 2546 Gilman Drive West, #3, Seattle, WA 98119.

THE FAMILY TREE by Karen Smith Vastola. Copyright 1997 by Karen Smith Vastola. Reprinted by permission of the author. All inquiries should be addressed to Karen Smith Vastola, 36 Greenmeadow Rd., Pleasantville, NY 10570.

FLAMINGO FANTASY by Linsey Hamilton. Copyright 1998 by Linsey Hamilton. Reprinted by permission of the author.

All inquiries should be addressed to Linsey Hamilton, 4660 Koval Ln., #23-D, Las Vegas, NV 89109.

FOOD IS LOVE by Sandra Fenichel Asher. Copyright 1998 by Sandra Fenichel Asher. Reprinted by permission of the author. All inquiries should be addressed to Sandra Fenichel Asher, 721 S. Weller Ave., Springfield, MO 65802.

FRIDAY by Carol Wright Krause. Copyright 1997 by Carol Wright Krause. Reprinted by permission of the author. All inquiries should be addressed to Carol Wright Krause, 9495 S. Constien Rd., Columbia, MO 65203.

THE GALLERY by Loretta Novick. Copyright 1998 by Loretta Novick. Reprinted by permission of the author. All inquiries should be addressed to Loretta Novick, 402 Westchester Ave., Fleetwood, NY 10552.

GAWK by Gary Garrison. Copyright 1997 by Gary Garrison. Reprinted by permission of the author. All inquiries should be addressed to Ian Kleinert, Fifi Oscard Talent & Literary Agent, 24 West 40th St., 17th Floor, New York, NY 10003.

THE GRAND MOMMY by Adam Kraar. Copyright 1992 by Adam Kraar. Reprinted by permission of the author. Excerpted from THE INFANT SOCIETY by Adam Kraar, copyright 1992. All inquiries should be addressed to Adam Kraar, 507 Henry St., Brooklyn, NY 11231.

GRAY MATTER by Jeanette Farr. Copyright 1997 by Jeanette Farr. Reprinted by permission of the author. All inquiries should be addressed to Jeanette D. Farr, 4080 N. Olive Ave., Turlock, CA 95382.

HAVING A GOOD TIME by Steve Allen. Copyright 1998 by Steve Allen. Reprinted by permission of the author. All inquiries should be addressed to Steve Allen, 15201 Burbank Blvd., Suite B, Van Nuys, CA 91411.

HIGH TRACK by Roger Cornish. Copyright 1998 by Roger Cornish. Reprinted by permission of the author. All inquiries should be addressed to Roger Cornish, 962 River Rd., Washington Crossing, PA 18977.

THE INHERITANCE by Vin Morreale, Jr. Copyright 1998 by Vin Morreale, Jr. Reprinted by permission of the author. All inquiries should be addressed to Vin Morreale, Jr., c/o VSM Productions, 1011 Colonel Anderson Pkwy., Louisville, KY 40222.

IT'S HALF-FULL by Michael Wright. Copyright 1998 by Michael Wright. Reprinted by permission of the author. All inquiries should be addressed to Michael Wright, University of Texas-El Paso, Theatre Arts, 500 W. University, El Paso, TX 79968-0549.

THE KEEPSAKE by Staci Swedeen. Copyright 1992 by Staci Swedeen. Reprinted by permission of the author. Adapted from MAKING HER MOAN by Staci Swedeen, copyright 1992. All inquiries should be addressed to Mary Harden, Harden Curtis Associates, 850 Seventh Ave., #405, New York, NY 10019.

KNEADING by Michael Wright. Copyright 1998 by Michael Wright. Reprinted by permission of the author. All inquiries should be addressed to Michael Wright, University of Texas-El Paso, Theatre Arts, 500 W. University, El Paso, TX 79968-0549.

LAST LAUGHS by Rachel Feldbin Urist. Copyright 1996 by Rachel Feldbin Urist. Reprinted by permission of the author. Excerpted from CLOWNS ON ICE by Rachel Feldbin Urist, copyright 1996 by Rachel Feldbin Urist. All inquiries should be addressed to Rachel Feldbin Urist, 310 Awixa, Ann Arbor, MI 48104.

THE LATE SHOW by Mike Thomas. Copyright 1998 by Michael Thomas. Reprinted by permission of the author. All inquiries should be addressed to Mike Thomas, 106 N. Olive, Fayetteville, AR 72701.

LATHER by Carleen R. Jaspers. Copyright 1998 by Carlene R. Jaspers. Reprinted by permission of the author. All inquiries should be addressed to Carkeeb Hasoersm, P.O. Box 71184, Las Vegas, NV 89170.

THE LOST PARTY by Hudson Plumb. Copyright 1998 by Hudson Plumb. Reprinted by permission of the author. Adapted from SALMON RETURN by Hudson Plumb, copyright 1996. All inquiries should be addressed to Hudson Plumb, 78 Irving Pl., Apt. 7B, New York, NY 10003.

MR. WONDERFUL by Olga Humphrey. Copyright 1998 by Olga Humphrey. Reprinted by permission of the author. Adapted from MR. WONDERFUL by Olga Humphrey, copyright 1997. All inquiries should be addressed to Olga Humphrey, 353 E. 76th St., #3W, New York, NY 10021.

MY GREATEST FAILING by Innes-Fergus McDade. Copyright 1992 by Innes-Fergus McDade. Reprinted by permission of the author. All inquiries should be addressed to Innes-Fergus McDade, 55 Carver Rd., Watertown, MA 02172.

N.I.M.B.Y. (NOT IN MY BACKYARD) by Leslie (Hoban) Blake. Copyright 1998 by Leslie (Hoban) Blake. Reprinted by permission of the author. All inquiries should be addressed to Chris Fish, 321 W. 24th St., Ste. 19A, New York, NY 10011.

OLD WOMAN by Joseph Robinette. Copyright 1998 by Joseph Robinette. Reprinted by permission of the author. All inquiries should be addressed to Joseph Robinette, Department of Theatre & Dance, Rowan University, 201 Mullica Hill Rd., Glassboro, NJ 08028.

THE OPEN WINDOW by Kent R. Brown. Copyright 1998 by Kent R. Brown. Reprinted by permission of the author. All inquiries should be addressed to Kent R. Brown, 122 Stillson Rd., Fairfield, CT 06432.

OUT ON THE ICE by Mark Steven Jensen. Copyright 1998 by Mark Steven Jensen. Reprinted by permission of the author. All inquiries should be addressed to Mark Steven Jensen, 2123 Co Rd., SW, Evansville, MN 56326.

PAIN AND PAINT by Nicholas Zagone. Copyright 1998 by Nicholas Zagone. Reprinted by permission of the author. All inquiries should be directed to Nicholas Zagone, 5010 Indian River Dr., #51, Las Vegas, NV 89103.

THE PICKUP by Kent R. Brown. Copyright 1998 by Kent R. Brown. Reprinted by permission of the author. All inquiries should be addressed to Kent R. Brown, 122 Stillson Rd., Fairfield, CT 06432.

PRIME TIME AGO by Steven Packard. Copyright 1994 by Steven Packard. Reprinted by permission of the author. All inquiries should be addressed to Steven Packard, A-flat, 437 W. 48th St., New York, NY 10036.

PROGRESSIVE PASSION by Mike Thomas. Copyright 1998 by Michael Thomas. Reprinted by permission of the author. All inquiries should be addressed to Mike Thomas, 106 N. Olive, Fayetteville, AR 72701.

QUE SERA, SERA by Katherine Snodgrass. Copyright 1998 by Katherine Snodgrass. Reprinted by permission of the author. All inquiries should be addressed to Katherine Snodgrass,

Boston Playwrights' Theatre, 949 Commonwealth Ave., Boston, MA 02215.

THE QUESTION by Mayo Simon. Copyright 1994 by Mayo Simon. Reprinted by permission of the author. Excerpted from LOVE by Mayo Simon, copyright 1994. All inquiries should be addressed to Wendy Streeter, The Joyce Ketay Agency, 1501 Broadway, Ste. 1908, New York, NY 10019.

RECORD HOLDER by Joseph Robinette. Copyright 1998 by Joseph Robinette. Reprinted by permission of the author. All inquiries should be addressed to Joseph Robinette, Department of Theatre & Dance, Rowan University, 201 Mullica Hill Rd., Glassboro, NJ 08028.

SCENES FROM THE PENITENTIARY by Anne Harris. Copyright 1998 by Anne Harris. Reprinted by permission of Helen Merrill, Ltd., on behalf of the author. Excerpted from SCENES FROM THE PENITENTIARY by Anne Harris. All inquiries should be addressed to Beth Blickers, Helen Merrill Ltd., 425 W. 23rd St., #1F, New York, NY 10011.

SNIFF by Jules Tasca. Copyright 1998 by Jules Tasca. Reprinted by permission of the author. All inquiries should be addressed to Jules Tasca, Gwynedd Mercy College, #901, Gwynedd Valley, PA 19437.

STARGAZER by Kent R. Brown. Copyright 1998 by Kent R. Brown. Reprinted by permission of the author. All inquiries should be addressed to Kent R. Brown, 122 Stillson Rd., Fairfield, CT 06432.

SUMMER'S LAST CALL by Bruce Post. Copyright 1998 by Bruce Post. Reprinted by permission of the author. Excerpted from SUMMER'S LAST CALL by Bruce Post, copyright 1998. All inquiries should be addressed to Bruce Post, Box 671, W. Redding, CT 06896.

SWEET TUESDAY FALLS by Julie Jensen. Copyright 1997 by Julie Jensen. Reprinted by permission of the author. Excerpted from SWEET TUESDAY FALLS by Julie Jensen, copyright 1997. All inquiries should be addressed to Julie Jensen, 4640 Koval Ln., #46C, Las Vegas, NV 89109.

THE TALKING BENCH by Kent R. Brown. Copyright 1998 by Kent R. Brown. Reprinted by permission of the author. All inquiries should be addressed to Kent R. Brown, 122 Stillson Rd., Fairfield, CT 06432.

THE TEA COZY by Joan Calof. Copyright 1998 by Joan Calof. Reprinted by permission of the author. All inquiries should be addressed to Joan Calof, c/o The Playwrights' Center, 2301 Franklin Ave., E., Minneapolis, MN 55406-1099.

THEY WERE ALL GOOD LOVERS by Mike Thomas. Copyright 1998 by Michael Thomas. Reprinted by permission of the author. All inquiries should be addressed to Mike Thomas, 106 N. Olive, Fayetteville, AR 72701.

THE THIRD SCOURGE by Vin Morreale, Jr. Copyright 1998 by Vin Morreale, Jr. Reprinted by permission of the author. All inquiries should be addressed to Vin Morreale, Jr., c/o VSM Productions, 1011 Colonel Anderson Pkwy., Louisville, KY 40222.

THE TIME-SHARE RAG by Kent R. Brown. Copyright 1998 by Kent R. Brown. Reprinted by permission of the author. All inquiries should be addressed to Kent R. Brown, 122 Stillson Rd., Fairfield, CT 06432.

WHOSE TURN IS IT? by Philip Potak. Copyright 1996 by Philip Potak. Reprinted by permission of the author. All inquiries should be addressed to Philip Potak, 186-B2 Nicholas Rd., Jefferson, NY 12093.

5727